radically simple

radically simple

Brilliant Flavors with Breathtaking Ease

Rozanne Gold

RODALE

Book design by Kara Plikaitis

Library of Congress Cataloging-in-Publication Data

Gold, Rozanne
    Radically simple : brilliant flavors with breathtaking ease / Rozanne Gold.
       p.   cm.
    Includes index.
    ISBN-13 978–1–60529–470–4   hardcover
    ISBN-10 1–60529–470–5 hardcover
    1. Cooking.   2. Quick and easy cooking.   I. Title.
  TX714.G5993   2010
  641.5'55—dc22   2010024994

Distributed to the trade by Macmillan
2   4   6   8   10 9 7 5 3   hardcover

We inspire and enable people to improve their lives and the world around them.

For Michael, Jeremy & Shayna
and for my parents, Marion Gold & Bill Gold—blessed be their names

WHAT IS **RADICALLY SIMPLE?**

"Good cooking is when things taste of what they are."
—Curnonsky

As a professional chef for decades, I believe that the best food in the world is often the simplest, and that simplicity, sophistication, and even authenticity can happily coexist.

With one hand in the restaurant world and the other in my home kitchen, my goal is to ramp up the ease of preparing great food every day without compromising the integrity of what I put on the table. No shortcuts or anything processed, just fresh ideas with a bit of "chef thinking" in every dish. I want to demonstrate that radically simple food and real cooking are, in fact, soul mates.

For years, my notion of simplicity had to do with limiting the number of ingredients in a recipe to three (not counting salt, pepper, and water), and I wrote a series of nine cookbooks using that principle as my guide. Today my idea has expanded to something broader and more liberating—where the *interplay* of time, technique, and essential ingredients becomes the focus. But more about that later.

Some of the things I love the most hardly qualify as "recipes": buttered bread with black olive paste; a hunk of crusty baguette dunked into a bowl of good vinaigrette; hot polenta poured over a slab of creamy Gorgonzola cheese; salty feta strewn with roasted peppers and a drizzle of wildflower honey; a soft-boiled egg with a dab of Sriracha crème fraîche, or wild arugula dressed with extra-virgin olive oil and sea salt. These ideas are too simple to be included in a book, yet they represent the essence of what simplicity means to me.

But more than 300 other radically simple recipes *are* here: Epiphanies like caramel-nuanced aged Gouda paired with sticky-sweet fresh black dates, and primal things like a beef rib roast (page 241), roasted unadorned at 500°F on a bed of salt. There's a one-ingredient soup, Pink Tomato Frappés (page 74), fashioned entirely from ripe tomatoes that have been whirled in a blender; a simple tranche of fresh salmon, perfectly broiled, with a grace note of blackened lemons (page 138); and an improbable three-ingredient pineapple flan that quivers with tropical intensity (page 305).

Just as importantly, I believe that cooking should be pleasurable, eliciting a feeling of abundance without the burden. You will find an entire chapter filled with exciting ideas for 10-minute salads; you'll discover soups that take less than 5 minutes to prepare and others that feel like they've been simmering all day; you'll want to try stunning main courses that are clearly more than the sum of their parts, and splendid desserts requiring just a handful of good ingredients.

Oh, yes: The procedures in virtually every recipe can be stated in fewer than 140 words—some with as few as 40. Not quite Twitter, but close!

COOKING IN THREE DIMENSIONS

I regard each radically simple recipe as a three-dimensional creation, with time, technique, and the number of ingredients making up the axes on which they are plotted. Some recipes may have lots of ingredients, but they're assembled and cooked in a jiffy. Some may require careful technique, but the shopping and cooking parts are easy. Others may reward an early effort in preparation with the alchemy of long and patient cooking while you do something else. I strive for a harmony of all three, and the result is a collection of recipes that evince an existential ease.

You might be surprised that a complex dish like Chicken Ras el Hanout with Tomato-Ginger Chutney (page 197) can be whipped up in less than 15 minutes. Or that a succulent Veal Roast with Fresh Thyme & Honey Mustard Jus (page 232), which takes $2\frac{1}{2}$ hours in the oven, consists of only four ingredients and requires almost no preparation at all. My "Whole Buttered" Onion Soup (page 86) deploys a radical technique that doesn't require you to slice onions, but relies on four hours in a slow oven for its creamy (though creamless) sophistication. Mahogany Short Ribs (page 246), a prized recipe, bathes in a radically simple marinade of prune juice and teriyaki sauce, which acts as both tenderizer and beneficent glaze. It is rather scrumptious on sweet potato puree and not bad at all with egg noodles tossed with rosemary butter. Try them both.

Or how about a slice of warm bittersweet chocolate cake (page 317) made with only *four* ingredients and baked in just 18 minutes. That's pretty radical.

THE ELEMENTS OF RADICAL SIMPLICITY

Rarely do recipes stand alone. I continue to be fascinated by the invisible connective tissue that holds a meal together and spend lots of time thinking about integrating a menu's components. I also take great pleasure in finding wines to match, and urge you to do the same—keeping in mind that everyone's taste is different and that no wine is "wrong" if you like the ways it goes with your food. In the same way, there's an inner logic to every recipe in the book that may not be apparent on the page, but certainly will be on your palate. Each one combines the following elements:

BEAUTY. I have always been attuned to how my dishes look. Over the course of a 30-plus-year career, I have developed recipes for magazines, cookbooks, and restaurants—all venues where the dishes must look as good as they taste. And what I've found is that the simplest recipes are usually the most striking. My Salmon with Lime Leaves, Poppy Rice & Coconut Sauce (page 139) is a stunner and, even with its additional fillip of curry oil, is astonishingly simple to prepare. In Blueberries with Hibiscus Spice, Sugar Syrup (page 290), blueberries are dusted with loose Red Zinger tea and a warm simple syrup gets poured over the top; the syrup turns red in front of you. The photographic style of *Radically Simple* is deliberately unadorned because I want you to see, in detail, how a dish is put together. I want you to look at the image and say to yourself: "I can do that."

CLARITY. In *Radically Simple*, the ingredients really do speak for themselves, as in An Opinionated Way to Roast a Chicken (page 203). Here I roast a chicken stark naked (the bird, that is) and serve the juices as the sauce. An optional foaming garlic-and-chive butter can be added, but I encourage you to experience the crystal-clear essence of a simple roasted bird. Taste-clarity is one of the most salient benefits of pared-down ingredient lists and straightforward cooking. Likewise, one ingredient can focus the flavor of another. For example, fresh basil makes peaches taste "peachier," and a drizzle of reduced pineapple juice dancing on warm asparagus soup makes its grassy flavor soar.

ECUMENISM. Radical simplicity is open to international influences. When the main ingredients and means of preparation are simple, a recipe becomes a wonderful showcase for unfamiliar ingredients such as Sriracha (Thai chili sauce), pimentón (Spanish smoked paprika), or ras el hanout (a North African spice mixture). My Summer Tomatoes with Za'atar Pesto (page 45), for example, would be a wonderful introduction to za'atar, the Middle Eastern seasoning blend of hyssop, toasted sesame seeds, and sumac that has long been a staple in my kitchen.

THE BEST INGREDIENTS. The simpler a dish is, the more it depends on the quality of its components. These recipes are based on fresh, unprocessed ingredients, and I encourage you to seek out the best—they are the critical tools in creating delicious meals. Often this means going beyond the supermarket and exploring ethnic groceries and specialty food stores. You will notice that many dishes have "grace notes"—wonderful microgreens or herbs, pea shoots or sprouts, edible flowers or Technicolor vegetables—that are now available in many farmers' markets. I encourage you to try them all.

In the ingredient lists you will not see salt, pepper, or water, but they are stated in the procedures—so it is best to read a recipe through before embarking on a culinary adventure. Sometimes a specific amount of salt or pepper is called for, but usually they are to be added "to taste." Salt means kosher salt, the choice of most professional chefs, who consider it less "salty" than iodized table salt. And you often need to use less of it. Coarse sea salt is sometimes required; I suggest you keep some in your pantry. I am also fond of a "flaked" salt called Maldon and often use it to "finish" a dish. Pepper, unless otherwise stated, means freshly ground black pepper, because once ground, pepper loses its perfume rapidly.

TECHNIQUE. I believe home cooks need to pay attention to technique, and that it is vitally important to read through the recipe and have a *mise en place* ready before starting to cook. Think of a painter: Everything is laid out before her—the colors on the palette, the brushes she'll need—so that she is free to create. Likewise, having all your ingredients measured and ready to go transforms the potentially frenetic business of cooking into a more lyrical experience. I am reminded of this every time I play hide-and-seek in my pantry during a crucial moment of a recipe!

Perhaps Curnonsky, France's most celebrated gastronome and food writer of the 20th century, said it best: "In cooking, as in all the arts, simplicity is the sign of perfection." I couldn't agree more.

BRUNCH

Weekday mornings hardly need a recipe book; that's what bagels, oatmeal, and frozen waffles are for. Trust me, I have a 14-year-old daughter. With the exception of some interesting *5-minute* juice blends, *10-minute* dishes such as Creamy, Lemony Eggs with Prosciutto, Peanut Butter–Granola Bruschetta, and a Breakfast "Surprise," you might just wait until Friday to use this chapter.

But on weekends and holidays—and birthdays, too—morning food should get the same respect given to food-after-dark. With pleasure aforethought, you will find here a handful of ideas meant for "the morning after." These are prepared the night before and practically make themselves in the morning. A multitalented Cheese Strata with Prosciutto, Basil & Spinach soaks up an eggy custard overnight. Morning Fruit Soup with Tapioca coalesces while you dream. Overnight Tabbouleh becomes a Mediterranean-Rim breakfast adorned with hard-boiled eggs. A specially formulated batter allows both you and Double-Rise Pancakes to rise slowly in the morning.

Some dishes need take no more than *20 minutes* to make and often just a handful of ingredients. Surprisingly, Homemade Turkey Sausage and Steak & Eggs with Salsa Verde & Fontina fit that criteria. While the first pot of coffee is brewing, you can also take advantage of my *30-Minute* Bakery, whipping up tender fruit muffins, a variety of scones, or Petit Pains au Chocolat, and feel deeply satisfied early in the day.

so easy

Seven Great Juice Blends 4

Apple-Ginger-Pear Martinis 6

"Bloody" Shrimp Cocktail 7

Creamy, Lemony Eggs with Prosciutto 8

Scrambled Eggs with Leeks & Sable 8

Frittata with Pancetta, Red Onion & Mint 9

Kimchee Frittata with Five-Spice Powder 9

Steak & Eggs with Salsa Verde & Fontina 10

Runny Eggs on Creamy Scallion-Bacon Grits 11

Zucchini, Fresh Mozzarella & Sun-Dried Tomato Tart 12

Smoked Trout on Frisée with Warm Bacon-Maple Vinaigrette 13

Smoked Salmon, Basil & Lemon Quesadillas 15

Herring Salad with Fennel, Crème Fraîche & Toasted Bread Crumbs 16

Glazed Salmon & Wok Eggs with Shiitakes 17

Homemade Turkey Sausage 17

Palacsintas with Apricot Jam & Powdered Sugar 18

Caramelized Almond Toasts 18

Warm Rhubarb Compote with Walnut-Coconut Crunch 20

Peanut Butter–Granola Bruschetta 21

Breakfast "Surprise" 21

set up overnight

Morning Fruit Soup with Tapioca 22

Homemade Cream Cheese 22

Carrot Marmalade 23

Double-Rise Pancakes with Strawberries, Bananas & Almonds 24

Overnight Tabbouleh with Hard-Boiled Eggs 25

Cheese Strata with Prosciutto, Basil & Spinach 26

30-minute bakery

Fresh Fruit Muffins: Blueberry, Cinnamon-Apple, or Pear 28

Petit Pains au Chocolat 29

Fruit Chaussons 29

Warm Buttermilk-Cheddar Scones 30

Golden Raisin–Fennel Scones 31

SEVEN GREAT JUICE BLENDS

Few things are better in the morning than freshly squeezed orange juice except, perhaps, these fabulous blends—one for every day of the week. Choose one combination; combine the ingredients in a large pitcher, chill until ready to serve. Each will serve 6. Add some prosecco for fun.

1
4 cups pear nectar
2 cups orange juice
¼ cup freshly squeezed lime juice

2
6 cups peach nectar
1 tablespoon freshly squeezed ginger juice*

3
4 cups watermelon juice**
3 cups mango or passion fruit nectar
2 tablespoons freshly squeezed lemon juice

4
4 cups watermelon juice**
2 cups freshly squeezed blood orange juice

5
6 cups banana or guava nectar
2 cups pink grapefruit juice

6
4 cups peach nectar
1 cup unsweetened cranberry juice
1 cup orange juice (tastes a little like Hawaiian punch)

7
2 cups pineapple juice
2 cups pear nectar
2 cups peach nectar

* Peel a 5-inch piece of ginger. Grate on the large holes of a box grater. Put the grated ginger in a paper towel and squeeze hard to extract juice.

** Process 2 pounds of seeded watermelon in a food processor to make 4 cups.

APPLE-GINGER-PEAR MARTINIS

Make these by the pitcher so that you don't need to be shaking and stirring when your guests arrive.

1$\frac{1}{2}$ cups pear nectar
2$\frac{1}{2}$ cups apple juice
4 limes
4 teaspoons honey
1$\frac{1}{4}$ cups vodka
4-inch piece fresh ginger, peeled

Stir the pear nectar and apple juice together in a pitcher. Squeeze 6 tablespoons lime juice into the pitcher. Add the honey and stir until it dissolves; stir in the vodka. Grate the ginger on the large holes of a box grater. Place the grated ginger in a paper towel and squeeze to extract 1 tablespoon juice; add to the pitcher. Stir, cover, and refrigerate until well-chilled.

Pour into chilled martini glasses or serve over ice. Garnish each with a slice of lime.
SERVES 6

"Bloody" Shrimp Cocktail

Part drink, part salad, this spin on a Bloody a Mary is chock-a-block with shrimp. Begin with ice-cold ingredients. Eat the shrimp, then drink up!

1 pound cooked peeled medium shrimp, about 32
3 cups tomato juice
6 tablespoons freshly squeezed lemon juice
3 tablespoons gin
1$\frac{1}{2}$ tablespoons orange juice
$\frac{3}{4}$ teaspoon Sriracha
$\frac{1}{4}$ cup freshly grated horseradish
4 short celery stalks with leaves

Divide the shrimp among 4 tall glasses. Combine the tomato juice, lemon juice, gin, orange juice, and Sriracha in a pitcher; stir well. Add salt to taste. Pour over the shrimp; top with as much horseradish as you like. Add a celery stalk to each glass. Place the filled glasses in the freezer for 3 minutes before serving. SERVES 4

CREAMY, LEMONY EGGS WITH PROSCIUTTO

Like hollandaise, these ultra-creamy scrambled eggs are made in the top of a double boiler,
giving them a voluptuous texture.

6 ounces thinly sliced prosciutto
6 extra-large eggs plus 3 egg whites
Grated zest and juice of 1 lemon
2 tablespoons unsalted butter
3 tablespoons chopped fresh chives

Line the centers of 4 large plates with overlapping slices of prosciutto. Combine the eggs
and whites and beat with an electric mixer or whisk until thoroughly mixed. Add the
lemon zest, 2 tablespoons lemon juice, and $\frac{1}{4}$ teaspoon salt and pepper. Mix well.

Bring several inches of water to a boil in the bottom of a double boiler. Reduce heat to a
simmer. Melt 1 tablespoon of the butter in the top of the double boiler; add the eggs.
Cook, stirring constantly with a rubber spatula, until the eggs have thickened into small
curds, about 10 minutes. Add the remaining butter in bits as you go along. Spoon the
hot eggs onto the prosciutto. Garnish with chives. SERVES 4

SCRAMBLED EGGS WITH LEEKS & SABLE

A more distinctive version of the classic lox, eggs, and onions, these eggs rest on slices of sable,
gently warming them. Sable, or smoked black cod, is available in upscale food stores.

8 thin slices smoked sable
2 cups chopped leeks, white and light green parts only
4 tablespoons unsalted butter
10 extra-large eggs

Overlap 2 slices of sable in the centers of 4 large plates. Wash the leeks; dry well. Melt
2 tablespoons of the butter in a very large frying pan. Add the leeks; cook, stirring,
until soft and golden, 10 minutes. Beat the eggs well with an electric mixer or whisk,
adding salt and pepper. Melt the remaining 2 tablespoons butter in the pan with the
leeks; add the eggs and continue to cook over medium heat, stirring constantly, until
just set, 2 minutes. Spoon the eggs atop the sable. SERVES 4

Frittata with Pancetta, Red Onion & Mint

Delicious served with room-temperature Italian White Bean Salad (page 69).

> 6 ounces pancetta in $\frac{1}{4}$-inch-thick slices
> 1$\frac{1}{2}$ tablespoons olive oil
> 1$\frac{1}{2}$ cups finely diced red onions
> 12 extra-large eggs
> 1 cup chopped fresh mint, plus sprigs for garnish

Preheat the broiler. Dice the pancetta into $\frac{1}{4}$-inch cubes. Heat the oil in a 10-inch ovenproof skillet. Add the pancetta and onions; cook over medium heat until the onions are soft, about 10 minutes.

Using an electric mixer or whisk, beat the eggs, $\frac{1}{4}$ cup cold water, and $\frac{1}{2}$ teaspoon salt and pepper in a bowl until thoroughly mixed. Pour the eggs into the hot pan with the pancetta. Cook over high heat for 1 minute, stirring constantly. Add the chopped mint; continue to cook and stir for 1 minute. Reduce heat to low; cook without stirring for 20 minutes. Cover; cook 5 minutes longer, or until the frittata is just set (the center will be a bit runny). Uncover and broil 30 seconds, until just firm. Cool 5 minutes; cut into wedges. Garnish with mint sprigs. SERVES 6

Kimchee Frittata with Five-Spice Powder

You'll want to serve this with a platter of smoky bacon or some tiny Chinese sausages. A dusting of five-spice powder at the end fills your nostrils with a wonderful perfume.

> 12 ounces very sharp yellow Cheddar cheese
> 2$\frac{1}{2}$ tablespoons olive oil
> 10 extra-large eggs
> $\frac{1}{2}$ cup slivered kimchee, plus 1 tablespoon brine
> $\frac{1}{2}$ teaspoon five-spice powder

Preheat the oven to 350°F. Grate the cheese on the large holes of a box grater. Oil a 9-inch springform pan with $\frac{1}{2}$ tablespoon of the oil. Cut a round of parchment and fit in the bottom of the pan. Sprinkle with one-third of the cheese.

With an electric mixer, beat the eggs with the remaining 2 tablespoons oil. Add the kimchee and brine and $\frac{1}{4}$ teaspoon salt; beat well. Pour the mixture into the pan; sprinkle evenly with the remaining cheese. Bake 20 to 25 minutes, until set. Sprinkle with the five-spice powder. SERVES 4

Steak & Eggs with Salsa Verde & Fontina

Skirt steak will do nicely here. Salsa verde is made from tomatillos. Some upscale food markets carry freshly prepared salsa verde, or you may use some from a jar.

1$^1\!/_2$ pounds skirt steak
1 teaspoon sweet or smoked paprika
3 cups medium-hot salsa verde
8 extra-large eggs
6-ounce piece imported Fontina cheese, coarsely grated
Fresh mint sprigs for garnish

Preheat the broiler. Rub the steak with the paprika and salt and pepper.

Put the salsa verde in a heavy 12-inch ovenproof skillet with a cover. Bring to a boil; lower heat to a simmer. Carefully break the eggs directly into the salsa. Mound the cheese over each egg. Cover and cook over medium heat for 6 to 8 minutes, until the whites are set and the yolks are runny. Meanwhile, broil the steak until medium rare, about 3 minutes per side. Let rest 5 minutes, then slice on the bias.

Serve the steak with the eggs, salsa verde, and mint springs. SERVES 4

RUNNY EGGS ON CREAMY SCALLION-BACON GRITS

You can either fry or poach your eggs; either way, make sure they have runny yolks to trickle into this dreamy stuff. Dedicated to my dear friend Chase Crossingham.

1½ cups instant grits
2 tablespoons unsalted butter, plus more for frying the eggs
⅓ cup freshly grated Parmigiano-Reggiano
¼ cup finely chopped scallions, white and green parts
4 slices bacon, cooked crisp and crumbled
8 extra-large eggs

In a medium saucepan, combine 5½ cups water and ½ teaspoon salt. Bring to a boil. Gradually whisk in the grits. Cover and cook over low heat, whisking often, until thick and creamy. Stir in the butter, cheese, scallions, and bacon. Cook 5 minutes longer. Add salt and pepper.

Fry the eggs in butter until the whites are set but the yolks are still runny. (Or poach the eggs: Bring a 14-inch skillet of water to a boil; add 2 tablespoons white vinegar and 1 teaspoon salt. Slip in the eggs and poach for about 3 minutes. Remove with a slotted spoon.) Spoon the grits into bowls. Top with the eggs. SERVES 4

ZUCCHINI, FRESH MOZZARELLA & SUN-DRIED TOMATO TART

According to People *magazine, this recipe, which I created for* Bon Appétit, *is country singer Martina McBride's favorite. It's great for company.*

1 sheet frozen puff pastry, thawed
6 ounces fresh mozzarella, shredded
½ cup freshly grated Parmigiano-Reggiano
1 tablespoon dried oregano
¼ cup finely minced scallions, white and light green parts
1 cup julienned sun-dried tomatoes in oil
½ cup finely julienned fresh basil
1 small zucchini, about 4 ounces
2 extra-large eggs
1 cup half-and-half

Preheat the oven to 400°F. Roll the pastry into a 12 × 12-inch square. Fit into an 11-inch tart pan with a removable bottom, pressing in firmly. Trim the edges.

Scatter the mozzarella cheese over the pastry. Sprinkle with 6 tablespoons of the Parmesan, the oregano, scallions, dried tomatoes, and basil. Slice the zucchini into very thin rounds. Arrange them over the basil in concentric circles. Beat together the eggs and half-and-half; add a large pinch salt and pepper. Pour the mixture into the pan. Sprinkle with the remaining Parmesan. Bake for 35 minutes, until just firm. SERVES 8

SMOKED TROUT ON FRISÉE WITH WARM BACON-MAPLE VINAIGRETTE

This is fabulous for brunch or an elegant dinner party; pop a bottle of bubbly for either occasion. The dressing can be made ahead and gently rewarmed.

8 slices bacon, cut into $1/2$-inch pieces
$1/2$ cup olive oil
$1/4$ cup maple syrup
3 tablespoons rice vinegar
2 teaspoons Dijon mustard
1 small garlic clove
2 tablespoons chopped fresh dill
2 large heads frisée or 1 large head escarole
30 grape tomatoes, halved lengthwise
4 large smoked trout halves, skin removed
1 small red onion, thinly sliced

In a medium skillet, cook the bacon until just crisp; drain on paper towels. Leave 3 tablespoons fat in the pan. Add the oil, maple syrup, vinegar, mustard, and garlic pushed through a press to the reserved bacon fat. Warm over low heat, whisking until emulsified. Add the dill and salt and pepper.

Cut the lettuce into large pieces and divide among 6 large plates. Scatter the tomatoes on top. Cut the trout crosswise into $3/4$-inch strips; arrange on the salads. Scatter the onion slices on top. Pour the dressing over the salads and top with the bacon. SERVES 6

SMOKED SALMON, BASIL & LEMON QUESADILLAS

There would be nothing wrong with topping these with a bit of salmon caviar. Or more.

8 (8-inch) flour tortillas
6 ounces whipped cream cheese
8 ounces good-quality smoked salmon
4 ounces goat cheese
½ cup julienned fresh basil
1 large lemon, zested and quartered
4 teaspoons olive oil

Preheat the oven to 250°F. Place 4 tortillas on a flat surface. Spread each with 3 tablespoons cream cheese to completely cover. Cut the salmon into 1-inch strips and scatter over the cream cheese. Crumble the goat cheese and sprinkle over the salmon. Scatter the basil over each; add a little grated lemon zest and black pepper. Top each with a second tortilla, pressing down firmly.

Heat 1 teaspoon oil in each of 2 large nonstick skillets. Place 1 quesadilla in each skillet. Cook over high heat, turning once, until golden, 2 minutes. Transfer to a baking sheet and keep warm in the oven. Repeat. Cut each quesadilla into quarters. Serve with wedges of lemon. SERVES 4

HERRING SALAD WITH FENNEL, CRÈME FRAÎCHE & TOASTED BREAD CRUMBS

This is unconventionally delicious. Serve with pumpernickel bread and slices of Havarti cheese.

24 ounces herring in wine sauce, chilled
1 medium fennel bulb with lots of fronds
1 tablespoon olive oil
$^1/_2$ cup panko
8 ounces crème fraîche
1 small red onion, thinly sliced
2 small yellow or red tomatoes, thinly sliced

Put the herring and wine sauce in a large bowl. Remove the fronds from the fennel and chop $^1/_4$ cup; set aside. Cut the fennel in half lengthwise, then slice thinly crosswise. Add to the herring and combine; let sit 10 minutes.

Heat the oil in a medium skillet; add the panko and a large pinch of salt. Cook, stirring over medium-high heat, until golden brown, 2 minutes. Using a slotted spoon, mound the herring mixture on each of 4 large plates. Spread several tablespoons crème fraîche on top to cover. Scatter the onion and chopped fronds on top. Sprinkle with the bread crumbs; top with the tomatoes. SERVES 4

Glazed Salmon & Wok Eggs with Shiitakes

This nifty combination of tastes is evocative of breakfast in Japan.

1 tablespoon soy sauce
1 tablespoon honey
1 tablespoon ketchup
¼ teaspoon plus 1 tablespoon Asian sesame oil
¼ teaspoon ground ginger
1 pound thick salmon fillet
7 extra-large eggs plus 3 egg whites
5 ounces sliced shiitake mushrooms
3 tablespoons chives snipped on the bias

Preheat the broiler. In a small bowl, mix together the soy sauce, honey, ketchup, ¼ teaspoon of the oil, and ginger. Cut the salmon into 4 square pieces. Brush with the glaze. Broil 3 to 4 minutes without turning, until rare. Glaze again.

With an electric mixer or whisk, beat the whole eggs and whites thoroughly. In a wok, briefly heat the remaining 1 tablespoon sesame oil over medium-high heat. Add the mushrooms and cook, stirring constantly, until soft, 2 minutes. Add salt and pepper; cook 1 minute longer. Add the eggs and cook, stirring with a flexible spatula, until creamy and set, several minutes longer. Serve the eggs alongside the salmon sprinkled with chives. SERVES 4

Homemade Turkey Sausage

You can make your own sausage in just 5 minutes. Here's how. Asafetida is a pungent spice used in India for centuries. When cooked it has a pleasant, oniony taste.

12 ounces ground turkey
3 garlic cloves
2 teaspoons ground cumin
¼ teaspoon ground coriander
Pinch of asafetida, optional
1 tablespoon olive oil

Put the turkey in a large bowl. Press the garlic through a press; add to the turkey. Add the cumin, coriander, asafetida, ½ teaspoon salt, and ¼ teaspoon black pepper. Using clean hands, mix thoroughly. Form the mixture into twelve 2-inch patties. Heat the oil in a large skillet. Add the patties and brown 2 minutes on each side. Do not overcook; they should be moist. SERVES 4

Palacsintas with Apricot Jam & Powdered Sugar

These Hungarian crepes are radically simple to make. The batter can be made a day in advance and whirled again before using.

1 cup whole milk
1 cup plus 2 tablespoons flour
2 tablespoons sugar
2 extra-large eggs
4 tablespoons unsalted butter
3⁄4 cup best-quality apricot jam
1⁄3 cup confectioners' sugar

Preheat the oven to 275°F. Blend the milk, flour, sugar, eggs, and a pinch of salt in a blender. Melt 2 tablespoons of the butter and add to the blender. Blend until smooth.

Melt 1 teaspoon of the butter in an 8-inch skillet. Coat the bottom of the pan with a very thin layer of batter; swirl to evenly spread the batter. Cook over medium heat until bubbles form on top and the crepe browns lightly on the bottom. Turn over; cook 30 seconds. While still in pan, put a heaping tablespoon of jam down the center of the crepe and roll up, pressing slightly. Transfer to a baking sheet. Cover with foil and place in the oven. Repeat to make 8 *palacsintas,* adding butter to the pan as you go. Sprinkle with confectioners' sugar pushed through a sieve. SERVES 4

Caramelized Almond Toasts

Lovely for breakfast or afternoon tea.

4 thick slices challah or brioche
2⁄3 cup sweetened condensed milk
1⁄2 teaspoon almond extract
1⁄2 cup sliced almonds
2 tablespoons confectioners' sugar

Preheat the oven to 375°F. Place the bread on a baking sheet. Stir together the condensed milk and almond extract. Spread a little on the bread to cover the surface. Sprinkle the surface evenly with the almonds; drizzle the remaining condensed milk on top. Bake 16 minutes, until golden. Cool; sprinkle with confectioners' sugar pushed through a sieve. MAKES 4

15 minutes

WARM RHUBARB COMPOTE WITH WALNUT-COCONUT CRUNCH

Radically delicious, this complex-sounding fruit-and-yogurt dish is ready to eat in 15 minutes and can either begin or end a special weekend brunch.

4 cups rhubarb, cut into $^1/_2$-inch pieces
$^2/_3$ cup plus 3 tablespoons sugar
$^1/_4$ cup crème de cassis or Chambord
$^1/_2$ cup walnut pieces
$^1/_2$ cup unsweetened organic flaked coconut
$^2/_3$ cup plain Greek yogurt
3 tablespoons wildflower honey

Wash the rhubarb; pat dry. In a medium saucepan, combine the rhubarb, $^2/_3$ cup of the sugar, and the cassis. Bring to a boil. Lower the heat and cover. Simmer, stirring occasionally, until soft, 10 minutes. Place saucepan in the freezer while you prepare the topping.

Combine the walnuts and remaining 3 tablespoons sugar in a medium skillet. Cook over high heat, stirring constantly with a wooden spoon, until the sugar melts and the nuts are crunchy, 3 minutes. Stir in the coconut and cook 30 seconds.

Transfer the rhubarb to 4 glasses. Sprinkle with the walnut-coconut mixture. Dollop with the yogurt; drizzle with the honey. SERVES 4

PEANUT BUTTER–GRANOLA BRUSCHETTA

This is embraced equally enthusiastically by kids, teens, and adults.

1¼ cups granola with raisins
⅓ cup honey
¼ cup creamy peanut butter
6 thick slices whole wheat baguette

Preheat the oven to 400°F. Combine the granola, honey, peanut butter, and a pinch of salt in a bowl and mix thoroughly. Toast the bread in the oven for 4 minutes, until golden. Spread each piece thickly with the granola mixture to cover completely. Return the bruschetta to the oven; bake for 5 minutes, until hot and gooey. Serve warm or at room temperature. MAKES 6

BREAKFAST "SURPRISE"

This is a trompe l'oeil—a trick of the eye—and a very pleasing way to end a morning meal. Be sure to buy a good brand of lemon curd.

3 cups plain Greek yogurt
4 heaping tablespoons lemon curd or orange marmalade
4 slices pound cake, cut ⅓ inch thick
2 tablespoons unsalted butter, melted

Put ¾ cup yogurt in the center of each of 4 large plates and smooth to make perfect flat circles (to resemble the whites of cooked eggs). Drop a tablespoon of lemon curd or marmalade dead center on each and shape to resemble an egg yolk.

Preheat a ridged grill pan. Brush the pound cake lightly with the melted butter. Grill the cake on both sides to resemble toast; cut in half on the diagonal. Serve alongside the "eggs." SERVES 4

MORNING FRUIT SOUP WITH TAPIOCA

This was taught to me by the incomparable food writer Gael Greene. A great way to start the day, it's both juice and fruit and very cool to look at. Make the base before you go to bed and stir in the diced fresh fruit in the a.m. Fun to eat with a side of Peanut Butter–Granola Bruschetta (page 21) or something from the 30-Minute Bakery (page 28).

2 tablespoons quick-cooking tapioca
$^1\!/_2$ cup frozen orange juice concentrate
1 tablespoon brown sugar
$^1\!/_2$ cup blueberries or chopped apple
$^1\!/_2$ cup finely diced peach or nectarine
$^1\!/_2$ cup finely diced strawberries or kiwifruits
$^1\!/_2$ cup finely diced banana or melon
2 tablespoons julienned fresh mint

Combine 1$^1\!/_2$ cups water and the tapioca in a small saucepan. Cook over medium heat, stirring constantly, until it comes to a full boil. Remove from the heat. Add the orange juice concentrate, sugar, and a pinch of salt. Let sit for 15 minutes. Stir well, cover, and refrigerate for 3 hours or overnight.

Stir in the fruit $^1\!/_2$ hour before serving. Ladle into flat soup bowls. Garnish with mint.
SERVES 4

HOMEMADE CREAM CHEESE ➤

Yogurt is to labneh as sour cream is to cream cheese: The same method used to make labneh can be used to make cream cheese from sour cream. Who knew?

1 cup sour cream

Put a large paper coffee filter in a large coffee filter cone or mesh sieve and place over a bowl to catch the liquid. Add the sour cream and drain overnight in the refrigerator. The mixture will be very thick. Add salt to taste. MAKES ABOUT $^3\!/_4$ CUP

Carrot Marmalade

This is a popular jam in Egypt. I adore it. Serve as you would any marmalade. It's delicious with butter, cream cheese, and goat cheese, too.

1 pound carrots, peeled
2 cups sugar
Grated zest and juice of 1 large lemon
$\frac{1}{4}$ teaspoon ground cardamom

Cut the carrots into 1-inch pieces. Pulse in a food processor until coarsely ground (about $\frac{1}{8}$-inch pieces). You will have about 3 cups. Put the carrots in a large saucepan. Add the sugar, lemon zest, 3 tablespoons lemon juice, the cardamom, and a large pinch of salt. Bring to a rapid boil. Stir and boil 1 minute. Reduce the heat to low and cook about 1 hour, stirring frequently. To test if it's ready, put 1 tablespoon of the mixture on a small plate. Put in freezer for 1 minute. If it becomes firm and doesn't flow, it's done (it will still look quite liquid in the pot). Let cool, cover, and refrigerate for up to 2 weeks. MAKES ABOUT 2 CUPS

Double-Rise Pancakes with Strawberries, Bananas & Almonds

Self-rising flour and extra baking powder levitate this batter to create the fluffiest pancakes imaginable. Use the batter within 15 hours of making.

2 extra-large eggs
1 cup buttermilk
3 tablespoons sugar
1 tablespoon baking powder
1 teaspoon vanilla extract
2 tablespoons olive oil, plus more for the griddle
1$\frac{1}{2}$ cups self-rising cake flour
1 cup pure maple syrup
1 cup finely diced bananas
1 cup finely diced strawberries
$\frac{1}{2}$ cup chopped roasted almonds

In a blender, combine the eggs, buttermilk, sugar, baking powder, vanilla, 2 tablespoons oil, flour, and $\frac{1}{2}$ teaspoon salt. Blend until smooth. Place the covered blender jar in the refrigerator overnight. Whirl the batter in the blender before using.

Combine the syrup, bananas, and strawberries in a medium saucepan. Cook 5 minutes over high heat, stirring often. Stir in $\frac{1}{4}$ cup of the almonds.

Heat a griddle; brush with oil. Stir the batter; ladle by $\frac{1}{4}$ cups onto the griddle, leaving space between the pancakes. Cook until browned, 3 minutes; turn, cook until golden, 2 minutes longer. Serve with the topping and remaining almonds. SERVES 4 TO 6 (MAKES ABOUT 14)

OVERNIGHT TABBOULEH WITH HARD-BOILED EGGS

When your morning meal is closer to noon, this is a terrific offering. It practically makes itself after you mix the ingredients together and chill overnight. Serve with feta cheese and a bowl of thick yogurt.

8 ounces coarse bulgur wheat
$1/4$ cup toasted sesame seeds
$1/2$ cup finely chopped carrots
$1/2$ cup finely chopped celery
$1/4$ cup finely chopped onion
1 ripe tomato, chopped
$1/2$ cup finely chopped red pepper
$1/2$ cup finely chopped green pepper
1 cup thick tomato juice
$1/2$ cup fresh lemon juice
$1/3$ cup extra-virgin olive oil
1 tablespoon fresh thyme leaves
9 hard-boiled eggs, halved

Combine all the ingredients except the eggs in a large bowl. Add 1 cup water and 1 teaspoon salt. Mix, cover, and refrigerate overnight.

Stir the tabbouleh; add salt and pepper. Mound on 6 plates. Serve each with 3 egg halves. SERVES 6

CHEESE STRATA WITH PROSCIUTTO, BASIL & SPINACH

This is the best kind of dish to serve for brunch. You assemble it the night before (or early in the morning) so that the layers—or striations—of bread, cheese, and spinach soak up the egg-and-milk base. Baked for 1 hour, the result is custardy, rich, and quiche-like.

3½ tablespoons unsalted butter
16 slices firm white sliced bread, crusts removed
8 ounces thinly sliced prosciutto
8 ounces feta cheese, crumbled
4 ounces provolone cheese, shredded
¼ cup finely minced scallions, white and green parts
4 ounces fresh baby spinach
½ cup finely julienned fresh basil
5 extra-large eggs
2 cups half-and-half
½ teaspoon Sriracha or hot sauce

Butter a 12 × 7-inch glass or ceramic dish with ½ tablespoon of the butter. Cover the bottom with 6 slices of bread, plus 1 slice cut in half to fill the spaces. Evenly cover the bread with half the prosciutto. Sprinkle with half of the feta, provolone, scallions, spinach, and basil. Repeat to make a second layer. Cut the remaining 2 bread slices into ¼-inch cubes; scatter over the top.

Beat together the eggs, half-and-half, and hot sauce. Pour over the strata; press down firmly with a spatula. Melt the remaining 3 tablespoons butter and drizzle over the top. Cover; refrigerate 5 hours or overnight.

Preheat the oven to 375°F. Uncover and bake 1 hour, until golden. SERVES 8

Before

After

FRESH FRUIT MUFFINS: BLUEBERRY, CINNAMON-APPLE, OR PEAR

These muffins are moist and delicate and can be made with ripe pears, tart apples, or fresh blueberries. They are a cinch to prepare and last several days in a covered tin.

1$\frac{1}{2}$ cups self-rising flour
$\frac{3}{4}$ cup granulated sugar
1 teaspoon ground cinnamon (1$\frac{1}{2}$ teaspoons if using apples)
1 extra-large egg
$\frac{1}{2}$ cup buttermilk
$\frac{1}{3}$ cup olive oil
1$\frac{1}{4}$ cups blueberries, diced peeled apples, or pears
3 tablespoons turbinado sugar

Preheat the oven to 350°F. Line 9 muffin cups with large paper liners.

Stir together the flour, granulated sugar, and cinnamon in a large bowl. In a medium bowl, beat together the egg, buttermilk, and oil. Stir the wet mixture into the dry mixture with a flexible rubber spatula until a batter forms. Gently stir in the fruit. Scoop the batter into the muffin cups. Sprinkle with the turbinado sugar. Bake for 25 minutes, until golden. Let cool. MAKES 9

PETIT PAINS AU CHOCOLAT

You could add a dab of raspberry preserves or a small piece of halvah to the filling.

1 sheet puff pastry, thawed until pliable but very cold
1 thin bar semisweet chocolate, about 4 ounces
1 large egg, beaten well with 1 tablespoon water
2 tablespoons sugar

Preheat the oven to 400°F. Line a baking sheet with parchment paper. Cut the cold pastry into 12 squares. Cut the chocolate into twelve 2 × ¾-inch rectangles. Place a chocolate piece on one edge of a piece of pastry and tightly roll up the pastry, keeping the seam on the bottom. Repeat.

Place the pastry bundles on the baking sheet seam side down and press the ends with the tines of a fork to seal tightly. Using a pastry brush, brush the pastry with the egg wash. Sprinkle very lightly with sugar. Bake 20 minutes, until puffed and golden brown. Transfer to a wire rack to cool. MAKES 12

FRUIT CHAUSSONS

Even if you've never worked with puff pastry before, making these will leave you feeling quite accomplished. They look like narrow envelopes with slits that slyly reveal their filling.

1 sheet frozen puff pastry, thawed
1 cup prune butter, apple or pear butter, or chunky fruit preserves
¼ cup sugar
½ teaspoon ground cinnamon
1 egg, beaten with 1 tablespoon water

Preheat the oven to 375°F. Roll out the pastry to a 12-inch square. Cut into 6 4 × 6-inch rectangles. Spread 2½ tablespoons fruit butter or preserves in a wide stripe down the length of each rectangle, a little to the right of dead center. Stir together the sugar and cinnamon. Sprinkle each filling with 1 teaspoon cinnamon-sugar. Fold the pastry over to make 2 × 6-inch rectangles. Press the edges together tightly and trim with a knife to make neat packages. Cut four 1-inch slits down the length of the folded edge of each pastry, about 1 inch apart. Brush the tops lightly with the egg wash. Sprinkle with the remaining cinnamon-sugar. Transfer to an ungreased baking sheet and bake 25 minutes, until golden. MAKES 6

WARM BUTTERMILK-CHEDDAR SCONES

Even if you don't have a magic touch making biscuits, this is a recipe that will help you succeed. Serve warm with sweet butter and a slick of apple jelly.

9 ounces very sharp Cheddar cheese
3 cups self-rising flour
2½ tablespoons sugar
10 tablespoons unsalted butter, room temperature
1 cup buttermilk
1 extra-large egg, beaten with 1 tablespoon water

Preheat the oven to 400°F. Shred the cheese on the large holes of a box grater. Combine the flour and sugar in the bowl of an electric mixer. Cut the butter into small pieces; add to the flour and mix until incorporated. While still beating, add the buttermilk and all but 1 tablespoon of the beaten egg. Mix briefly; add two-thirds of the cheese. Mix until the dough comes together.

Divide the dough in half. On a floured board, pat the dough into two 7-inch circles, about ½ inch thick. Using a pastry brush, "paint" the tops with the remaining beaten egg; scatter with the remaining cheese. Cut each circle into 6 wedges. Place the wedges 1 inch apart on an ungreased baking sheet. Bake 18 to 20 minutes, until golden. Let cool in the pan 10 minutes. MAKES 12

GOLDEN RAISIN–FENNEL SCONES

Lovely with sweet butter and marmalade.

$^{1}/_{3}$ cup chopped walnuts
2 cups all-purpose flour
$^{1}/_{3}$ cup sugar
2 teaspoons baking powder
$6^{1}/_{2}$ tablespoons unsalted butter, cut in small pieces
2 extra-large egg yolks plus 1 whole egg
$^{1}/_{2}$ cup buttermilk
$^{1}/_{2}$ cup golden raisins
1 tablespoon fennel seeds

Preheat the oven to 400°F. Grease a baking sheet with $^{1}/_{2}$ tablespoon of the butter. Lightly toast the walnuts in a small skillet over medium heat until fragrant, about 3 minutes.

Combine the flour, sugar, baking powder, and $^{1}/_{2}$ teaspoon salt in a large bowl. Mix well. Using your fingertips, blend in the butter until the mixture resembles fine crumbs. In a small bowl, whisk together 2 yolks and the buttermilk. Stir into the flour mixture. Mix in the walnuts, raisins, and fennel seeds until a dough forms. Knead several times on a floured board. Pat the dough into a 6-inch circle. Cut into 8 wedges. Place on the baking sheet 1 inch apart. Beat the egg with 1 tablespoon water. Brush the scones with the egg wash. Bake 16 to 18 minutes, until golden. Cool on a rack. MAKES 8

10-MINUTE SALADS

In traditional European kitchens, the salad—a simple hillock of dressed greens—always comes after the main course to avoid "interfering with the wine." When Californians began asserting their gastronomic selves, salads "launched" the meal. In the 1970s, the heyday of nouvelle cuisine, chefs showered hot things—nuggets of foie gras, clots of melting cheese, sizzling shrimp—onto chilled greens and in doing so signaled a culinary free-for-all.

Today a salad is a salad if you say it is. It can be warm. It can be cold. It can contain all manner of vegetables, fruit, meat, and fish. It doesn't even require lettuce anymore. At the Rainbow Room in New York, where I was consulting chef for many years, we served a 1-pound heirloom tomato, carved tableside, and capriciously called it: a salad.

The crux of this chapter is extreme freshness and purity. Because each of these salads can be prepared in less than 10 minutes, nothing loses its bouquet or texture. You pinch and pluck some herbs for pinpoint flavor bursts; you tear some tender leaves of market-fresh lettuce and dress them just-like-that; you sprinkle grappa on slivers of autumn pears to welcome a coverlet of rosy prosciutto—even that's a salad. You make Parmesan crisps and prosciutto "bacon" as crunchy accessories; you whirl a whole lemon and good olive oil for an instant vinaigrette—all these are radically simple approaches to creating stunning salads. Within moments, the colors and shapes of nature coalesce into small works of edible impressionism.

And the newly trendy raw fish preparations that a generation ago might have been alarming—crudo, seviche, *tiradito,* sashimi—these, fundamentally, are radical salads, too, since they require no cooking and only modest skills with a sharp knife.

My salads are streamlined in both time and effort. There are spins on classics, such as substituting Asian fish sauce for anchovies in a lightened Caesar salad; frying leaves of fresh basil to accompany sliced tomatoes and buffalo mozzarella; or making gravlax, usually a two-day process, in 10 minutes. You may redirect a salad's flavor and add complexity by adding snippets of Thai basil (for great mystery and perfume), sprinkles of fennel pollen, or chopped garlic chives.

Most of the salads in this chapter are meant for the beginning of a meal. These preludes are divided into two categories: The first is composed salads that are, for the most part, devoid of lettuce and instead fashioned from fresh vegetables or fish. The second group contains salads made with leafy greens such as mesclun, wild arugula, local greens (that you find seasonally in your farmers' market), and microgreens that one thankfully can find in most good supermarkets. And then there are my simple side salads, global in nature, meant to accompany—or transform— a hunk of protein. I've also included a quintet of 5-minute dressings, but no matter what salad you choose, or how you choose to dress it, the better the ingredients, the less need to fuss.

composed salads

Scallop Carpaccio with Seaweed Salad & Lemon Oil **36**

Tiradito **37**

Smoked Salmon with Petite Salade, Goat Cheese & Lime Vinaigrette **38**

Spooned Avocado, Lime & Smoked Paprika **38**

Last-Minute Gravlax **39**

Spiced Salmon on a Moroccan Salad **40**

Watermelon Salad with Feta & Black Olives **42**

A Pair of Prosciutto Salads **43**

Tomato, Buffalo Mozzarella & Fried Basil Salad **44**

Heirloom Tomatoes with Lemony Tahina **45**

Summer Tomatoes with Za'atar Pesto **45**

Beets with Balsamic Syrup, Mint & Walnuts **46**

Chilled Asparagus Tonnato with "Confetti" **46**

Asparagus, Bok Choy & Radicchio Salad **48**

Shaved Fennel with Parmigiano & Hot Pepper **48**

Warm Wild Mushrooms on Hummus **49**

little side salads

Eggplant and Roasted Pepper Salad with Feta **62**

Two-Cabbage Slaw **62**

Moroccan Carrots **63**

Couscous with Dates & Almonds **63**

Magic Beets **64**

Apple Cider Cucumbers **64**

Turkish Cucumbers **64**

Russian Red Bean Salad **65**

Italian White Bean Salad **65**

leafy green salads

Spring Mix with Carrot-Ginger Dressing & Prosciutto "Bacon" **50**

Salade Normande **50**

Pea Shoots & Greens with Goat Cheese & Cumin Vinaigrette **53**

Watercress, Endive & St. Agur Blue Cheese **53**

Endive, Mâche & Cranberry Salad with Parmesan Frico **54**

Lemony Arugula & Sun-Dried Tomato Salad with Smoked Mozzarella **55**

Baby Romaine & Crispy Chickpeas with Hazelnut Vinaigrette **56**

Grapefruit, Date & Arugula Salad with Parmesan Shards **57**

Fig, Fennel & Endive Salad with Pistachio Vinaigrette **58**

Grilled Romaine with Roquefort & Deviled Pecans **58**

Eggless Caesar Salad with Green Apple "Croutons" **59**

Arabic Orange Salad with Nasturtiums **61**

simple dressings

Carrot-Ginger Dressing **66**

Beet Vinaigrette **66**

Maple-Mustard Vinaigrette **66**

Lebanese Pomegranate Dressing **67**

Caesar-ette Dressing **67**

SCALLOP CARPACCIO WITH SEAWEED SALAD & LEMON OIL

This dish looks like something from a four-star restaurant. Jade strands of hiyashi wakame, *a Japanese seaweed salad that you can buy packaged from an Asian market, form a dramatic backdrop for gossamer slices of raw scallops. Buy the biggest scallops you can find and use only "dry" scallops, rather than the usual chemically dipped and waterlogged specimens; their surface should be matte, not shiny.*

$^1/_2$ cup olive oil
1 lemon, zested and halved
1 cup *hiyashi wakame* (seaweed salad)
4 or 5 huge sea scallops, about 10 ounces total

Put the oil in a small pitcher. Stir in the lemon zest; add a large pinch of salt. On each of 4 large plates, scatter $^1/_4$ cup seaweed salad to cover the entire interior of the plate in wisps. Slice the scallops paper-thin horizontally to form large circles. Squeeze a little lemon juice on the salad. Arrange the scallop slices over the salad, leaving spaces between them. Sprinkle with coarse sea salt. Drizzle with the lemon oil. SERVES 4

TIRADITO

Tiradito is the Peruvian equivalent of sashimi—except that tiradito *is glossed with a dressing or briefly marinated in assertive pepper purees. It is no coincidence that the innovative sushi chef Nobu Matsuhisa got his start in Lima, Peru, where such things are common. My* tiradito *begins with thin slices of impeccably fresh raw fish that get bathed in a tart elixir of a whole pureed lemon, olive oil, and garlic.*

12 ounces raw halibut or red snapper, sliced paper thin
1 small lemon
$^1/_2$ cup olive oil
1 medium garlic clove
3 tablespoons finely minced fresh chives
Handful tender mesclun or pea shoots

Arrange the fish slices in a tight circle without overlapping in the centers of 4 large plates. Sprinkle the fish lightly with salt. With a small sharp knife, cut the rind and pith from the lemon; quarter the flesh and remove the seeds. Process the lemon (including the rind and pith), oil, garlic, and $^1/_4$ teaspoon salt in a blender until very smooth. Spoon the dressing lightly over the fish to coat completely. Sprinkle with chives and coarsely cracked pepper. Garnish the plates with mesclun or pea shoots. SERVES 4

SMOKED SALMON WITH PETITE SALADE, GOAT CHEESE & LIME VINAIGRETTE

This is a sexy way to serve smoked salmon. A more radical approach would be to just put it on a plate with a wedge of lemon . . . but this is a show-off dish for company.

3 tablespoons extra-virgin olive oil
Grated zest and juice of 1 large lime
12 ounces thinly sliced smoked salmon
1 large handful microgreens or mesclun
3 ounces firm goat cheese
1 tablespoon pink peppercorns or fresh lemon thyme leaves

Put the oil in a cup. Stir in the lime zest, 1½ teaspoons lime juice, and a pinch of salt. Arrange the salmon slices on 4 large plates. Put a little mound of greens in the center of each. Cut 4 thin slices of cheese and place on the greens; crumble the remaining cheese over the salmon. Drizzle the salad and salmon with the lime oil. Sprinkle with pink peppercorns or thyme. SERVES 4

SPOONED AVOCADO, LIME & SMOKED PAPRIKA

This is a radically simplified version of guacamole that is very impromptu. Serve it almost as soon as you spoon it. Nice to serve with "batons" of crunchy jicama or Tortilla Ribbons (page 102).

4 very ripe medium avocados
2 to 4 large limes
20 grape tomatoes
¼ large red onion, slivered
¼ teaspoon smoked paprika, or more to taste
2 handfuls baby arugula
¼ cup olive oil

Cut the avocados in half; remove the pits. Using a large spoon, scoop large pieces into a large bowl. Squeeze the juice of 2 limes over the avocado. Cut the tomatoes in half lengthwise. Add the tomatoes and slivered onion to the bowl. Add the smoked paprika and salt. Add the arugula; drizzle oil over everything. Toss, adding more lime juice, salt, and smoked paprika to taste. SERVES 4

LAST-MINUTE GRAVLAX

This is a radically simple way to make gravlax. The traditional concept is to bury the salmon for 24 hours in a cover of dill, salt, and sugar. My version takes minutes and results in an ethereal texture and similar flavor notes. It's nice to drizzle this with a bit of Swedish mustard sauce, which takes only one minute to make (see below).

12 ounces center-cut fresh salmon, in one piece
1 teaspoon sugar
4 tablespoons finely chopped fresh dill
2 tablespoons mirin (sweet rice wine)
2 teaspoons rice vinegar

Cut the salmon in long paper-thin, horizontal slices, holding your knife parallel to the work surface. Divide the slices among 4 large round plates, overlapping, to cover the entire surfaces. Trim the edges to form a perfect circle. In a small bowl, mix the sugar with $^1\!/_2$ teaspoon salt; sprinkle on the fish. Sprinkle each plate with 1 tablespoon dill, then splash each with $1^1\!/_2$ teaspoons mirin and $^1\!/_2$ teaspoon rice vinegar. Sprinkle with a little salt and pepper. Let sit 5 minutes. Serve with the mustard sauce. SERVES 4

1-MINUTE MUSTARD SAUCE

1 tablespoon sugar
1 tablespoon distilled white vinegar
1 tablespoon Dijon mustard
2 tablespoons extra-virgin olive oil

Stir together the sugar and vinegar in a small bowl until the sugar dissolves. Stir in the mustard, then whisk in the oil. MAKES $^1\!/_4$ CUP

Spiced Salmon on a Moroccan Salad

Evocative flavors, colors, and textures all in one, and all in 10 minutes.

2 large juice oranges
$^1\!/_2$ cup torn fresh basil leaves
$^1\!/_2$ small red onion, slivered
10 large oil-cured black olives, pitted
2 cups torn escarole or mesclun
6 tablespoons extra-virgin olive oil
1 teaspoon chili powder
1 teaspoon ground cumin
$^1\!/_4$ teaspoon ground cinnamon
2 teaspoons salt
4 pieces fresh salmon without skin, 3 ounces each

With a sharp knife, remove the rind and pith from the oranges. Slice the oranges very thin; arrange on 4 large plates. Top with the basil and onion; scatter the olives around. Place greens on top. Drizzle each salad with a little oil.

In a small bowl, mix together the chili powder, cumin, cinnamon, and 2 teaspoons salt; rub the mixture onto one side of each piece of fish. Heat 1 tablespoon of the oil in a medium skillet. Add the fish, spice side down and cook 2 minutes over high heat. Turn over and cook until rare, 2 minutes longer. Arrange a piece of fish on each salad and drizzle with the remaining oil. SERVES 4

WATERMELON SALAD WITH FETA & BLACK OLIVES

In June 1997, a recipe for a savory watermelon salad first appeared in the food section of the New York Times. The salad was mine; the rest is history.

1¼-pound piece ripe red watermelon
6 ounces feta cheese, thinly sliced or crumbled
6 ounces oil-cured black olives, pitted and roughly chopped
3 tablespoons roughly chopped fresh basil
3 tablespoons extra-virgin olive oil
Handful of microgreens, optional

Remove the rind from the watermelon, then seed and thinly slice the flesh. Layer or toss it with the feta and olives. Top with the basil and black pepper. Drizzle with the oil; sprinkle with salt. Garnish with greens. SERVES 4 TO 6

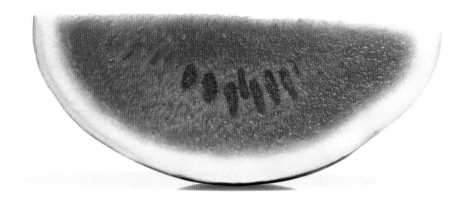

A Pair of Prosciutto Salads

Two classic salads, each with a twist. Either one is an occasion to splurge on the best imported prosciutto you can find; San Daniele is a terrific choice.

Prosciutto with Figs & Mint

12 fresh ripe small black figs
12 ounces thinly sliced prosciutto
Droplets of mild honey
¼ cup slivered fresh mint

Remove the stems from the figs. Cut each into 4 wedges. Drape 3 ounces prosciutto over the centers of 4 large plates. Place 12 fig wedges around the circumference of each plate. Drizzle droplets of honey on the figs and stud with bits of slivered mint. Add black pepper. SERVES 4

Prosciutto with Pears & Parmigiano

2 very ripe medium pears
Few drops grappa
12 ounces thinly sliced prosciutto
2-ounce chunk Parmigiano-Reggiano

Peel the pears; cut into very thin wedges and remove any seeds. Scatter the pears in the centers of 4 large plates. Add a few drops of grappa. Drape each serving with 3 ounces of prosciutto. Using a vegetable peeler, scrape shards of Parmesan over the prosciutto. Add black pepper. SERVES 4

TOMATO, BUFFALO MOZZARELLA & FRIED BASIL SALAD

This is a simple spin on the usual Salad Caprese. The fried basil stays crispy for a while, but it's best to fry it as close to serving as possible. Use fresh buffalo mozzarella, if you can find it.

5 very ripe large tomatoes
12 ounces best-quality fresh mozzarella
6 tablespoons olive oil plus $\frac{1}{2}$ cup for frying
2 teaspoons sherry vinegar
1 small garlic clove
20 fresh large basil leaves

Slice the tomatoes $\frac{1}{2}$ inch thick. Slice the mozzarella a bit thinner. Arrange overlapping slices of the tomatoes and cheese on 4 large plates or one large platter. In a small bowl, whisk together the 6 tablespoons oil, vinegar, and garlic pushed through a press.

Heat the remaining $\frac{1}{2}$ cup oil in a medium skillet until very hot. In several batches, fry the basil leaves for 1 to 2 minutes, until crispy. Transfer to paper towels; sprinkle with salt. Spoon the dressing over the tomatoes; top with crispy basil. SERVES 4

leaves of fried basil

Heirloom Tomatoes with Lemony Tahina

What's radical is that the dressing for this summer salad contains neither oil nor vinegar. The more varied the tomato colors, the more interesting the salad.

$^1/_2$ cup well-stirred tahina
Grated zest and juice of 2 large lemons
8 ripe medium heirloom tomatoes
$^1/_3$ cup torn fresh flat-leaf parsley or cilantro leaves

Put the tahina in a food processor. Add half of the zest and 5 tablespoons juice. Process, adding up to $^1/_2$ cup water, until smooth and thick (between heavy cream and mayonnaise). Add a generous amount of salt and pepper. Cut the tomatoes into wedges. Arrange on 4 large plates or a platter. Sprinkle with salt. Spoon the dressing over the tomatoes. Sprinkle the remaining zest on top and scatter with parsley. SERVES 4

Summer Tomatoes with Za'atar Pesto

You can make this even when it isn't summer—just find the best tomatoes possible. Campari tomatoes are nice, as are tomatoes on the vine from Israel. I always keep za'atar, a heady spice blend of dried hyssop, ground sumac, and sesame seeds, in my fridge, and you will find it used elsewhere in this book. It looks like marijuana, smells like Jerusalem, and is available in Middle Eastern markets.

$^1/_4$ cup pine nuts
3 tablespoons za'atar
3 tablespoons freshly grated Parmigiano-Reggiano
6 tablespoons extra-virgin olive oil
4 large ripe tomatoes

Lightly toast the pine nuts in a small skillet over medium heat until fragrant, about 3 minutes. In a medium bowl, stir together the za'atar, cheese, and oil. Cut the tomatoes in $^1/_4$-inch-thick slices. Arrange on a platter overlapping. Salt lightly. Spoon the za'atar pesto over the tomatoes; scatter the pine nuts on top. SERVES 4

BEETS WITH BALSAMIC SYRUP, MINT & WALNUTS

The radical idea here is my balsamic syrup, which adds a level of elegance to commodity canned beets. Vibrant bits of mint, preferably spearmint, tie all the flavors together.

  1 cup walnut halves
  $^1/_2$ cup balsamic vinegar
  2 medium garlic cloves
  2 (14-ounce) cans small beets, drained well
  2 tablespoons olive oil
  $^3/_4$ cup coarsely chopped fresh mint
  4 ounces firm goat cheese, coarsely crumbled

Lightly toast the walnuts in a small skillet over medium heat until fragrant, about 2 minutes. Remove from the pan and set aside. Put the vinegar in the skillet; add 1 garlic clove pushed through a press. Bring to a boil; boil until reduced to 3 tablespoons. Cut the beets in half; put in a large bowl. Add the reduced vinegar and walnuts. Put the oil in a small bowl; add the remaining garlic clove pushed through a press. Toss the garlic oil with the beets. Add salt and pepper. Transfer to a platter. Top with the mint and goat cheese. SERVES 4

CHILLED ASPARAGUS TONNATO WITH "CONFETTI" ➤

The inspiration for this dish comes from vitello tonnato—*the Italian preparation of cold sliced veal covered with a creamy tuna sauce and sprinkled with capers.*

  1$^1/_2$ pounds medium asparagus, trimmed
  $^1/_4$ cup extra-virgin olive oil
  5-ounce can oil-packed Italian tuna
  1 large garlic clove
  1 large lemon
  Handful mesclun, torn into tiny "confetti" pieces
  2 tablespoons capers, drained

Bring a large skillet of salted water to a boil; fill a bowl with ice water. Place the asparagus in boiling water. Cook until crisp-tender, 6 minutes. Drain immediately and plunge into the ice water; let sit for 3 minutes. Drain, pat dry, and divide the asparagus among 4 plates. Drizzle with 2 tablespoons of the oil.

Combine the tuna and its oil, the garlic, the remaining 2 tablespoons olive oil, and 2 thin lemon slices with rind (without seeds) in a food processor. Process until *very* smooth, adding enough water and lemon juice so that the texture resembles thick heavy cream. Add salt and pepper. Pour the dressing over the asparagus; sprinkle with the mesclun "confetti" and capers. SERVES 4

don't forget the capers

Asparagus, Bok Choy & Radicchio Salad

Sharp, salty provolone perched atop a hill of vaguely Asian ingredients is a mixed metaphor of flavors that tastes truly new. It's a nice salad alongside to my New Asia Steak (page 240).

> 1 pound thin asparagus, trimmed
> 2 tablespoons olive oil
> 1 large garlic clove, smashed and peeled
> 2 large heads baby bok choy
> 1 small head radicchio
> 1 tablespoon rice vinegar
> 4-ounce piece provolone cheese

Cut the asparagus on the bias into $1/3$ inch pieces. Heat the oil and garlic in a large skillet. Add the asparagus; cook over high heat 1 minute. Transfer the asparagus, oil, and garlic to a large bowl. Push the garlic through a press back into the bowl.

Separate the bok choy leaves from the bulbs. Thinly slice the bulbs and tear the leaves into large pieces. Cut the radicchio leaves into 1-inch pieces. Toss the radicchio and bok choy in the bowl with the warm asparagus. Add the vinegar and salt and pepper. Using a vegetable peeler, shave shards of provolone on top. SERVES 4

Shaved Fennel with Parmigiano & Hot Pepper

I love this as an unusual starter to precede a hefty main course, but it is also a nice side salad. The little nubbins of cheese are unexpected. Sometimes I add fresh orange segments, too.

> 1 large fennel bulb, about $1\frac{1}{2}$ pounds
> 2 tablespoons extra-virgin olive oil
> 1 tablespoon white balsamic vinegar
> Large pinch red-pepper flakes
> 4-ounce piece Parmigiano-Reggiano
> 2 big handfuls baby arugula

Trim the feathery fronds from the fennel bulb; chop to make $1/4$ cup and set aside. Cut the fennel in half lengthwise and cut crosswise as thinly as possible. Place in a bowl. Add the oil, vinegar, pepper flakes, and salt. Break the cheese into very small pieces; add to the salad and toss. Stir in the arugula. Transfer to 4 large plates and scatter the chopped fronds on top. SERVES 4

WARM WILD MUSHROOMS ON HUMMUS

This is a lovely main course for vegetarians. The "instant" hummus—made with Asian sesame oil instead of tahina—is a radically simple idea from my sister-in-law, Gail, and it's great.

2 cups canned chickpeas, rinsed and drained
4 1/2 tablespoons freshly squeezed lemon juice
2 teaspoons ground cumin
1 teaspoon Asian sesame oil
1 small garlic clove
1/2 cup olive oil
6 ounces sliced shiitake mushrooms
6 ounces sliced cremini or baby portobello mushrooms
1/2 cup slivered fresh basil

Put the chickpeas, 3 tablespoons of the lemon juice, cumin, sesame oil, and garlic in a food processor; process briefly. Add 1/4 cup of the olive oil and 3 tablespoons water and process until smooth. Add salt. Divide the hummus among 4 large plates. Smooth into large circles and make a depression in the center of each.

Heat the remaining 1/4 cup oil in a large skillet. Add the mushrooms and 1/4 cup of the basil. Cook over high heat until the mushrooms are soft, 3 minutes. Add salt and pepper. Mound into the centers of the hummus; squeeze a few drops of lemon on tops. Garnish with the remaining 1/4 cup basil. SERVES 4

SPRING MIX WITH CARROT-GINGER DRESSING ➤ & PROSCIUTTO "BACON"

This dressing uses very little oil and has loads of fresh flavors. In addition to the spring mix here, it is lovely spooned over sliced cucumbers or poured over chilled steamed broccoli. My daughter dips strawberries in it! There is great synergy among the flavors.

12 thin slices prosciutto
$^1/_2$ cup diced carrot
$^1/_3$ cup orange juice
4 teaspoons sugar
4 teaspoons rice vinegar
1 tablespoon chopped onion
1 quarter-size slice peeled fresh ginger
2 tablespoons olive oil
5 ounces spring mix

Preheat the oven to 400°F. Lay the prosciutto on a rimmed baking sheet in a single layer. Bake for 8 minutes, until crispy. Cool for 2 minutes on the sheet.

Combine the carrot, orange juice, sugar, rice vinegar, onion, and ginger in a food processor and process until very smooth. Stir in the oil and $^1/_2$ teaspoon salt. Put the greens in a large bowl and toss with the dressing. Add salt and pepper. Divide the greens among 4 large plates and top each salad with two slices of crisped prosciutto. SERVES 4

SALADE NORMANDE

This radical dressing comes from the classic French repertoire and is improbably good.

2 large heads Boston lettuce
$^2/_3$ cup heavy cream
2 tablespoons freshly squeezed lemon juice
$^1/_4$ cup chopped fresh chives
4 teaspoons chopped fresh tarragon

Tear the lettuce in large pieces and put in a large bowl. Whisk together the cream and lemon juice. Toss the dressing with the greens and add salt and pepper. Add the chives and tarragon and toss again. SERVES 4

prosciutto "bacon"

spring mix with carrot-ginger dressing

◄ Pea Shoots & Greens with Goat Cheese & Cumin Vinaigrette

A garden of earthy delights. You can find pea shoots at local farmers' markets in spring, early summer, and fall.

3$\frac{1}{2}$ ounces pea shoots
4 ounces mesclun
$\frac{1}{3}$ cup olive oil
1 teaspoon Dijon mustard
1 teaspoon red wine vinegar
$\frac{1}{2}$ teaspoon ground cumin
1 medium garlic clove
6-ounce log fresh goat cheese
$\frac{1}{4}$ cup salted shelled sunflower seeds

Discard the bottom inch of the pea shoots. Toss the shoots with the mesclun in a large bowl. Whisk together the olive oil, mustard, vinegar, and cumin. Push the garlic through a press into the dressing and stir. Toss the salad with the vinaigrette and add salt and pepper. Divide the salad among 4 large plates. Slice the cheese into 4 disks and place 1 on each salad. Sprinkle with sunflower seeds. SERVES 4

Watercress, Endive & St. Agur Blue Cheese

While I have never had a blue cheese I didn't love, I am particularly enamored of St. Agur from France. It is distinctively creamy and worth the splurge.

$\frac{2}{3}$ cup walnut halves
3 large heads endive, about 12 ounces
2 small bunches watercress
$\frac{1}{4}$ cup walnut oil
4 teaspoons rice vinegar
4 ounces St. Agur or creamy Danish blue cheese

Lightly toast the walnuts in a small skillet over medium heat until fragrant, about 2 minutes. Transfer to a small bowl and let cool. Trim the bottoms of the endive; cut in half lengthwise. Separate the leaves and place in a large bowl. Remove the stems from the watercress and discard; wash the leaves, dry well, and add to the bowl. Add the oil and vinegar and toss. Add the walnuts and crumble in the cheese. Toss again; add salt and pepper. SERVES 4

ENDIVE, MÂCHE & CRANBERRY SALAD WITH PARMESAN FRICO

This is a very impressive salad for company. The lacy Parmesan wafers, or fricos, *can be made as you toast the walnuts. Raspberry vinegar is a blast from the past but it ties all these flavors together with great finesse.*

$^1/_2$ cup freshly grated Parmigiano-Reggiano
2 teaspoons flour
$^1/_2$ cup walnut halves
2 large heads Belgian endive, about 8 ounces
$2^1/_2$ ounces mâche
2 teaspoons sugar
1 tablespoon raspberry vinegar
1 tablespoon Dijon mustard
1 teaspoon mustard seeds
$^1/_3$ cup olive oil
$^1/_2$ cup unsweetened dried cranberries

Preheat the oven to 400°F. Stir together the cheese and flour. Line a baking sheet with parchment paper or a silicone liner. Make 4 mounds of cheese on the lined baking sheet. Using your fingers, spread each into a thin 3-inch circle. Put the walnuts in a pie tin. Bake both for 8 minutes, until the nuts are fragrant and the *fricos* are golden and crisp; cool for 2 minutes.

Trim the bottoms of the endive. Cut crosswise into $^1/_2$-inch pieces; place in a large bowl. Add the mâche. Combine the sugar and vinegar in a small bowl; whisk in the mustard, mustard seeds, and oil until creamy. Toss the salad with the dressing. Add the walnuts, cranberries, and salt and pepper and toss again. Divide among 4 large plates; top each salad with a *frico*. SERVES 4

LEMONY ARUGULA & SUN-DRIED TOMATO SALAD WITH SMOKED MOZZARELLA

For this dressing, small pieces of a peeled lemon get whirled in a blender with garlic and good olive oil until emulsified. That's it! It deliciously unifies a salad of many flavors.

1 small lemon
2 medium garlic cloves, chopped
$\frac{1}{2}$ cup extra-virgin olive oil
3 large bunches arugula
2 small heads radicchio
12 ounces smoked mozzarella, in one piece
$\frac{3}{4}$ cup oil-packed sun-dried tomatoes
6 tablespoons pine nuts

Using a small knife, remove the rind and pith from the lemon and discard. Cut the lemon into small pieces, removing the seeds. Place in a blender. Add the garlic, oil, and salt and pepper. Process until very smooth.

Wash the arugula; dry well. Place in a large bowl. Slice the radicchio paper-thin; add to the bowl. Toss with all but 3 tablespoons of the dressing. Cut the cheese into 12 thin slices; cut each in half. Divide the salad among 6 salad plates. Place 4 overlapping cheese half slices on each salad. Cut the dried tomatoes into strips; scatter on top. Drizzle with the remaining dressing. Lightly toast the pine nuts in a small skillet over medium heat until golden, about 2 minutes. Scatter on the salads. SERVES 6

Baby Romaine & Crispy Chickpeas with Hazelnut Vinaigrette

Chickpeas fried in hazelnut oil become crispy "croutons" for a simple salad. You may add a pinch of cumin or smoked paprika as they cook. Delicious with roast chicken.

$\frac{1}{2}$ cup hazelnut oil
1 cup canned chickpeas, rinsed, drained, and patted dry
1 medium garlic clove
Grated zest and juice of 1 lemon
5 ounces baby romaine and mesclun mix
1 very ripe large tomato

Heat 2 tablespoons of the oil in a large skillet. Add the chickpeas with a large pinch of salt. Cook over high heat, stirring, until crispy, 3 minutes.

Put the remaining oil in a large bowl. Add the garlic pushed through a press. Add the lemon zest and 1$\frac{1}{2}$ tablespoons lemon juice. Whisk; add salt and pepper. Add the lettuces and toss. Divide the salad among 4 large plates. Quarter the tomato and cut each quarter into 4 thin wedges. Tuck 4 wedges into each salad. Scatter the warm chickpeas on top of each. SERVES 4

GRAPEFRUIT, DATE & ARUGULA SALAD WITH PARMESAN SHARDS

This is a lovely merger of tastes. Although there is no vinegar in the dressing, it gets punctuations of acidity from the grapefruit. Sometimes I collect a little of the juice to drizzle on top.

2 large grapefruit
8 very large moist Medjool dates
5 ounces wild arugula or baby arugula
⅓ cup olive oil
3-ounce chunk Parmigiano-Reggiano
Extra-virgin olive oil for drizzling

Grate the zest of 1 grapefruit and set aside. Remove the rind and pith from both grapefruit; cut between the membranes to release the segments. Quarter the dates lengthwise; remove the pits. Toss the arugula with the olive oil and salt. Divide the arugula among 4 large plates. Sprinkle with the zest and arrange the grapefruit segments and dates on top. Using a vegetable peeler, cut shards of cheese and scatter over the dates. Add coarsely cracked pepper and drizzle with olive oil. SERVES 4

FIG, FENNEL & ENDIVE SALAD WITH PISTACHIO VINAIGRETTE

Here's a lush salad made with juicy fresh figs against a background of bitter, salty, pungent, and sweet flavors. It's a great start to a meal or served after the main course with a slice of Roquefort cheese.

9 large fresh purple figs
1 large fennel bulb
3 cups baby arugula
3 large heads Belgian endive
$\frac{1}{4}$ cup olive oil
$2\frac{1}{2}$ tablespoons pure maple syrup
3 tablespoons rice vinegar
1 tablespoon Dijon mustard
1 small garlic clove
$\frac{1}{2}$ cup shelled roasted pistachios, coarsely chopped

Trim the figs and cut lengthwise into quarters. Remove the fronds from the fennel; chop to make $\frac{1}{4}$ cup and set aside for garnish. Halve the fennel bulb lengthwise. Place cut side down on a board; slice very thinly across its width. Place in a large bowl with the arugula. Slice the endive $\frac{1}{4}$ inch thick on the bias; add to the bowl.

Whisk together the oil, maple syrup, vinegar, and mustard; add the garlic pushed through a press. Process $\frac{1}{4}$ cup of the pistachios in a food processor until finely ground. Add to the dressing. Pour the dressing over the salad; toss and add salt and pepper. Top with the remaining pistachios, figs, and chopped fennel fronds. SERVES 6

GRILLED ROMAINE WITH ROQUEFORT & DEVILED PECANS

Add a level of complexity to any salad by lightly grilling or broiling the lettuce before assembling.

$\frac{1}{2}$ cup pecan halves
$1\frac{1}{2}$ teaspoons Worcestershire sauce
12 ounces Roquefort cheese, crumbled
$\frac{1}{2}$ cup mayonnaise
$\frac{1}{2}$ cup plain Greek yogurt
$\frac{1}{2}$ teaspoon hot-pepper sauce
4 large romaine lettuce hearts
$\frac{1}{4}$ cup extra-virgin olive oil

Combine the pecans and Worcestershire sauce in a small skillet. Cook over medium heat, stirring, until dry, 2 minutes. Add salt and pepper. Let cool. Put half of the cheese, the mayonnaise, and yogurt in a food processor; process until smooth. Add the pepper sauce and $1/4$ cup water and process until creamy.

Preheat the broiler. Quarter each romaine heart lengthwise. Using a pastry brush, brush the romaine with the oil. Place on a rimmed baking sheet. Broil several minutes on each side, until lightly browned and wilted. Alternatively, lightly "grill" the lettuce in a hot grill pan. Arrange the lettuce side by side on a large platter. Spoon dressing over the lettuce and top with the pecans and remaining cheese. SERVES 6

EGGLESS CAESAR SALAD WITH GREEN APPLE "CROUTONS"

This version of Caesar salad—one of the simplest imaginable—was formulated with kids in mind. It is light and airy and made without eggs or anchovies. Instead I sneak in a little Thai fish sauce. Granny Smith apples take the place of croutons.

$1/2$ cup chopped pecans
$1/2$ cup olive oil
1 small garlic clove
2 tablespoons freshly squeezed lemon juice
1 teaspoon Dijon mustard
1 teaspoon Thai fish sauce
2 romaine hearts
1 cup freshly grated Parmigiano-Reggiano
2 large green apples, cut into $1/3$-inch cubes

Lightly toast the pecans in a small skillet over medium-high heat until fragrant, about 2 minutes. Be careful not to burn them! Cool on a plate.

In a medium bowl, whisk together the oil, garlic pushed through a press, lemon juice, mustard, and fish sauce. Set aside. Wash the romaine and cut into $3/4$-inch pieces. Dry well with paper towels and put in a large bowl. Add $1/2$ cup of the cheese. Pour in the dressing and toss gently to coat. Add $1/4$ cup of the cheese, the apples, and pecans and toss again. Divide among 6 plates. Sprinkle with the remaining $1/4$ cup cheese. SERVES 6

ARABIC ORANGE SALAD WITH NASTURTIUMS

Savory, tart, and sweet, this Moroccan-inspired salad can begin a meal or come after the main course with fresh goat cheese or a hard sheep's milk cheese. Almonds or walnuts may be used instead of pistachios.

1/4 cup shelled pistachios, coarsely chopped
2 large navel oranges
2 large blood oranges
1 tablespoon confectioners' sugar
1/4 teaspoon ground cinnamon
6 large radishes
3 large handfuls mâche
1/4 cup extra-virgin olive oil, plus more for drizzling
2 teaspoons pomegranate molasses
16 nasturtium flowers

Lightly toast the pistachios in a small skillet over medium heat until fragrant, about 2 minutes. Set aside. With a sharp knife, cut away the rind and all the white pith from all 4 oranges. Cut the oranges into thin slices. Arrange on 4 large plates or on a platter. Stir together the sugar and cinnamon and sprinkle on the oranges. Trim the radishes; slice very thin and arrange over the oranges. Distribute the mâche over the oranges. Whisk together the oil and pomegranate molasses; add salt. Drizzle the dressing over the salad. Distribute the pistachios and nasturtiums on the salad. Drizzle with more oil. SERVES 4

EGGPLANT AND ROASTED PEPPER SALAD WITH FETA

This tastes like an elemental ratatouille. Add capers, olives, or tomato paste, if you like.

    1 large eggplant, 1 pound
    4 tablespoons olive oil
    12 ounces jarred roasted peppers
    1 small garlic clove
    3 ounces feta cheese
    3 tablespoons fresh basil chiffonade

Preheat the broiler. Peel the eggplant; cut into $\frac{1}{2}$-inch cubes. Put on a rimmed baking sheet; toss with 3 tablespoons of the oil. Broil 4 minutes; turn with a spatula and broil 4 to 5 minutes longer, until lightly browned.

Meanwhile, drain the peppers, saving 3 tablespoons of the liquid. Rinse the peppers under cold water; pat dry and coarsely chop. Transfer the hot eggplant to a large bowl. Add the peppers, the reserved pepper liquid, the remaining 1 tablespoon oil, and garlic pushed through a press. Add salt and pepper; toss. Cover and chill for 1 hour or up to 1 day. Top with the feta cheese and basil. SERVES 4

TWO-CABBAGE SLAW

Although I like to cut my own green cabbage, for simplicity's sake I sometimes buy preshredded red cabbage. The addictive dressing can be made 2 days ahead. For real indulgence, crumble in some blue cheese or cooked bacon.

    1 medium green cabbage, about 2 pounds
    10 ounces shredded red cabbage
    $\frac{1}{3}$ cup rice vinegar
    $\frac{1}{3}$ cup sugar
    $\frac{2}{3}$ cup mayonnaise
    $\frac{1}{2}$ cup dried cranberries
    $1\frac{1}{2}$ teaspoons celery seed

Cut the green cabbage in half through the core. Remove the core. Place cut side down on a board and slice $\frac{1}{8}$ inch thick. Place in a large bowl; add the red cabbage. In another bowl, stir together the vinegar and sugar until the sugar dissolves. Stir in the mayonnaise, cranberries, celery seed, and 1 teaspoon salt. Pour over the cabbage; mix thoroughly. Chill for 1 hour or up to 1 day. Add salt and pepper. SERVES 6 TO 8

Moroccan Carrots

I make this often to serve as a tapa *with drinks or as a delicious side dish.*

1½ pounds slender carrots, peeled
6 tablespoons extra-virgin olive oil
5 tablespoons red wine vinegar
1 tablespoon ground cumin
1 tablespoon sweet paprika
Large pinch ground cinnamon
1 large garlic clove
⅓ cup julienned fresh flat-leaf parsley

Cut the carrots on the bias ¼ inch thick. Bring a pot of water fitted with a steamer basket to a rapid boil. Add the carrots, cover, and steam for 8 minutes, until just tender. In a large bowl, whisk together the oil, vinegar, cumin, paprika, and cinnamon. Push the garlic through a press and add to the dressing with 1 teaspoon salt. Add the hot carrots to the dressing. Toss well and add salt and pepper. Chill for several hours or up to 1 day. Stir in the parsley before serving. SERVES 4 OR MORE

Couscous with Dates & Almonds

⅓ cup slivered almonds
Scant 2 cups couscous
1½ cups canned chickpeas, rinsed and drained
¼ cup extra-virgin olive oil
2 scallions, finely chopped, white and green parts
10 large dates, pitted and finely diced
1 teaspoon ground cardamom
Grated zest and juice of 2 lemons
⅓ cup coarsely chopped cilantro

In a large saucepan, bring 2 cups salted water to a boil. Lightly toast the almonds in a small skillet over medium heat until fragrant, about 2 minutes. Set aside. Add the couscous to the boiling water and stir. Cover and remove from the heat. Let sit for 4 minutes. Uncover and fluff with a fork. Transfer to a large bowl. Add the almonds, chickpeas, olive oil, scallions, dates, cardamom, lemon zest, and 3 tablespoons lemon juice. Stir in the cilantro and salt and pepper. SERVES 6

MAGIC BEETS

I call these magic beets because they can be made in 3 minutes.

14-ounce can small whole beets
3 tablespoons rice vinegar
3 tablespoons pure maple syrup
1 teaspoon olive oil
$\frac{1}{4}$ teaspoon ground coriander

Slice the beets about $\frac{1}{8}$ inch thick. Put in a container with a tight-fitting lid, such as a large jam jar. Pour in the vinegar, maple syrup, oil, coriander, and $\frac{1}{2}$ teaspoon salt. Cover tightly and shake. Serve right away, or chill for up to 2 days. SERVES 2 OR 3

APPLE CIDER CUCUMBERS

Fat-free, refreshing, and crisp. You may also add slivers of red onion.

$\frac{1}{2}$ cup apple cider vinegar
$\frac{1}{3}$ cup pure maple syrup
$1\frac{1}{2}$ seedless hothouse cucumbers, about 1 pound
3 tablespoons chopped fresh dill

In a medium bowl, whisk together the vinegar and maple syrup. Peel the cucumbers; slice into thin rounds and add to the dressing. Add salt and pepper. Stir in the dill. Cover and chill for 1 hour or up to 1 day. SERVES 4

TURKISH CUCUMBERS

This is a version of a Turkish cucumber salad known as cacik.

2 medium cucumbers
1 cup plain Greek yogurt
1 teaspoon Asian sesame oil
2 teaspoons black sesame seeds or onion seeds
3 tablespoons slivered cilantro or mint

Peel the cucumbers and cut in half lengthwise. Remove the seeds using a small spoon. Slice into $\frac{1}{4}$-inch half-moons. Place in a bowl. Stir in the yogurt, oil, salt, and pepper and refrigerate for 2 to 24 hours. Sprinkle with the sesame seeds and cilantro. SERVES 4

TAKE THE "CAN" OUT OF CANNED BEANS

The red bean version is adapted from a Russian salad called lobio. *Make it part of a global antipasto to begin a meal or take it on a picnic. The surprise in the white bean variation is freshly grated ginger—you hardly taste it, but it makes the flavor of fresh lemon reverberate and it seems to firm up the beans.*

RUSSIAN RED BEAN SALAD

2 (19-ounce) cans red kidney beans
¾ cup walnut pieces
⅓ cup finely chopped cilantro
¼ cup finely minced scallions, white and green parts
3 tablespoons extra-virgin olive oil
2½ tablespoons red wine vinegar
1 teaspoon ground cumin

Rinse the beans in a colander under cold water. Pat dry; place in a large bowl. Process the walnuts in a food processor until very finely ground. Add to the bowl with the cilantro, scallions, oil, vinegar, and cumin. Add salt and pepper and toss. Chill for 1 hour or up to 2 days; adjust seasonings before serving. SERVES 4

ITALIAN WHITE BEAN SALAD

19-ounce can white cannellini beans
1 cup wild arugula
½ cup torn fresh basil leaves
¼ cup paper-thin sliced red onion
12 grape tomatoes, halved lengthwise
½-inch piece peeled fresh ginger
¼ cup extra-virgin olive oil
1 tablespoon freshly squeezed lemon juice, or more to taste
3 tablespoons freshly grated Parmigiano-Reggiano

Rinse the beans under cold water; drain and pat dry. Put in a large bowl. Add the arugula, basil, onion, and tomatoes. Grate the ginger on a Microplane grater and put in a medium bowl. Add the oil, lemon juice, and grated cheese and mix well. Toss with the beans and add salt, pepper, and more lemon juice if needed. SERVES 4

Carrot-Ginger Dressing

$1/2$ cup diced fresh carrot
$1/3$ cup orange juice
2 tablespoons sugar
1 tablespoon chopped onion
1 tablespoon olive oil
4 teaspoons rice vinegar
1 teaspoon chopped peeled fresh ginger

Combine all the ingredients in a food processor and process until very smooth. MAKES 1 CUP

Beet Vinaigrette

1 cup chopped canned beets
$1/2$ tablespoons balsamic vinegar
$1/4$ cup olive oil

Put the beets in a food processor with the vinegar and $1/3$ cup water and process until smooth. Continue to process, slowly adding the oil, until very smooth. Add salt and pepper. MAKES 1¼ CUPS

Maple-Mustard Vinaigrette

$1/3$ cup olive oil
2 tablespoons pure maple syrup
2 tablespoons rice vinegar
2 teaspoons Dijon mustard
1 small garlic clove

Whisk together the oil, maple syrup, vinegar, and mustard in small bowl. Add the garlic pushed through a press. Add salt and pepper. MAKES ½ CUP

Lebanese Pomegranate Dressing

$1/2$ cup extra-virgin olive oil
3 tablespoons pomegranate molasses

Whisk together the oil and molasses until blended. Add a large pinch of salt.
MAKES $2/3$ CUP

Caesar-ette Dressing

$1/2$ cup olive oil
1 small garlic clove
2 tablespoons freshly squeezed lemon juice
1 teaspoon Dijon mustard
1 teaspoon Thai fish sauce
2 tablespoons freshly grated Parmigiano-Reggiano

Whisk together the oil and the garlic pushed through a press. Whisk in the lemon juice, mustard, fish sauce, and cheese. Add salt and pepper. MAKES $3/4$ CUP

SOUPS

There I was, giving a cooking demonstration in New York City's vibrant Union Square Market, when I ran out of food. The line for "free tastes" was growing ominously that sultry summer afternoon. What to do? I begged a farmer for a bushel of beefsteak tomatoes and started pureeing the heck out of them in a blender that teetered atop a rickety table. In minutes, the natural pectin bound the tomatoes into a mousse-y froth worthy of a snapshot in *Molecular Gastronomy Digest.* A touch of *fleur de sel* made the flavor soar. Everyone wanted a taste of Pink Tomato Frappé.

You will find that recipe here, along with dozens of other soups that are, in one way or another, radically simple. They just taste complicated.

Some of the soups are lean and sexy (Ginger Bouillon with Enoki Mushrooms) and take no longer than 5 minutes to prepare; some are rough-hewn (a lusty Split Pea Soup with Soppressata) but require only a handful of ingredients. Some exploit a new (or very old ingredient)—e.g., chickpea flour to make a new-fangled "hummus" soup. And some defy centuries-old approaches to classics, like my "extreme" onion soup made with whole buttered onions that bake for 4 hours.

A few are unlikely as can be but serve an important function, for they are made with ingredients you might have in your pantry but would never consider offering as "soup" to sophisticated guests. For example, Tomato-Anisette Soup is based on V8 and contemporized with Thai fish sauce. The combination is riveting, especially under a coverlet of lightly salted whipped cream. Beet Soup with Lemon Crème Fraîche, based on canned beets, is goosed up with vinegar and lemon zest. These are exquisite "emergency" soups.

There are chilled soups that make great preludes to any meal—no matter the season. What makes them so appealing is that they can be prepared a day or two in advance to let the alchemy of their flavors deepen. What makes them so peculiar is that many of them are also delicious served hot! Jade Soup, made from little more than boiled zucchini mixed with fresh crab and perfumed with dill, is a great example, as is Cauliflower Vichyssoise, which is luxurious at both temperatures.

Nor did I overlook gazpacho, perhaps the best-known chilled soup. I propose two variations: One is the color of lipstick and thickened with a leftover breakfast bagel instead of bread; another is verdant green, sporting bright Asian flavors and thickened with Japanese bread crumbs. It also makes a great sauce for simply grilled halibut.

Many soups might sound familiar but are accessorized in inventive new ways. Green Pea–Wasabi Soup gets a flounce of crunchy wasabi peas; Parsnip-Apple Soup gets "bacon candy"; Truffled Asparagus Soup is drizzled with a syrupy reduction of pineapple juice. These are radically simple ways to make a statement. No doubt you'll devise a few of your own.

5-minute soups

Sweet Tomato–Watermelon Soup 72

Avocado Soup with Fino Sherry 72

Pink Tomato Frappés 74

Tomato-Anisette Soup with Tarragon 76

Cucumber-Coconut Bisque 76

Beet Soup with Lemon Crème Fraîche 77

Chickpea Flour Soup from Provence 79

Ginger Bouillon with Enoki Mushrooms 79

cold soups

Fragrant Asian Gazpacho 80

Plum Tomato Gazpacho 81

Cauliflower Vichyssoise with Chive Flowers 82

Jade Soup with Lump Crab & Dill 82

Asparagus Bisque with a Touch of India 84

Green Pea–Wasabi Soup with Mint 84

hot soups

Tortellini in Pesto Broth 85

Onion Soup with Apple Cider & Thyme 86

"Whole Buttered" Onion Soup 86

Carrot Soup with Ginger & Crispy Carrot Tops 87

Silky Corn Soup with Scallions & Green Apple 88

Sweet Garlic-Fennel Bisque with Toasted Pine Nuts 89

Broccoli Soup with Lemon-Pistachio Butter 90

Sweet Potato–Rutabaga Soup with Toasted Pecans 90

Split Pea Soup with Soppressata & Fresh Oregano 91

Brie and Pear Soup, Brandied Cherries & Pears 92

Parsnip-Apple Soup with "Bacon Candy" 93

Pappa al Pomodoro 94

Truffled Asparagus Soup with Pineapple Reduction 95

Calabaza Soup with Celery & Crispy Sage 96

elemental broths

Corn Cob Broth 98

Double-Strength Beef Broth 98

Golden Chicken Broth 99

"Beet" Broth 99

grace notes: things that go well with soup

Olive Oil Biscuits 100

Buttery Oatcakes 100

Walnut-Onion Muffins 101

Pappadams 101

Tortilla Ribbons 102

Basil-Scrubbed Toasts 102

Barcelona Bread 102

Fennel-Cumin Flatbreads 103

Emergency Crackers 103

Sweet Tomato–Watermelon Soup ➤

The combination of tomatoes and watermelon has become popular in salads, so why not in soup? Served cold, the perfume of the watermelon lifts the soup with an elegant sweetness; served hot, the watermelon provides depth beneath a tomato-y base.

> 1 pound ripe red watermelon, after trimming
> 1 pound grape tomatoes
> 1 tablespoon basil pesto or finely snipped fresh lavender

Remove the seeds from the watermelon. Combine the tomatoes and watermelon in a blender and process until completely smooth. Add salt to taste; the amount will depend completely on the flavor and ripeness of the fruit. Top with the pesto or lavender.
SERVES 4

To Serve the Soup Hot

Heat the soup in a large saucepan over medium heat until hot. Add **4 tablespoons butter** and cook for 5 minutes, until the soup thickens a bit. Stir in $\frac{1}{2}$ teaspoon Asian sesame oil, or more to taste. Serve hot, garnished with snippets of fresh basil or mint leaves.

Avocado Soup with Fino Sherry

This soup has a mesmerizing flavor and velvety texture. If making the soup ahead of time, chill well and add the sherry (and optional garlic) at the very end. More awesome still: Crumble blue cheese on top! Serve with Marcona almonds.

> 2 medium-large ripe avocados
> 3 cups chicken broth, chilled
> 2 cups buttermilk, chilled
> 2 tablespoons fino sherry
> 1 small garlic clove, optional

Cut the avocados in half and remove the pits. Scoop the flesh into a food processor. Add the broth and $1\frac{1}{2}$ cups of the buttermilk. Process until *very* smooth. Stir in the sherry and garlic pushed through a press. Add salt to taste. Ladle into bowls and drizzle each serving with a bit of the remaining buttermilk. SERVES 4

fennel-cumin flatbread

serve hot or cold

PINK TOMATO FRAPPÉS

Nothing expresses the idea of summer better than this one-ingredient recipe. Each pound of tomatoes makes 2 cups of soup.

3 pounds very ripe red tomatoes
Fleur de sel

Wash and core the tomatoes. Cut in half through the equator and squeeze out the seeds. Cut half the tomatoes into chunks and put in a blender. Process until completely smooth and foamy. Transfer to a bowl. Repeat with the remaining tomatoes. Add fleur de sel to taste. Sprinkle more on top before serving. SERVES 6

After a few minutes, the pectin in the tomatoes firms it up, making a kind of mousse.

TOMATO-ANISETTE SOUP WITH TARRAGON

This fabulous soup, meant to jump-start the appetite, is a great last-minute hors d'oeuvres when served in demitasse cups and passed on a tray. It has a haunting flavor that no one can identify but is very sexy. Please try it.

1/2 cup heavy cream
4 cups tomato-vegetable juice cocktail, such as V8
1/4 cup anisette liqueur
1 teaspoon Thai fish sauce
Fresh tarragon for garnish

Using a wire whisk, whip the cream with a pinch of salt until thick. Set aside.

Bring the vegetable juice just to a boil in a medium saucepan. Reduce the heat and stir in the anisette. Simmer for 2 minutes. Stir in the fish sauce; add lots of freshly ground black pepper. Pour into soup bowls. Top with the whipped cream and snippets of tarragon. SERVES 6

CUCUMBER-COCONUT BISQUE

This is incredibly refreshing and lasts, surprisingly, up to 5 days in the fridge. Even kids love it. Make sure all the ingredients are chilled.

2 large cucumbers, peeled
1 1/2 cups plain Greek yogurt
1/2 cup coconut milk, chilled
4 scallions
1/4 cup chopped fresh mint, plus julienned mint for garnish
1 1/2 teaspoons cumin
2 tablespoons olive oil, plus more for drizzling
1/3 cup finely minced red bell pepper

Cut the cucumbers in half lengthwise and scrape out the seeds with a spoon. Cut the flesh into pieces and put in a blender with the yogurt and coconut milk. Sliver the dark green parts of the scallions and set aside for garnish. Chop the white and light green parts and add to the blender with the chopped mint, cumin, and oil. Process for several minutes, until smooth; add salt. Ladle into bowls. Garnish with slivered scallion greens, julienned mint, bell pepper, and a drizzle of oil. SERVES 4

BEET SOUP WITH LEMON CRÈME FRAÎCHE

The color of rubies, this soup dazzles. It can be made in 60 seconds and eaten right away if the ingredients are well-chilled. If not, pop the soup in the freezer until ice cold.

2 (14-ounce) cans small whole beets
¹⁄₃ cup olive oil
¹⁄₄ cup balsamic vinegar
1 large garlic clove
¹⁄₂ cup crème fraîche
1 large lemon

Put the beets and liquid in a food processor; begin to process. Add ³⁄₄ cup water, the oil, vinegar, and garlic. Process until *very* smooth. Stir in salt and pepper. Top each serving with the crème fraîche and grate lots of lemon zest on top. SERVES 4

an unusual soup

made from chickpea flour

◄ CHICKPEA FLOUR SOUP FROM PROVENCE

The soup, known as fournade, *is an adaptation of an old French recipe from Provence. It is made from chickpea flour (which you can find at any Middle Eastern market or health food store) and great extra-virgin olive oil. Thick, creamy, and nutty, it tastes like it's been cooking all day. A friend once called it "hummus soup." Don't forget to squeeze lemon into the soup before you eat!*

2 large garlic cloves
$\frac{1}{4}$ cup extra-virgin olive oil, plus more for drizzling
2 teaspoons ground cumin
1 cup chickpea flour
1 scallion, green top only
1 lemon, cut in wedges

Put 6 cups water in a 4-quart pot. Add the garlic pushed through a press, the oil, cumin, and 1 teaspoon salt. Whisk, bring to a boil, and boil for 1 minute. Reduce the heat and whisk in the chickpea flour. Whisk 3 minutes over high heat until as thick as heavy cream. If it is still lumpy, puree in a blender or food processor, then reheat. Ladle into bowls. Thinly slice the scallion and scatter on top. Drizzle with the oil and serve with lemon wedges. SERVES 4

GINGER BOUILLON WITH ENOKI MUSHROOMS

Instead of miso soup, try this elegant bit of wizardry. It has a similar sensibility but is less tricky to deal with and the result is clear instead of cloudy.

2 ounces candied ginger, about $\frac{1}{4}$ cup
4 cups chicken broth
2 scallions, roots removed
2-inch piece fresh ginger, peeled
$3\frac{1}{2}$ ounces enoki mushrooms
1 teaspoon Asian sesame oil

Wash the candied ginger to remove the sugary coating and cut into thin julienne.

Bring the broth to a boil in a medium saucepan over high heat; boil 1 minute. Reduce the heat to medium. Slice the scallions very thinly on the bias; add to the saucepan. Grate the fresh ginger on the large holes of a box grater; place in a paper towel and squeeze to get 1 tablespoon juice. Add to the saucepan. Remove the bottom inch from the mushrooms. Add the candied ginger and mushrooms to the saucepan; cook 2 minutes, until hot. Ladle into bowls. Add droplets of oil. SERVES 4

FRAGRANT ASIAN GAZPACHO

*Unorthodox perhaps but this tastes refreshingly Asian and
partners well with a glass of chilled sake. Panko, the
Japanese equivalent of bread crumbs, gives the soup body.*

$^{1}/_{2}$ cup panko
$^{1}/_{4}$ cup olive oil
3 tablespoons rice vinegar
2 large garlic cloves
1 large green bell pepper, seeded
2 medium zucchini, about 12 ounces
2 cups fresh baby spinach
1 cup chopped fresh cilantro
$^{1}/_{3}$ cup chopped fresh mint
3 scallions, cut in 1-inch pieces
1-inch piece fresh ginger, peeled and
    chopped
Few drops green hot-pepper sauce

Combine the panko, oil, vinegar, and garlic in a food
processor; process briefly. Cut the pepper and zucchini
into large pieces. Add to the processor. Add the
spinach, cilantro, mint, scallions, and ginger. Process
until just blended. Add 2 cups water and the hot sauce;
process until smooth. Transfer to a bowl. Add a
generous amount of salt to taste. Chill until very cold.
SERVES 4

PLUM TOMATO GAZPACHO

I invented this delicious gazpacho, which starts with half of a large toasted bagel, after breakfast one morning. This is not far-fetched, for any red gazpacho worth its salt is made from an amalgam of bread, tomatoes, and olive oil.

$^1/_2$ large plain bagel, lightly toasted
$^1/_4$ cup extra-virgin olive oil, plus more for drizzling
1 tablespoon sherry vinegar
4 large ripe plum tomatoes
1 large red bell pepper, seeded
$^1/_4$ small yellow onion
1 large cucumber, peeled and seeded
2 cups strained tomatoes (such as Pomi) or thick tomato juice
$^1/_2$ teaspoon hot-pepper sauce
Handful of fresh basil, julienned

Tear the bagel into pieces and put in a food processor. Add the oil and vinegar. Cut the tomatoes, pepper, onion, and cucumber into $^1/_2$-pieces. Add to the food processor. Process until coarsely ground. Add the strained tomatoes and process until fairly smooth but still with a discernible texture. Add 1 cup cold water to loosen, then season with the hot sauce and salt. Cover and refrigerate for 2 hours. Ladle into bowls and garnish with basil. Drizzle with additional oil. SERVES 4

CAULIFLOWER VICHYSSOISE WITH CHIVE FLOWERS ➤

This more healthful riff on classic vichyssoise is still luxuriously suave. For a stunning presentation, blanch a bunch of parsley and puree in a blender with 2 tablespoons olive oil and $1/4$ cup water; add a swirl to each serving to dance on the white velvet background.

$2^1/_2$ pounds cauliflower, or $1^3/_4$ pounds florets
2 large leeks
1 cup light cream
Chive flowers, petals of other edible flowers, or snipped chives

Break the cauliflower into small pieces and put in a 4-quart pot. Add 5 cups water (water will not cover the cauliflower) and 2 teaspoons salt. Chop the white parts of the leeks to get $1^1/_2$ cups. Wash well; add to the pot. Bring to a rapid boil; reduce the heat to medium. Cover and cook until the vegetables are very soft, 25 minutes. Cool 5 minutes. In 2 batches, puree in a food processor until *very* smooth, adding $1/2$ cup cream to each batch. Transfer to a bowl; add salt and pepper. Cover; refrigerate until very cold. Add water or additional cream if too thick. Garnish as desired. **SERVES 6**

JADE SOUP WITH LUMP CRAB & DILL

The jade green color of this velvety soup comes, unexpectedly, from pureed zucchini. You'll love it cold; you'll love it hot. If you can't find lump crabmeat, use snow crab.

$2^1/_4$ pounds medium zucchini
$1/2$ cup finely chopped fresh dill, plus sprigs for garnish
16 ounces jumbo lump crabmeat
4 large shallots, chopped
2 tablespoons unsalted butter

Cut the zucchini into $1/2$-inch pieces. Place in a large saucepan with the dill, three-quarters of the crabmeat, the shallots, and $3^1/_2$ cups water. Bring to a boil. Reduce the heat to medium and cover. Cook until very soft, 20 minutes. Cool 5 minutes.

In 2 batches, puree the soup in a blender. Add the butter; process until very smooth, 2 minutes. Add $1^1/_2$ teaspoons salt. Transfer to a bowl, cover, and refrigerate until very cold. If serving hot, bring soup just to a boil. Ladle into bowls. Garnish with the remaining crab and dill sprigs. **SERVES 6**

swirl on parsley oil

Asparagus Bisque with a Touch of India

Garam masala, a magical mixture of spices that includes cumin, coriander, cinnamon, and cardamom, takes this soup in an exotic direction. Serve with Pappadams (page 101).

    2 cups chopped leeks, white part only
    2 teaspoons garam masala
    2$\frac{1}{2}$ pounds medium asparagus, trimmed
    2 tablespoons chopped fresh tarragon, plus more for garnish
    8 ounces crème fraîche
    1 tablespoon pink peppercorns

Put 4$\frac{1}{2}$ cups water in a 4-quart pot. Add the leeks, 1 teaspoon garam masala, and $\frac{1}{2}$ teaspoon salt. Bring to a boil; boil 5 minutes. Lightly peel asparagus and cut into 1-inch pieces. Add to the pot and reduce the heat. Cover and cook until the asparagus is tender but still green, 15 minutes. Cool 5 minutes.

Puree the soup in a blender until smooth. Add the remaining garam masala, tarragon, and all but 2 tablespoons of the crème fraîche. Blend on high until *very* smooth. Cover and refrigerate until cold. Add salt and ladle into bowls. Garnish with the remaining crème fraîche, chopped tarragon, and pink peppercorns. SERVES 4

Green Pea–Wasabi Soup with Mint

Peas and wasabi tap dance really well together, both in those crunchy wasabi-coated peas you eat as a snack and now in this exuberant soup.

    4 cups fresh shelled peas or thawed frozen peas
    $\frac{1}{2}$ cup finely chopped shallots
    1$\frac{1}{4}$ cups buttermilk
    2 teaspoons wasabi powder dissolved in 1 tablespoon water
    $\frac{1}{4}$ cup slivered fresh mint, plus more for garnish
    $\frac{1}{2}$ cup wasabi peas

Combine the peas and shallots in a large saucepan. Add 3 cups water and 1 teaspoon salt. Bring to a boil. Reduce the heat and cook until the peas are tender but still bright green, about 5 minutes (the timing will vary depending on the type of pea). Let cool for 5 minutes. Puree in a blender until smooth, slowly adding 1 cup of the buttermilk. Add the dissolved wasabi and mint; process until *very* smooth. (You may strain the soup at this point, but I like it as is.) Add salt to the soup, cover, and refrigerate for several hours, until cold. Ladle into bowls and drizzle with the remaining buttermilk poured from a spoon. Garnish with mint and wasabi peas. SERVES 4 OR 5

TORTELLINI IN PESTO BROTH

My teenage daughter loves this soup. Is there a better recommendation? The whole thing comes together in 10 minutes, including the homemade pesto! Sprinkle with additional cheese at the table.

> 4 cups chicken broth
> 2 cups fresh basil leaves
> $1/3$ cup freshly grated Parmigiano-Reggiano, plus more for sprinkling
> 6 tablespoons olive oil
> 2 tablespoons pine nuts
> 1 large garlic clove
> 32 fresh or frozen cheese tortellini

Heat the broth until boiling. Wash the basil and dry well. Put the basil in a food processor with half the Parmesan, oil, pine nuts, and garlic; process until smooth. (Makes about 1 cup.) Whisk $1/3$ cup of the pesto into the hot broth. (Save the remaining pesto for another use.) Reduce the heat to medium and add the tortellini. Cook until tender, about 7 minutes. Ladle into bowls and sprinkle with the remaining cheese. SERVES 4

Onion Soup with Apple Cider & Thyme

This soup is dark and brooding and very reminiscent of the French classic. It tastes great as is, but is especially pleasing when pureed until smooth.

    1½ pounds large onions
    4 tablespoons unsalted butter
    1½ cups chicken broth
    1¼ cups fresh apple cider
    5 sprigs fresh thyme, plus more leaves for garnish
    1 cup freshly grated Parmigiano-Reggiano

Cut the onions in half through the stem end. Cut lengthwise into thin slices. Melt the butter in a 4-quart pot. Add the onions and cook over high heat, stirring, until softened and very dark brown, about 10 minutes. Add the broth, cider, and thyme sprigs; scrape the bottom of the pot and bring to a rapid boil. Reduce heat and cook, stirring often, until the onions are very soft, 25 minutes. Add salt and pepper. Leave as is, or puree in a food processor until smooth. Sprinkle with the Parmesan and thyme leaves. SERVES 6

"Whole Buttered" Onion Soup

Here's a radical new way to make onion soup: There's no slicing, dicing, or stirring. Instead, whole buttered onions bake for 4 hours, oozing luscious juices that caramelize like toffee.

    3 pounds medium yellow onions, about 10
    6 tablespoons unsalted butter, sliced thin
    3 tablespoons Madeira
    1½ tablespoons wildflower honey or truffle honey
    Sprigs of fresh chervil for garnish

Preheat the oven to 275°F. Peel the onions. Place in a 6-quart Dutch oven. Top with the butter. Cover and bake 4 hours, until very soft, turning the onions after 2 hours. Transfer to a large bowl. Pour 4 cups water into the casserole and scrape up the browned bits. Add to the onions. In 2 batches if necessary, puree the onion mixture in a food processor until *very* smooth. Pour through a sieve placed over a medium saucepan. Mash down to extract all the juices. Save the pulp.

Bring the soup to a boil. Reduce the heat and add the Madeira and honey. Simmer 10 minutes. Add salt and pepper. Ladle into bowls and garnish with a dollop of onion pulp and chervil. SERVES 4

Carrot Soup with Ginger & Crispy Carrot Tops

There are many versions of carrot soup, but none easier to make or more delicious than this one. The carrot tops will stay crispy for up to 1 hour, maybe longer.

1¹⁄₂ pounds carrots with ¹⁄₃ cup green tops
¹⁄₂ teaspoon five-spice powder
¹⁄₂ teaspoon curry powder
4-ounce piece fresh ginger, peeled and grated
¹⁄₂ cup coconut milk or heavy cream
¹⁄₄ cup olive oil for frying

Peel the carrots and cut into 1-inch pieces. Put in a large saucepan with 5 cups water, the five-spice powder, curry powder, and 1 teaspoon salt. Bring to a boil. Reduce the heat, cover, and cook 35 minutes, until very soft. With a slotted spoon, transfer the carrots to a food processor. Process until *very* smooth, slowly adding the cooking liquid. Squeeze the grated ginger in a paper towel to extract 2 tablespoons juice. Add to the processor with the coconut milk. Process until smooth. Return the soup to the saucepan and add salt.

Wash and dry the carrot tops. Heat the oil in a small skillet until hot. Fry the carrot tops until crispy and bright green, 30 seconds. Transfer to paper towels and sprinkle with salt. Reheat the soup and garnish with the carrot tops. SERVES 4

SILKY CORN SOUP WITH SCALLIONS & GREEN APPLE

Save the corn cobs for a delicious elemental broth (page 98).

6 large ears sweet yellow corn
2 bunches scallions
3 tablespoons unsalted butter
$^1/_4$ teaspoon Sriracha
6 tablespoons very finely diced Granny Smith apple

Cut the corn kernels from the cobs to get 5 cups. Chop the white and light green parts only of the scallions to get $^2/_3$ cup.

Melt the butter in a 4-quart pot. Add the scallions and cook over medium heat for 3 minutes. Add $^1/_2$ cup water and bring to a boil. Add the corn, 5 cups water, and 2 teaspoons salt. Bring to a rapid boil and reduce the heat. Cover and simmer until tender, 15 minutes. Cool 5 minutes. Puree the soup in batches in a blender or food processor until *very* smooth. Pass through a sieve, pressing down hard on the solids; discard the solids. Reheat the soup, adding Sriracha and salt to taste. Garnish with diced apple. SERVES 4

SWEET GARLIC-FENNEL BISQUE WITH TOASTED PINE NUTS

A profusion of garlic cloves and fresh fennel sweetens in simmering cream to become a wondrous soup that might rival oyster bisque as a new holiday favorite. It can be made early in the day and reheated. You can slip in some shucked oysters and heat briefly.

24 large garlic cloves, peeled
1 cup half-and-half
1 cup heavy cream
2 very large fennel bulbs with fronds
$1/3$ cup pine nuts, lightly toasted

Place the garlic in a 4-quart pot. Add the half-and-half, cream, 4 cups water, and 1 tablespoon salt. Bring to a boil and reduce the heat. Cover and simmer for 25 minutes, until the garlic is very soft.

Chop $1/2$ cup of the fennel fronds. Cut the fennel into $1/2$-inch pieces. Add to the pot the fennel with half of the chopped fronds. Bring to a boil. Reduce heat. Cover and simmer 30 minutes, until the fennel is *very* soft.

In batches, puree the soup in a food processor until *very* smooth. Return to the pot. Add salt and pepper. Reheat and top with pine nuts and chopped fronds. SERVES 6

BROCCOLI SOUP WITH LEMON-PISTACHIO BUTTER

No part of the humble broccoli is wasted in making this soup; both florets and stalks are boiled and pureed into a velouté. Pistachio butter tastes as good as it sounds.

3 tablespoons chopped salted pistachios
6 tablespoons unsalted butter, room temperature
Grated zest of 1 lemon
1 very large head broccoli, about 1½ pounds
4 large garlic cloves
⅓ cup chopped fresh basil

Lightly toast the pistachios in a small skillet until fragrant, 3 minutes. Put 4 tablespoons of the butter in a bowl. Mix in the pistachios and lemon zest. Roll the mixture in a piece of parchment to make a 1-inch diameter log. Freeze.

Remove the broccoli florets from the stalks. Peel the stalks; discard the bottom inch and cut into small pieces. Place in a 4-quart pot with the garlic, 6 cups water, and 1 teaspoon salt. Bring to a boil. Boil 10 minutes and add the florets. Cook 8 minutes. Add the basil and cook 2 minutes.

Transfer the broccoli, garlic, and 3 cups cooking liquid to a food processor. Process until smooth. Add the remaining 2 tablespoons butter. Process until *very* smooth. Reheat and serve topped with thin slices of frozen butter. SERVES 4

SWEET POTATO–RUTABAGA SOUP WITH TOASTED PECANS

This simple soup has lots of complexity and is worthwhile all by itself, but toasted pecans add a bit of magic. Try serving with a glass of Prosecco.

5 slices bacon, diced
1½ pounds sweet potatoes
1 large rutabaga, about 1½ pounds
1 large red onion, diced
1½ teaspoons ground coriander
¾ cup chopped pecans

In a large pot, cook the bacon over medium heat for 5 minutes, until the fat is rendered; do not crisp. Peel the potatoes and rutabaga. Cut into 1-inch pieces and add to the pot. Add the onions and toss with the bacon fat and cook over high heat for 2 minutes. Add 5 cups water, the coriander, and 1 teaspoon salt. Bring to a boil; reduce the heat to medium, cover, and cook for 45 minutes, until the vegetables are *very* soft. Cool 10 minutes.

Toast the pecans in a small skillet over medium heat until fragrant, about 3 minutes. In 2 batches, puree the soup in a food processor until *very* smooth. Reheat the soup, adding salt and pepper. Ladle into bowls and garnish with the toasted pecans. SERVES 6

SPLIT PEA SOUP WITH SOPPRESSATA & FRESH OREGANO

This soup has a homey kitchen table charm. It gets a layer of sweetness from lots of onions that melt into obscurity. Little cubes of carrot are added toward the end so that they retain their shape, becoming textural buoys in a sea of earthiness.

$\frac{1}{4}$ cup olive oil
1 heaping cup very finely chopped onions
4 ounces soppressata, thinly sliced
1 tablespoon chopped fresh oregano, plus more for garnish
8 ounces dried split green peas
1 cup finely diced carrots

Heat the oil in a 4-quart pot. Add the onions and cook over high heat for 5 minutes. Stack the soppressata and roll up like a cigar; slice into $\frac{1}{8}$-inch ribbons. Set aside $\frac{1}{4}$ cup for garnish and add the rest to the pot. Add the oregano and cook, stirring, until the onions are very soft and golden, 10 minutes. Add the split peas and 6 cups water. Bring to a boil with the cover askew. Reduce the heat and simmer 45 minutes, stirring frequently. Add the carrots and cook 20 minutes longer, until soft. Add salt and pepper. Ladle the hot soup into bowls. Garnish with the reserved soppressata and oregano. SERVES 4

BRIE AND PEAR SOUP, BRANDIED CHERRIES & PEARS

This is one of my signature soups to which I have added a special touch: a relish of tart dried cherries rehydrated with a splash of brandy and tossed with finely diced pears. Be sure to use a ripe, double-crème Brie, one that really smells like cheese.

$^1/_4$ cup unsweetened dried cherries
3 large ripe pears, peeled and halved
1 tablespoon brandy
2 cups chicken broth
$^1/_4$ cup finely diced yellow onion
8 ounces ripe Brie, well-chilled
2 tablespoons finely minced fresh chives

Dice the cherries and put in a bowl. Core the pears. Finely dice 1 pear half; add to the cherries along with the brandy and 1 tablespoon water. Set the relish aside.

Cut the remaining pear halves into $^1/_2$-inch pieces. Place in a large saucepan. Add the broth and onion. Bring just to a boil. Reduce the heat, cover, and simmer until the pears are very soft, 20 minutes. Cool 5 minutes.

Trim and discard the rind from the cheese; cut the cheese into small pieces. Puree the soup in a food processor until smooth. Add the cheese and process until *very* smooth. Reheat the soup and add salt and pepper. Garnish with the relish and chives. SERVES 4

PARSNIP-APPLE SOUP WITH "BACON CANDY"

This soup can be made up to 3 days in advance. If you want to serve this to vegetarians, eliminate the bacon and garnish with smoked almonds.

4 packed cups chopped leeks, white and light green parts
2 pounds parsnips, peeled
3 large Fuji apples, $1\frac{1}{4}$ pounds, peeled
4 tablespoons unsalted butter
8 strips thick-sliced bacon
$\frac{1}{4}$ cup turbinado sugar

Preheat the oven to 375°F. Wash leeks and dry. Cut the parsnips and apples into 1-inch pieces. Melt 3 tablespoons of the butter in a medium pot. Add the leeks; cook 5 minutes over medium heat. Add the parsnips and apples; cook 5 minutes. Dice 2 bacon strips and add to the pot with $6\frac{1}{2}$ cups water and 1 teaspoon salt. Bring to a boil. Reduce heat and cook until the vegetables are *very* soft, 25 minutes.

Meanwhile, place 6 bacon slices on a parchment-lined baking sheet. Rub the sugar evenly onto the top of each slice. Bake 10 minutes; drain the fat. Bake 10 minutes longer, until crisp. Cut into $\frac{1}{4}$-inch pieces.

In batches, puree the soup in a blender until *very* smooth. Reheat the soup with the remaining tablespoon of butter. Serve garnished with the bacon candy. SERVES 8

Pappa al Pomodoro

This famously soupy dish, thickened with bread instead of pasta, is much like a pasta course—deeply satisfying and a great way to begin a meal. It's a good excuse to use your best extra-virgin olive oil, which should be drizzled on right before serving. A tip: The best way to "chop" canned tomatoes is to use scissors to snip them right in the can.

$^1/_3$ cup extra-virgin olive oil, plus more for drizzling
3 large garlic cloves, thinly sliced
28-ounce can plum tomatoes in puree, chopped
2 cups chicken stock
4 ounces baguette, cut into small pieces, about 5 packed cups
$^1/_3$ cup chopped fresh basil
Large pinch hot-pepper flakes
$^3/_4$ cup freshly grated Parmigiano-Reggiano or Pecorino Romano, or a mixture

Heat the oil in a 4-quart pot. Add the garlic and cook until soft but not brown, 1 minute. Add the tomatoes and stock; bring to a boil and cook 10 minutes over high heat. Add the bread and cook 8 minutes, mashing with a potato masher until the ingredients are integrated and the bread is very soft. Add the basil, pepper flakes, and salt. Cook 2 minutes longer. Stir in $^1/_2$ cup of the cheese. Ladle into bowls and drizzle with additional oil. Sprinkle with the remaining $^1/_4$ cup cheese. SERVES 4

TRUFFLED ASPARAGUS SOUP WITH PINEAPPLE REDUCTION

This soup is asparagus to the second power, made from boiled stalks and garnished with roasted tips. But the real surprise is a syrupy reduction of pineapple juice: It all makes a compelling flavor match that is among my favorites. Although there are several steps, this is a radically simple means toward a radically complex end.

1 cup unsweetened pineapple juice
2½ pounds medium asparagus, peeled
1 tablespoon olive oil
4 tablespoons unsalted butter, sliced
1½ teaspoons white truffle oil

Preheat the oven to 450°F. Put the juice in a small skillet and boil over high heat until reduced to ¼ cup. Set aside.

Discard the bottom inch from each asparagus spear. Cut off the tips and place in a pie pan; toss with the olive oil. Roast 8 minutes, until just tender. Cut the asparagus stalks into 2 inch pieces. Place in a 4 quart pot with the butter and 2 cups water. Bring to a boil; reduce the heat and cover. Cook until just tender, 10 minutes. Transfer to a food processor. Process, adding as much cooking liquid as needed to make a smooth, thick puree. Add the truffle oil and salt and pepper and reheat. Ladle into bowls and top with the roasted asparagus tips. Drizzle with the pineapple reduction. SERVES 4

CALABAZA SOUP WITH CELERY & CRISPY SAGE

This has an air of the West Indies about it, with its earthy flavors of ginger, scotch bonnet pepper, celery, thyme, and sage. Butternut squash may be substituted for the calabaza.

3½ pounds calabaza, in one wedge
6 tablespoons olive oil
2 cups finely chopped onions
1 cup finely chopped celery, plus leaves for garnish
2 tablespoons finely chopped peeled fresh ginger
½ small scotch bonnet pepper, finely minced
1 teaspoon dried thyme leaves
20 medium-large fresh sage leaves
1 tablespoon dark brown sugar

Preheat the oven to 400°F. Remove seeds from the squash. Place in a roasting pan. Drizzle with 1 tablespoon of the oil. Pour 1 inch water into the pan and bake 1¼ hours, until very soft. Scoop out the flesh.

Heat 3 tablespoons of the oil in a 4-quart pot. Add the onions, celery, ginger, minced pepper, thyme, 2 sage leaves, and 1 teaspoon salt. Cook 15 minutes over medium heat. Add the sugar and 4 cups water. Bring to a boil, reduce the heat, and add the squash. Cover and cook 15 minutes. In batches, puree the soup in a food processor until *very* smooth.

Fry the remaining sage leaves in 2 tablespoons hot oil until crispy. Drain on paper towels and sprinkle with salt. Reheat the soup if necessary; garnish with the fried sage and celery leaves. SERVES 6

delicious

CORN COB BROTH

The perfect vegetarian backdrop to any soup, this light broth is faintly sweet. I drink it as "tea."

3 large ears fresh corn
1 thick slice onion, optional

Husk the corn and remove the silk. Using a sharp knife, cut the corn kernels from the cobs and save for another use. Break the cobs in half and put in a 2-quart saucepan. Add 6 cups water and the onion. Bring to a boil, reduce the heat, and cover. Simmer for 30 minutes. Strain the broth and add salt to taste. MAKES ABOUT 5 CUPS.

DOUBLE-STRENGTH BEEF BROTH

This rich broth takes hours of simmering yet only minutes to prep. I have tasted this broth against many on the market and I must say that, even without any bone-roasting, 20-gallon stockpot or clarifying, the result is exquisitely credible. Beefy and crystal clear. If you add $\frac{1}{4}$ cup of Madeira at the end, you have something very special to sip either before a meal or as an intermezzo between courses at a fancy dinner party.

3 large leeks
3 tablespoons olive oil
3-pound beef shin on the bone, cut into 2 pieces
$1\frac{1}{2}$ pounds marrow bones
8 fresh thyme sprigs
1 teaspoon whole black peppercorns

Slice off the top 3 inches of the leeks, then cut into $\frac{1}{2}$-inch pieces; wash thoroughly and dry. Heat the oil in 6-quart pot. Brown the meat well on all sides, about 6 minutes. Lightly salt. Add the leeks and cook until wilted, 5 minutes. Add the marrow bones, thyme, 1 teaspoon salt, peppercorns, and enough water to cover by 2 inches, about 15 cups. Bring to a boil, skimming foam from the surface. Reduce the heat, cover, and simmer 3 hours.

Pour the broth through a sieve into a clean pot, discarding the solids. Set aside for 20 minutes, then skim off as much fat as possible. (Or chill the broth until solidified and scrape off fat from the surface.) Return the broth just to a boil, then simmer, uncovered, until reduced to $4\frac{1}{2}$ cups, about 1 hour. Add salt. MAKES $4\frac{1}{2}$ CUPS

GOLDEN CHICKEN BROTH

The intensity of this chicken broth comes from saffron, bay, and—a trick I learned in Israel—onion skins. It makes a great base for matzoh balls. Collect the onion skins that inevitably accumulate in the bottom of your fridge.

6 pounds chicken wings
$1/2$ teaspoon whole black peppercorns
3 fresh bay leaves
2 teaspoons saffron threads
1 pound onions plus onion skins from 2 more pounds

Put the wings in a large pot. Add 4 quarts water, the peppercorns, bay leaves, saffron, and 1 tablespoon salt. Cut the onions into quarters, reserving the skins, and add to the pot. Add all the onion skins. Bring to a rapid boil, stirring. Reduce the heat and place the cover askew. Simmer for 2 hours. Strain the broth through a sieve and save the wings for another use.* Return the broth to the pot and boil over high heat until reduced to 12 cups. Add salt to taste. Let cool and skim off fat. MAKES 3 QUARTS

*You can broil the wings and splash them with black vinegar and soy sauce, or pick off the meat.

"BEET" BROTH

No, this is not a typo for beef broth. This garnet-hued broth is made by infusing water with fresh beets and spices. It is an excellent vegetarian broth with a vibrant color.

1 small fennel bulb
2 medium beets, without leaves or stems
1 cup finely chopped red onion
2 carrots, peeled and finely chopped
1 teaspoon caraway seeds
1 teaspoon fennel seeds
$1/2$ teaspoon ground allspice
1 tablespoon red wine vinegar

Core the fennel and finely dice the bulb to get 1 cup. Peel the beets and cut into $1/4$-inch pieces. Put 8 cups water in a 4-quart pot. Add the chopped fennel, beets, onion, carrots, caraway and fennel seeds, allspice, and $1/2$ teaspoon salt. Bring to a boil and reduce the heat. Simmer for 1 hour with the cover askew. Add the vinegar and cook 5 minutes longer. Strain through a sieve. Add salt and pepper to taste. MAKES ABOUT 4 CUPS

OLIVE OIL BISCUITS

These take about 2 minutes to prepare and 14 minutes to bake, so you can make them while your soup is simmering.

6 tablespoons milk
7 tablespoons olive oil
1 cup self-rising flour
3 tablespoons freshly grated Parmigiano-Reggiano

Preheat the oven to 400°F. Combine milk and 5 tablespoons of the oil in a small cup. Mix the flour and cheese in a large bowl; make a well in the center. Pour in the milk mixture; mix with a fork until a smooth, damp dough forms. Turn the dough onto a lightly floured surface; pat to a ¼-inch thickness. Using a 1½-inch cookie cutter, cut out 15 biscuits. Place on an ungreased baking sheet. Bake 14 minutes, until just firm. Mix the remaining 2 tablespoons oil with a large pinch of salt. Brush the hot biscuits with the salted oil. Serve warm. MAKES 15

BUTTERY OATCAKES

These are my favorite "go-withs" to accompany any creamy soup with a bit of inherent sweetness. They're also a terrific afternoon snack when spread with some creamy blue cheese.

Vegetable oil, for greasing the pan
3 cups old-fashioned rolled oats
8 tablespoons unsalted butter, room temperature
½ cup sweetened condensed milk

Preheat the oven to 350°F. Lightly oil a rimmed baking sheet. Process the oatmeal and 1 teaspoon salt in a food processor until it looks like flour. Cut the butter into pieces and add to the oats; process until mixed. Add the condensed milk. Process until blended; the mixture will be sticky.

Spread the mixture on the baking sheet in a very thin layer (with your hands or a rolling pin). Trim the edges to make a 10x8-inch rectangle. With a small sharp knife, score into 24 rectangles. Prick each 4 times with fork tines. Bake 20 minutes. Reduce the heat to 300°F; separate the crackers with a metal spatula. Bake 12 minutes longer, until golden. MAKES 24

WALNUT-ONION MUFFINS

In the 1980s, I helped create a three-star restaurant in New York called the Hudson River Club, whose menu was based on the region's local bounty. My friend Wendy Dubit, who had a farm in the Hudson Valley, found this recipe in an old cookbook. I just made it radically simple.

> 1 large yellow onion, coarsely chopped
> 2 extra-large eggs
> 8 tablespoons unsalted butter, melted
> 6 tablespoons sugar
> 1½ cups self-rising flour
> 1 cup shelled walnuts, about 4 ounces, finely chopped

Preheat the oven to 425°F. Coat 16 muffin cups with cooking spray. Process the onion in a food processor until finely ground. Measure out 1 cup.

Beat the together the onion, eggs, butter, and sugar. Blend in the flour and ground walnuts to make a smooth batter. Fill the muffin tins and bake 18 minutes, until just firm and golden. Serve warm. MAKES 16

PAPPADAMS

Pappadams are translucent round wafers made from lentil and rice flours. You find them in Indian or Middle Eastern food stores, and in supermarkets with good ethnic-food sections. To serve, they can be fried in oil, but I prefer to crisp them over an open fire.

> 8 pappadams

Using long tongs, grasp the edge of a pappadam and hold it over a medium-high gas flame on the stovetop so that the flame just touches it. Turn it constantly until tiny bubbles form on each side and the pappadam turns an off-white color. There will be some blackened spots. Each pappadam should take 30 to 45 seconds to crisp. MAKES 8

TORTILLA RIBBONS

Radically cool to float atop gazpacho (page 80), Sweet Tomato–Watermelon Soup (page 72), or Silky Corn Soup with Scallions & Green Apple (page 88).

3 corn tortillas
3 tablespoons vegetable oil

Cut the tortillas into ⅛-inch-wide ribbons. Heat the oil in a medium skillet. In batches, fry the ribbons over high heat for several minutes until crisp. Drain on paper towels and sprinkle lightly with salt. Let cool. MAKES 4 CUPS

BASIL-SCRUBBED TOASTS

Rubbing a fistful of fresh basil onto toast turns it slightly green.

½ thin crisp baguette
1 large garlic clove
1 cup fresh basil leaves

Preheat the oven to 350°F. Cut the baguette slightly on the bias into ½-inch-thick slices. Arrange on a baking sheet. Toast in the oven 5 minutes, until golden and crisp. Cut the garlic in half. Rub one side of each toast with the garlic, then with a handful of basil leaves until fragrant and green. MAKES ABOUT 12

BARCELONA BREAD

In Spain this is called pan au tomaquet.

½ ciabatta loaf
1 large ripe tomato
¼ cup extra-virgin olive oil

Preheat the oven to 350°F. Cut the ciabatta into ½-inch-thick slices and arrange on a baking sheet. Toast in the oven for about 8 minutes, until golden and crisp. Cut the tomato in half and rub the cut side all over one side of each toast. Drizzle with oil and sprinkle with sea salt. MAKES ABOUT 8

FENNEL-CUMIN FLATBREADS

You'll feel proud when you make these professional-looking flatbreads. The texture is almost silky, thanks to crème fraîche stirred into the flour.

> 1 cup flour
> 1 teaspoon fennel seeds
> 1 teaspoon cumin seeds
> 3 tablespoons crème fraîche

Preheat the oven to 425°F. Adjust the oven rack to the center position. Combine the flour, fennel and cumin seeds, and 1 teaspoon salt in the bowl of a standing mixer. Begin to mix on slow, adding the crème fraîche and $^1/_4$ cup water. Mix until the dough forms a ball. On a lightly floured surface, knead the dough several times to incorporate. Divide the dough into 6 portions. Using a rolling pin, roll each piece paper-thin so that it is about 8 inches long and 3 inches wide. Place on a rimmed baking sheet. Bake 8 minutes. Turn over and bake 4 minutes longer, until firm and golden in patches. MAKES 6

EMERGENCY CRACKERS

This is the best way to make lots of crackers quickly. I always keep lavash in my freezer for this purpose.

> 1 very large ultra-thin lavash bread
> $^1/_4$ cup olive oil
> Fine sea salt

Preheat the oven to 375°F. Using a pastry brush, brush the lavash lightly with oil and sprinkle with salt. Place directly on an oven rack and bake 6 minutes, until golden and just firm. Let cool and break into irregular 2-inch pieces. MAKES A LOT!

PASTA

This chapter is divided into three themes: fresh pasta dishes that can be prepared in 10 minutes; dried pasta recipes with five ingredients or fewer; and pasta-and-sauce combos that are prepared in less than 20 minutes. Although these dishes are quick to prepare, remember that 4 quarts of salted water, covered, will take almost 20 minutes to reach a rolling boil, so plan accordingly.

Here's my favorite kind of menu for entertaining: a small portion of pasta served as a prelude to a more substantial protein, followed by a simple salad and sometimes cheese. It eliminates the need for a starchy accompaniment to the protein and lets me concentrate on fabulous vegetable sides. But the following recipes also can make grand main courses—many perfect for vegetarians. Simply begin the meal with a soup, a salad, or something unexpected from the vegetable chapter!

Many of my dishes are riffs on Italian classics. For example, I sprinkle crushed pork rinds on fresh pasta. They provide a two-fer: the taste of *guanciale* (cured pork jowl) or pancetta, plus the crunchy flourish typically provided by bread crumbs in rustic pasta dishes. Similarly, fettuccine gets glamorized with a sauce of smoked salmon, crème fraîche, and lemon.

While studying cooking in Florence with Giuliano Bugialli in 1978 (while I was chef to New York City Mayor Ed Koch), I was taught the dictum of "coupling"—that is, finding the saucy soul mate for each variety of pasta—whether it was fresh or dried, short and stubby, or long and slinky. While I respect tradition as much as the next guy, that sort of orthodoxy is out and the transmogrification of pasta into global self-expression is at an all-time high.

So fly to the moon with some new ideas. A radically simple rendition of mac-and-cheese in which hot pasta is tossed with freshly made pimiento cheese; "golden" fettuccine made so by boiling fresh pasta in turmeric-infused salt water; tahina as an unlikely yet simple saucing agent; Thai fish sauce incorporated into an unusual marinara; or capellini flavored with Chinese chili paste, Thai basil, and orange zest with a runny egg perched on top to become the "sauce." These global ingredients have become change agents for what pasta could, and *should*, be.

You'll also find a few surprise techniques here. Dried pasta "marinates" in olive oil *before* cooking—an absorption process that makes the pasta really toothsome. Another technique has you boiling pasta in a bottle of wine and then dousing it with extra-virgin olive oil.

Good-quality ingredients can make all the difference in the outcome. Choose the best fresh and dried pastas, excellent extra-virgin olive oil, and cheeses from authentic sources—the most important being Parmigiano-Reggiano (a cow's milk cheese from Parma, Italy) and Pecorino Romano (made from sheep's milk near Rome).

10-minute fresh pasta

Linguine with Zucchini, Lemon Zest & Basil **108**

Pasta with Pepper, Pecorino & Pork Rinds **108**

Linguine with Pesto Rosso **109**

Fettuccine with Smoked Salmon, Crème Fraîche & Lemon **110**

Fettuccine with Tahina, Pine Nuts & Cilantro **110**

Capellini with Spicy Fish Sauce Marinara **111**

Pumpkin Ravioli with Crispy Sage & Walnut Butter **111**

Golden Fettuccine with Sardines, Fennel & Saffron **113**

Capellini with Chili Paste & Crispy Egg **114**

Angel Hair with Ginger Butter & Chives **114**

Tortellini with Yogurt, Mint & Smoked Paprika Oil **116**

5-ingredient dried pasta

Spaghetti with Aged Gouda & Frozen Olive Oil **118**

Pimiento Mac **119**

Pasta Cooked in a Bottle of Wine **119**

A Recipe from 1841: Macaroni & Tomatoes **120**

Baked Ziti in Bianco with Fontina & Salami **120**

Perciatelli with French Breakfast Radishes, Bacon & Greens **123**

20-minute dried pasta

Short Rigatoni with Cauliflower, Anchovies & Raisins **124**

"Thunder & Lightning" **126**

Castellane with Ricotta & Tomato-Marsala Sauce **126**

Pasta Rustica with Sole, Greek Olives & White Wine **127**

Campanelle with Caramelized Onions, Peas & Mint **128**

Fusilli with Braised Escarole, Garlic & Ricotta Salata **131**

Gemelli with Sausage, Leeks & Barely Wilted Spinach **132**

Warm Sesame Noodles with Ginger & Snow Peas **133**

LINGUINE WITH ZUCCHINI, LEMON ZEST & BASIL

When thin slices of lightly floured zucchini are fried, then tossed with bits of crispy basil and showered with fragrant lemon zest, you get lots of complexity for something quite simple.

2 medium zucchini, trimmed
6 tablespoons olive oil
1 large garlic clove, peeled and smashed
1/4 cup Wondra flour
1/3 cup chopped fresh basil
12 ounces fresh linguine
1 lemon
1/2 cup freshly grated Parmigiano-Reggiano

Bring a large pot of salted water to a boil. Slice the zucchini into thin rounds. Heat 3 tablespoons of the oil in a very large skillet. Add the garlic and discard when brown. Dust the zucchini with the flour. Add to the skillet and cook over high heat until dark golden and soft, about 6 minutes. Add the basil and cook for 1 minute.

Cook the pasta in the boiling water, 3 minutes, or until tender. Drain the pasta and toss with the remaining oil. Spoon the zucchini and pan juices over the pasta. Grate the zest of the lemon on top and squeeze a little juice over all. Sprinkle with the cheese. SERVES 4

PASTA WITH PEPPER, PECORINO & PORK RINDS

This triptych of flavors—sharp pecorino, a profusion of black pepper, and something porky—is the hallmark of the classic pasta alla gricia. *It usually is made with pancetta or* guanciale *(cured pork jowl), but is radically delicious made with crumbled pork rinds, also known as* chicharrones! *You can find them in the snack section of supermarkets and bodegas.*

1/4 cup olive oil
1 large garlic clove, peeled and smashed
8 or 9 ounces fresh linguine
1 cup freshly grated Pecorino Romano
1/2 teaspoon finely cracked black peppercorns
1 1/2 ounces fried pork rinds (1 cup crushed)

Bring a large pot of salted water to a rapid boil. Heat the olive oil in a small skillet; add the garlic and cook over medium heat until golden, 3 minutes. Remove from the heat and discard the garlic. Cook the pasta in the boiling water 3 minutes, or until tender. Drain well, saving $1/4$ cup cooking liquid. Transfer the pasta to a large bowl. Add the garlic-flavored oil, $2/3$ cup of the cheese, the reserved cooking liquid, and the pepper. Toss well. Crush the pork rinds with your hands and sprinkle on the pasta along with the remaining cheese. SERVES 4

LINGUINE WITH PESTO ROSSO

Pesto based on fresh tomatoes and almonds ori ginated in the town of Trapani, Sicily. This is my take made with ingredients gathered from the four corners of my refrigerator.

> 1 cup loosely packed fresh flat-leaf parsley
> 1 cup loosely packed fresh basil leaves
> $1/2$ pint grape tomatoes
> $1/3$ cup extra-virgin olive oil
> $1/4$ cup almonds or pine nuts
> 1 medium garlic clove
> $1/3$ cup freshly grated Parmigiano-Reggiano
> $2/3$ cup freshly grated Pecorino Romano
> 12 ounces fresh linguine

Bring a large pot of salted water to a boil. Combine the parsley, basil, tomatoes, oil, nuts, garlic, and Parmesan in a food processor. Add $1/3$ cup of the pecorino and process until very smooth. Add salt and pepper. Transfer to a large bowl. Cook the pasta in the boiling water 3 minutes, or until tender. Drain well and shake dry. Add the pasta to the pesto and toss thoroughly. Sprinkle with the remaining pecorino. SERVES 4

Fettuccine with Smoked Salmon, Crème Fraîche & Lemon

My husband, the globe-trotting restaurant consultant, complains that this dish rarely lives up to its hype—but this version does. Often I dollop it with pearls of salmon caviar.

8 ounces fresh fettuccine
4 ounces smoked salmon, thinly sliced
8 ounces crème fraîche
6 tablespoons freshly grated Parmigiano-Reggiano
¼ cup finely chopped fresh chives
Grated zest of 1 large lemon

Bring a large pot of salted water to a boil. Add the pasta and cook 3 to 4 minutes, until tender. Meanwhile, cut the salmon into ½-inch-wide strips. Drain the pasta well; shake dry. Immediately return the pasta to the warm pot. Add the smoked salmon, crème fraîche, cheese, and salt. Warm gently for 1 minute over low heat, but do not cook. Transfer to 4 bowls. Top with chives and lemon zest. SERVES 4

Fettuccine with Tahina, Pine Nuts & Cilantro

It's radically delicious to coat hot strands of pasta in silky tahina. You can play up its Middle Eastern flavor by browning ground lamb and strewing it on top. It then becomes a red wine–worthy main course for dinner.

6 tablespoons pine nuts
3 tablespoons tahina
2 tablespoons olive oil
1 small garlic clove
12 ounces fresh fettuccine
½ cup freshly grated Parmigiano-Reggiano
6 tablespoons torn cilantro leaves

Bring a large pot of salted water to a boil. Lightly toast the pine nuts in a small skillet over medium heat until fragrant, about 3 minutes. In a large bowl, stir together the tahina and oil. Push the garlic through a press and add to the bowl. Cook the pasta in the boiling water 3 minutes, or until tender. Drain the pasta, saving ½ cup cooking water. Add the pasta to the bowl and toss well. Add the cheese and cooking water and toss until creamy. Add salt and pepper. Sprinkle with the toasted pine nuts and cilantro. SERVES 4

CAPELLINI WITH SPICY FISH SAUCE MARINARA

Lemon, fresh ginger, Thai fish sauce, and honey coalesce into an exceptional marriage of flavors in this quick pasta sauce. It can double as a fabulous adornment for grilled fish and steak—just swirl 2 tablespoons of unsalted butter into the finished sauce.

28-ounce can whole tomatoes in puree
3 tablespoons extra-virgin olive oil
1 tablespoon honey
2 teaspoons Thai fish sauce
3 large garlic cloves
1 lemon slice, about $\frac{1}{4}$ inch thick
2 nickel-size pieces peeled fresh ginger
$\frac{1}{4}$ teaspoon hot-pepper flakes
12 ounces fresh capellini

Bring a large pot of salted water to a boil. Combine the tomatoes and puree, oil, honey, fish sauce, garlic, lemon, ginger, and pepper flakes in a food processor. Process until very smooth. Transfer to a large saucepan and bring to a boil. Reduce the heat to medium and cook until thick, 8 minutes. Cook the pasta in the boiling water 1 minute, or until tender. Drain well and shake dry. Transfer to bowls and spoon the sauce on top. SERVES 4

PUMPKIN RAVIOLI WITH CRISPY SAGE & WALNUT BUTTER

If you're lucky enough to find fresh ravioli or tortelloni stuffed with pumpkin or squash, then use it! Otherwise, use ravioli or ra violini stuffed with cheese.

16 ounces fresh pumpkin or cheese ravioli
4 tablespoons unsalted butter
2 tablespoons olive oil
$\frac{1}{4}$ cup finely chopped sage
$\frac{1}{2}$ cup finely chopped walnuts
$\frac{1}{2}$ cup freshly grated Parmigiano-Reggiano

Bring a large pot of salted water to a boil. Cook the pasta 8 minutes, or until tender. Meanwhile, melt the butter and oil in a very large skillet over medium-high heat. Add the chopped sage and walnuts and cook until both are crispy but not dark brown, about 3 minutes. Drain the pasta and shake dry. Toss the pasta with the sage-walnut butter and salt and pepper. Sprinkle with cheese. SERVES 4

good-for-you sardines

Golden Fettuccine with Sardines, Fennel & Saffron

A happy accident: Boiling pasta in turmeric-dyed water imparts a glorious goldenrod hue. It makes a beautiful nest for a Riviera-inspired sauce of tomatoes, sardines, and fennel. Sometimes, I add a splash of anisette to the sauce as it simmers, and once I tried limoncello! Not bad at all.

28-ounce can plum tomatoes in puree
$3^1/_2$ ounces skinless boneless sardines in olive oil
1 large garlic clove
Large pinch cayenne
1 teaspoon fennel seeds
Heaping $^1/_4$ teaspoon saffron threads
1 tablespoon turmeric
8 ounces fresh fettuccine
$^1/_2$ cup freshly grated Parmigiano-Reggiano or Pecorino Romano

Bring a large pot of salted water to a boil. Combine the tomatoes with the puree, sardines and their oil, garlic (pushed through a press or grated on a Microplane), and cayenne in a large saucepan. Add $^1/_2$ teaspoon of the fennel seeds and half of the saffron. Stir and bring to a boil. Cook 10 minutes over high heat, stirring and breaking up the tomatoes with a potato masher.

Meanwhile, add the turmeric and remaining saffron to the boiling water and simmer 5 minutes. Add the pasta and cook 5 minutes, until tender. Drain well, shake dry, and transfer to a serving bowl. Pour the hot tomato sauce over the pasta. Sprinkle with the cheese and remaining $^1/_2$ teaspoon fennel seeds. SERVES 4

CAPELLINI WITH CHILI PASTE & CRISPY EGG ➤

This fanciful dish has become a favorite supper-for-two in our house—we even like it as breakfast-in-bed. I cook the eggs over high heat so that the edges get frilly and crisp. Freshly grated orange zest adds a jolt of perfume and ties the flavors together.

3 tablespoons unsalted butter, room temperature
1/2 teaspoon Chinese chili paste with garlic
4 ounces fresh capellini
2 extra-large eggs
1/4 cup freshly grated Parmigiano-Reggiano or Pecorino Romano
1 medium orange
2 tablespoons slivered fresh Thai basil

Bring a pot of salted water to a boil. Combine 2 tablespoons of the butter and the chili paste in a large bowl. Add the pasta to the boiling water and cook 3 to 5 minutes, until tender. Meanwhile, melt the remaining 1 tablespoon butter in a small skillet. Break the eggs into the pan and cook until the edges are crispy but the yolks are still runny; sprinkle with salt. Drain the pasta, shake dry, and add to the bowl. Toss with the cheese. Divide between bowls. Top with grated orange zest, a fried egg, and slivers of basil. SERVES 2

ANGEL HAIR WITH GINGER BUTTER & CHIVES

Turn this dish into a fabulous main course by simply placing a few slices of rare seared tuna on top, or under the pasta, to gently warm the fish.

4 tablespoons unsalted butter, room temperature
3-inch piece fresh ginger
1/2 teaspoon Asian sesame oil
12 ounces fresh angel hair pasta
1/2 cup freshly grated Parmigiano-Reggiano
1/4 cup minced fresh chives

Bring a large pot of salted water to a boil. Put the butter in a large bowl. Peel the ginger and grate on the large holes of a box grater into a paper towel. Squeeze the ginger juice (about 2 teaspoons) into the bowl. Add the oil and a large pinch of salt. Add the pasta to the boiling water and cook 2 minutes, until tender. Drain well, saving 1/4 cup cooking liquid. Add the pasta to the bowl and toss gently. Stir in the cheese and cooking water; add salt and pepper. Sprinkle with chives. SERVES 4

runny yolk

Tortellini with Yogurt, Mint & Smoked Paprika Oil

This is an exotic riff on a Turkish pasta dish called manti, *which is topped with yogurt and melted butter. Sometimes I serve it with an untraditional dusting of grated pecorino, which lends a desirable aroma. It's a lovely dish to serve before a lamb entrée.*

1 pound fresh cheese or meat tortellini
$\frac{1}{2}$ cup olive oil
$\frac{1}{2}$ teaspoon sweet smoked paprika
1 large garlic clove, peeled and smashed
1 cup plain Greek yogurt, room temperature
$\frac{1}{3}$ cup torn fresh mint leaves

Bring a large pot of salted water to a boil. Add the tortellini and cook 8 minutes, until tender. Meanwhile, in a small bowl, combine 5 tablespoons of the olive oil, the smoked paprika, garlic, and a large pinch of salt. In another bowl, whisk together the yogurt, 2 more tablespoons oil, and salt to taste. Drain the pasta well, shake dry. Toss the pasta with the remaining 1 tablespoon oil and add salt and pepper. Divide among 4 bowls. Top with the yogurt and mint, and drizzle with the smoked paprika oil. SERVES 4

SPAGHETTI WITH AGED GOUDA & FROZEN OLIVE OIL

Long ago, I came up with the idea of using frozen olive oil instead of butter when I wanted to emulsify a sauce in a healthier way. Now I use it in this version of spaghetti aglio e olio *(garlic-and-oil pasta) because the oil carries the garlic flavor beautifully without actually having to cook it (garlic burns easily and becomes bitter!) and also because it coats the pasta in a more clingy way than warm oil. Aged Gouda adds a level of caramel-like complexity that is quite different from using Parmesan.*

⅓ cup olive oil
1 medium garlic clove
12 ounces dried spaghetti
Large pinch red-pepper flakes
3-ounce chunk aged Gouda cheese

Put the oil in a ramekin. Push the garlic through a press and stir into the oil with a large pinch of salt. Freeze until solid, at least 4 hours.

Bring a large pot of salted water to a boil. Add the pasta and cook 10 minutes, or until tender. Drain well and shake dry. Break the frozen oil into pieces; put in a large bowl and add the pepper flakes. Add the pasta and toss well. Add salt. Using a Microplane grater, grate the cheese on top and toss again before serving. SERVES 4

PIMIENTO MAC

*Tossed with steaming hot pasta, my homemade version of humble pimiento cheese—a favorite
Southern sandwich spread—rivals more familiar versions of the classic mac and cheese.*

12 ounces dried pasta such as shells, elbows, or spaghetti
8 ounces very sharp yellow Cheddar cheese, cut into small pieces
6$\frac{1}{2}$-ounce jar roasted peppers
2 tablespoons mayonnaise
1 large garlic clove

Bring a large pot of salted water to a boil. Add the pasta and cook 12 minutes, or until
tender. Meanwhile, combine the cheese, roasted peppers (including brine from the jar),
mayonnaise, and garlic in a food processor and process until smooth. Drain the pasta
well and toss with the cheese mixture. Add salt and pepper. SERVES 4 TO 6

PASTA COOKED IN A BOTTLE OF WINE

This recipe was adapted from Colman Andrews's wonderful book, Flavors of the Riviera. *In
this unusual recipe, pasta is cooked in dry white wine that reduces to a wonderful glaze. I add a
coverlet of thinly sliced prosciutto that is gently warmed atop the pasta. The dish was meant to
celebrate the first pressing of the olives, so be sure to use your best olive oil.*

1 bottle dry white wine (3$\frac{1}{2}$ cups)
1 pound dried penne rigate
$\frac{1}{2}$ cup extra-virgin olive oil
$\frac{1}{2}$ cup freshly grated Parmigiano-Reggiano
18 paper-thin slices prosciutto

In a large saucepan, bring the wine, 2 cups water, and 1 teaspoon salt to a boil. Add
the pasta and reduce the heat to medium. Cook, uncovered and stirring often, until
the liquid is almost completely absorbed, about 20 minutes. Drain well and shake
dry. Transfer the pasta to a large bowl. Stir in the oil and cheese. Add salt and
pepper. Divide the pasta among 6 bowls and drape 3 slices of prosciutto over each
serving. SERVES 6

A Recipe from 1841: Macaroni & Tomatoes

Time lends enchantment to many dishes. I adapted this Neapolitan recipe from one found in an Italian cookbook from 1841 by cooking teacher Giuliano Bugialli. Its method is fascinating: Dried pasta marinates in olive oil before cooking. Rather than boiled, the pasta is then baked, resulting in a soft, dense, slightly chewy texture.

8 ounces dried ziti
7 tablespoons extra-virgin olive oil or garlic oil
28-ounce can plum tomatoes in puree
1 tablespoon fresh thyme leaves
$\frac{1}{2}$ cup freshly grated Parmigiano-Reggiano

Preheat the oven to 400°F. Put the ziti in an 8-cup soufflé dish. Add the oil and stir. Cover and let sit for 20 minutes.

Process the tomatoes and puree in a food processor until almost smooth. Pour the tomatoes over the pasta and stir in $\frac{1}{2}$ teaspoon salt. Mix well. Bake 45 minutes, stirring 3 times, until softened and slightly chewy. Stir in half the thyme and half the cheese. Transfer to bowls and sprinkle with the remaining thyme and cheese. SERVES 4

Baked Ziti in Bianco with Fontina & Salami ➤

This is not the tomato-y baked ziti we all know. This, its alter ego, is a tad more sophisticated.

3 tablespoons unsalted butter, room temperature
8 ounces dried ziti or cellentani
6-ounce piece Italian Fontina
3 ounces Genoa salami, sliced very thin
3 tablespoons finely chopped fresh oregano

Preheat the oven to 400°F. Grease an 8-cup soufflé dish with 1 tablespoon of the butter. Bring a large pot of salted water to a boil. Add the pasta and cook 12 minutes. Drain well and shake dry.

Shred the cheese on the large holes of a box grater. Finely julienne the salami. Arrange one-third of the pasta in the dish; top with one-third of the cheese, half of the salami, dabs of butter, 1 tablespoon of the oregano, and salt and pepper. Repeat layering, ending with pasta and cheese on top. Bake, uncovered, 15 minutes, until bubbly and golden. Stir well; mound onto plates and sprinkle remaining oregano. SERVES 4

Ziti "in bianco"

PERCIATELLI WITH FRENCH BREAKFAST RADISHES, BACON & GREENS

I love everything about this dish: the peppery bite of the radishes smacked up against smoky bacon and strong-willed cheese; the color; the use of both the radish bulbs and their leaves; the very name of the dish; and that I invented it quite by accident.

6 ounces dried perciatelli or spaghetti
Several large bunches large French breakfast radishes, greens included
4 strips bacon
2 tablespoons olive oil
$^1/_3$ cup freshly grated Pecorino Romano

Bring a large pot of salted water to a boil. Cook the pasta 12 minutes, until just tender. Separate the radishes from the greens and slice enough radishes $^1/_8$ inch thick to yield 1 cup. Measure out 3 cups of packed radish greens and coarsely chop. Cut the bacon into $^1/_3$-inch strips. Cook in a very large sauté pan over high heat for 3 minutes, until the fat is rendered and the bacon is soft, not crispy. Add the oil, chopped radish leaves, and sliced radishes. Cook over high heat until the greens wilt and the radishes soften, 5 minutes.

Drain the pasta; add to the pan and cook 2 minutes. Toss with half the cheese, lots of coarsely cracked black pepper, and salt. Sprinkle with the remaining cheese. SERVES 2

SHORT RIGATONI WITH CAULIFLOWER, ANCHOVIES & RAISINS

You'll find recipes like this in Sicily, where sweet, salty, and aromatic meet in joyful harmony.

4 cups small cauliflower florets
12 ounces dried mezzi rigatoni or radiatore
$1/3$ cup olive oil
2 tablespoons unsalted butter
8 anchovy fillets
$1/4$ cup golden raisins, chopped
2 large garlic cloves, minced
$1/4$ cup finely chopped fennel fronds
$1/2$ cup freshly grated Parmigiano-Reggiano

Bring a large pot of salted water to a boil. Add the cauliflower and cook 6 minutes, until soft; transfer to a colander with a slotted spoon. Return the water to a boil. Cook the pasta 12 minutes, until just tender. Drain well, reserving $1/3$ cup cooking water.

Meanwhile, heat the oil and butter in a very large skillet. When the butter melts, add the anchovies and mash into the hot oil. Add the cooked cauliflower, raisins, garlic, and $1/4$ teaspoon salt. Cook over high heat, stirring, for 5 minutes. Add the reserved pasta water and cook, stirring up browned bits, about 1 minute. Stir in the cooked pasta; add the fennel fronds and salt and pepper. Cook until hot, spoon into bowls, and sprinkle with cheese. SERVES 4

"Thunder & Lightning"

This is adapted from an old Italian cookbook, translated for me by a chef in Hoboken, New Jersey. Thunder *refers to the profusion of fried chickpeas and* lightning *to the excessive amount of cracked black peppercorns. Sometimes I add a tiny bit of fresh rosemary, too.*

12 ounces dried orecchiette
¼ cup olive oil
2 cups cooked chickpeas or 1 drained 19-ounce can
2 large garlic cloves, minced
1 cup chicken broth
1 tablespoon dried sage leaves
1½ teaspoons cracked black peppercorns
2 tablespoons unsalted butter
⅔ cup freshly grated Parmigiano-Reggiano

Bring a large pot of salted water to a boil. Cook the pasta 12 minutes, until tender. Meanwhile, heat the oil in a large skillet. Add the chickpeas and garlic and cook over high heat until the chickpeas begin to pop, 4 minutes. Add the broth, sage, and peppercorns. Cook until the broth has reduced by one-quarter, 10 minutes.

Drain the pasta well. Put in a large bowl with the butter. Add the chickpeas and broth and toss well. Add half the cheese and salt. Toss. Divide evenly among 4 warm bowls and top with the remaining cheese. SERVES 4

Castellane with Ricotta & Tomato-Marsala Sauce

This meatless sauce tastes like it's been cooking all day and, because of the Marsala, hints at the complexity of a slow-simmered veal stew. It's really homey.

28-ounce can crushed tomatoes in puree
3 tablespoons dry Marsala
3 large garlic cloves
2 tablespoons extra-virgin olive oil
1 pound dried castellane or cavatelli
1 cup fresh ricotta, room temperature
1 cup freshly grated Parmigiano-Reggiano

Bring a large pot of salted water to a boil. Process the tomatoes, Marsala, and garlic in a food processor until *very* smooth. Transfer to a medium saucepan and add the olive oil. Bring to a boil, reduce the heat, and simmer until thick, 18 minutes. Add salt and pepper; a pinch of sugar might be necessary if it is too acidic.

Meanwhile, add the pasta to the boiling water and cook 12 minutes, until tender. Drain well and shake dry. Return the pasta to the pot and stir in 2 cups of the sauce. Heat gently, stirring. Transfer to bowls and top each with more sauce, the ricotta, and Parmesan. SERVES 4 TO 6

Pasta Rustica with Sole, Greek Olives & White Wine

Here's the whole Mediterranean diet rolled up into one quick little meal—pasta, wine, olive oil, olives, garlic, lemon zest, and fish: perhaps the world's healthiest dish. Sometimes I make it in a wok, where it cooks up really quickly.

8 ounces dried penne rigate
3 large ripe plum tomatoes
2 large yellow tomatoes
$1/4$ cup extra-virgin olive oil
2 large garlic cloves, minced
$1/2$ cup dry white wine
$1/2$ cup finely chopped fresh curly parsley
$1/3$ cup slivered fresh basil leaves
1 tablespoon grated lemon zest
12 ounces lemon sole, cut in $1/2$-inch strips
16 pitted kalamata olives

Bring a large pot of salted water to a boil. Cook the pasta 12 minutes, until tender. Drain well. Meanwhile, cut all the tomatoes into $1/2$-inch pieces. Heat the oil in a wok or large skillet. Add the garlic and cook 30 seconds but do not brown. Add the tomatoes, wine, half the parsley, the basil, lemon zest, and 1 teaspoon salt. Cook 3 minutes over high heat. Add the fish and olives. Cook until the fish is just cooked through, 2 minutes.

Add the cooked pasta to the skillet and heat 2 minutes, until hot. Divide among 4 bowls. Garnish with the remaining chopped parsley. SERVES 4

CAMPANELLE WITH CARAMELIZED ONIONS, PEAS & MINT

This is an exuberant way to dress up any short pasta. Thai fish sauce adds a dose of umami . . . and intrigue. Sometimes I use edamame instead of peas.

4 large yellow onions, about 1½ pounds
⅓ cup extra-virgin olive oil
12 ounces dried farfalle
1 cup frozen peas
3 tablespoons white balsamic vinegar
1 tablespoon Thai fish sauce
1 cup coarsely chopped fresh mint
⅓ cup freshly grated Parmigiano-Reggiano plus a 2-ounce piece

Bring a large pot of salted water to a boil. Cut the onions in half through the roots. Place cut side down on a board. Thinly slice lengthwise (not into half-circles). Heat the oil in a very large skillet. Add the onions and cook over high heat, stirring, until dark brown, about 15 minutes. Meanwhile, cook the pasta in the boiling water for 12 minutes, until tender. Add the peas for the last 5 minutes of cooking. Drain well, saving ½ cup cooking liquid.

Add the vinegar and fish sauce to the onions; cook 2 minutes. Add the drained pasta and peas, reserved cooking water, mint, and grated cheese. Cook 2 minutes, until hot. Add salt and pepper. Serve in bowls; use a vegetable peeler to shave shards of cheese on top. SERVES 6

caramelized onions

FUSILLI WITH BRAISED ESCAROLE, GARLIC & RICOTTA SALATA

This is earthy and robust. Instead of ricotta salata to finish the dish, you might use sheep's milk feta. Another substitution note: Once I used iceberg lettuce instead of escarole, and it was delicious!

8 ounces dried fusilli
1 large head escarole
6 tablespoons extra-virgin olive oil
4 large garlic cloves, thinly sliced lengthwise
$1/3$ cup freshly grated Pecorino Romano
4 ounces ricotta salata or sheep's milk feta

Bring a large pot of salted water to a boil. Add the pasta and cook 12 minutes, until just tender. Drain well; save $1/3$ cup cooking liquid. Meanwhile, wash the escarole and dry; tear into medium pieces. Heat 3 tablespoons of the oil in a very large skillet. Add the escarole and garlic; cook over high heat, stirring often, until the escarole wilts and browns in spots, 10 minutes.

Add the pasta to the pan with the escarole and cook over high heat, tossing, for several minutes. Add the pecorino, remaining 3 tablespoons oil, and cooking water if the pasta is dry. Add salt and pepper to taste. Top with slices or crumbles of ricotta salata or feta. SERVES 4

GEMELLI WITH SAUSAGE, LEEKS & BARELY WILTED SPINACH

You might encounter this dish in an old-fashioned Italian restaurant, had it not been modern-ized with scotch bonnet pepper for heat and baby spinach, which barely needs cooking. A splash of grappa is a nice touch; add while the cream is simmering, if you wish.

8 ounces dried gemelli
2 tablespoons olive oil
1 cup finely minced leeks
8 ounces fennel sausage
$^3/_4$ cup heavy cream
$^1/_2$ scotch bonnet pepper, seeded and slivered
5 ounces baby spinach

Bring a large pot of salted water to a boil. Cook the pasta 12 minutes, until tender. Drain well, saving $^1/_2$ cup cooking liquid. Meanwhile, heat the oil in a very large skillet. Add the leeks and cook, stirring, until soft, 5 minutes. Remove the sausage from the casings and crumble into the pan. Cook over high heat until browned, 5 minutes. Add the cream and slivered pepper. Cook until the cream has thickened, 3 minutes.

Add the pasta to the skillet and heat through. Add the spinach and cooking liquid and cook, stirring, until the spinach just wilts, 2 minutes. Add salt and transfer to bowls. SERVES 4

WARM SESAME NOODLES WITH GINGER & SNOW PEAS

Asian sesame noodles are generally eaten cold, but they are also delicious hot. The sauce takes only minutes to prepare.

8 ounces dried linguine
6 ounces snow peas, trimmed and julienned
1/4 cup smooth peanut butter
2 tablespoons chopped peeled fresh ginger
1/4 cup chopped scallions, white and green parts
2 tablespoons soy sauce
1 tablespoon Asian sesame oil
1 tablespoon rice vinegar
1 tablespoon honey
1 large garlic clove, chopped
1/4 teaspoon Sriracha
3 tablespoons julienned fresh cilantro or mint or both

Bring a large pot of salted water to a boil. Add the linguine and cook 10 minutes. Add the snow peas and cook 3 minutes longer, until the pasta is tender. Drain well and shake dry. Meanwhile, combine the peanut butter, ginger, scallions, soy sauce, oil, rice vinegar, honey, garlic, Sriracha, and 2 tablespoons water in a food processor. Process until very smooth.

Transfer the pasta and snow peas to a large bowl. Add the sauce and toss. Top with the herbs. Serve warm. SERVES 4

FISH

Although many home cooks think there is inherent daring in preparing fish, every recipe in this chapter is manageable and most take less than 15 minutes to make! Because fish is a fabulous source of healthy protein and a great way to get dinner on the table in a hurry, I have become a zealot for finding new ways to prepare it. You'll find nearly three dozen of my favorite ways with fish here.

The goal is to maximize the unique flavor and the singular texture of a particular fish, not to overwhelm its virtues. So one begins with great ingredients and treats them simply. Cooking technique may be key to the success of the dish, but there is also skill involved in the purchasing of seafood. So apply these simple rules when buying fish: 1) Look first. If it's a whole fish, make sure it has clear, shiny eyes, an unblemished layer of scales, and bright red gills. For steaks and fillets, the surface of the fish should be glistening, not dull, and the flesh should be firm and compact, not flaking apart. 2) Smell. Fish should never smell fishy or "off"; you can smell bad fish even through a supermarket package. Great, fresh fish smells like the sea. 3) Ask questions. You want to develop trust with your purveyor. Don't be afraid to ask questions like "How fresh is this?" "How long can I keep it?" "Where does it come from?"

It is hard to give exact cooking times for fish, so you must also rely on your intuition—and your finger. You want the fish to be firm yet yielding to the touch.

Fish is good for you. Inherently low in calories and saturated fats, fish contains many beneficial nutrients, including vitamins A and D and omega-3 fatty acids, which can help lower blood levels of the harmful low-density lipoproteins (LDL) that contribute to heart disease. Omega-3 fatty acids can also help boost the body's immune system.

Thankfully, many supermarkets now sell top-quality fresh fish and even have their own fishmongers to cut and fillet dozens of varieties—both farmed and wild—right before your eyes. Do, however, support your local fish store or, better yet, buy directly from fishermen in season and buy wild fish when possible.

The following main-course recipes feature 18 varieties of fish and shellfish. Served in half portions, many of them make wonderful starters. Cold preparations of fish and shellfish, for hors d'oeuvres or first courses, can also be found in the salad chapter.

salmon

Salmon with Cucumbers & Blackened Lemons **138**

3-Minute Wasabi Salmon **138**

Salmon with Lime Leaves, Poppy Rice & Coconut Sauce **139**

Salmon & Mint in Crispy Grape Leaves **140**

Smoked & Fresh Salmon en Chemise **143**

Ginger's No-Ginger Salmon **144**

"Golden Robe" Salmon with Snow Peas & Red Cabbage **145**

Korean-Style Salmon "Bulgogi," Bok Choy & Shiitakes **147**

flat fish & halibut

Sole Provençal with Petit Ratatouille **152**

"Silver Packet" Flounder with Miso Mayo **152**

Red Snapper with Pop-Pop Tomatoes **153**

Oven-Steamed Halibut with Carrots, Lemon & Thyme **155**

Roasted Halibut with Tomatoes & Saffron Vinaigrette **156**

Halibut in Prosciutto Wrappers, Red Onions & Crispy Basil **156**

tuna & swordfish

Seared Tuna with Fresh Corn & Wasabi "Cream" **162**

Black & Blue Tuna with Garlic Asparagus & Yogurt-Caper Sauce **163**

Charred Tuna, Mizuna & Pear with Black Vinaigrette **165**

Grilled Tuna with Lemony Tahina, Greens & Pomegranate Seeds **166**

Swordfish Steaks with Sardine "Bolognese" **168**

Green Curry Swordfish with Shiitakes & Basil **168**

Roasted Swordfish with Tomatoes-on-the-Vine & Rosemary Tartare Sauce **169**

mod cod

Sautéed Cod with Chorizo, Orange & Wild Arugula, Sherry Vinaigrette **148**

Crunchy Crumbed Cod with Frozen Peas **150**

Braised Cod with "Sliced Tomato" Sauce & Fresh Oregano **150**

500-Degree Cod with Macadamia Butter & Radicchio **151**

bass & blues

Fennel-Roasted Striped Bass, Tiny Tomatoes & Crispy Capers **157**

Chilean Sea Bass with Pistachio-Pesto Crust & Green Bean "Fries" **158**

Braised Black Sea Bass on Pancetta-Studded Cabbage **159**

Holy Mackerel **160**

Bluefish Salmoriglio with Red Pepper Julienne **162**

crustaceans

Sheet-Pan Mussels with Red Curry–Garlic Broth **170**

Steamed Clams with Sake & Chilies **170**

Shrimp Escabeche with Blood Orange Mojo **172**

Riso in Bianco with Shrimp Scampi **173**

Seared Scallops on Sweet Pea Puree **174**

Salt-Water Lobsters, Healthy Drawn Butter **175**

SALMON WITH CUCUMBERS & BLACKENED LEMONS

Is there anything more radically simple than a succulent piece of broiled salmon? Alone, it's a one-ingredient recipe that's hard to beat. Gussied up with unexpected accessories—buttery cooked cucumbers and blackened lemons that provide warm acidity—it's even better.

1 large cucumber, peeled
1 tablespoon unsalted butter
2 tablespoons finely chopped fresh dill
4 thick salmon steaks, 8 ounces each
2 large lemons

Preheat the broiler. Halve the cucumber lengthwise and remove seeds. Slice crosswise into $\frac{1}{4}$-inch half moons. Melt the butter in a large skillet. Add the cucumbers; cook over high heat until softened, 3 minutes. Add the dill, salt, and pepper and cook until just tender, about 2 minutes.

Season the salmon with salt and pepper. Halve the steaks lengthwise, removing the center bones. Cut the lemons in half crosswise. Cut a small piece from each end so they can stand upright. Arrange the fish and lemons, cut sides up, on a broiler pan. Broil 5 minutes, until the lemons blacken and the fish is rare. Arrange 2 pieces of fish crossed on each plate, with the cucumbers and lemons alongside. SERVES 4

3-MINUTE WASABI SALMON

This is a dish for company that is much more than the sum of its parts. Three minutes refers to the time it takes to prep; the rest all happens in the oven.

$3\frac{1}{2}$- to 4-pound side of salmon with skin, bones removed
6 tablespoons wasabi powder
$1\frac{1}{2}$ cups mayonnaise
1 tablespoon black sesame seeds
Purple basil sprouts, micro-herbs, or mizuna

Preheat the oven to 450°F. Use tweezers to remove any bones from the fish. Season the salmon side with salt and pepper. Mix the wasabi powder with $\frac{1}{3}$ cup water to make a smooth paste. Stir in the mayonnaise. Spread on the fish to cover completely. Place on a rimmed baking sheet and roast for 20 minutes, until the fish is just firm and the top is slightly puffy and golden. Sprinkle with sesame seeds and sprouts. Serve hot. SERVES 8

Salmon with Lime Leaves, Poppy Rice & Coconut Sauce

This is an all-in-one dish—protein, starch, sauce, and flavored oil—that's exotic, too, and can be made in no time at all. Kefir lime leaves can be found in Indian and Middle Eastern food stores; they freeze beautifully and have an amazing perfume.

1 cup basmati rice
2 teaspoons poppy seeds
2 tablespoons unsalted butter
2 tablespoons olive oil
$1/4$ teaspoon curry powder
4 salmon fillets, $6\frac{1}{2}$ ounces each, skin removed
8 large kefir lime leaves
$\frac{1}{2}$ cup coconut milk
2 teaspoons sake

Bring the rice, 4 cups water, and 1 teaspoon salt to a boil in a saucepan. Boil until tender, 12 minutes; drain well. Add the poppy seeds and $\frac{1}{2}$ tablespoon of the butter; cover and keep warm. In a small bowl, stir together the oil, curry powder, and a pinch of salt. Set aside.

Meanwhile, season the fish with salt. Place 2 lime leaves on top of each fillet; wrap each tightly in plastic. Place the fish in a steamer basket set in a large pot of boiling water. Cover and steam 8 minutes, until just firm.

In a medium saucepan, bring the coconut milk to a boil, whisking constantly. Whisk in the remaining $1\frac{1}{2}$ tablespoons butter, sake, salt, and pepper. Cook 1 minute. Unwrap the fish. Serve atop the rice with the coconut sauce and drizzles of curry oil. SERVES 4

SALMON & MINT IN CRISPY GRAPE LEAVES

Crispy salty grape leaves, fresh mint, and a divine sauce of crème fraîche and garlic signal a very hip Greek-inspired dish.

1/2 cup crème fraîche
1 small garlic clove
4 thick salmon fillets, 6 ounces each, skin removed
2 medium bunches fresh mint
8 large grape leaves in brine, rinsed and dried
3 tablespoons olive oil

Preheat the oven to 450°F. Mix the crème fraîche with the garlic pushed through a press. Add salt. Season the fish with salt and pepper. Top each fillet with 6 mint leaves. Wrap each piece of fish tightly in 2 overlapping grape leaves, tucking in the ends as you go.

Heat the oil in a large nonstick skillet. Add the packets and cook over high heat until crispy, 2 minutes on each side. Transfer the fish to a rimmed baking sheet and scatter with mint sprigs. Bake 8 minutes, until the fish is just firm. Serve with the crème fraîche and crispy mint. SERVES 4

a robe of smoked salmon

Smoked & Fresh Salmon en Chemise

Fresh salmon enrobed in a layer of smoked salmon and roasted at a high temperature is rich and elegant with a subtle smoky perfume. An instantaneous room-temperature sauce, made from tomatillos, basil, cilantro, and lime, is a striking accompaniment.

6 salmon fillets with skin, 6 ounces each
9 ounces thinly sliced smoked salmon
16 ounces tomatillos, at room temperature
$1/2$ cup extra-virgin olive oil
$1/2$ cup packed fresh basil leaves
$1/2$ cup packed fresh cilantro leaves
$1/4$ cup chopped onion
1 tablespoon fresh lime juice
Large handful of pea shoots or microgreens for garnish

Preheat the oven to 475°F. Season the salmon fillets with salt and pepper; place on a rimmed baking sheet. Completely enrobe the top and sides of each fillet with a thin layer of smoked salmon, pressing down firmly and tucking ends under the fish. Roast 12 to 14 minutes, until just firm. Do not overcook.

Meanwhile, cut the tomatillos into 1-inch pieces. Add to a food processor with the oil, basil, cilantro, onion, lime juice, and $1\frac{1}{2}$ teaspoons salt. Process until very smooth. Spoon a puddle of sauce onto 6 large plates. Top with the salmon and garnish with pea shoots. SERVES 6

GINGER'S NO-GINGER SALMON

I stole this from my friend Ginger Brown, a producer for Sesame Street *for decades, who entertains often. I love it for a romantic dinner for two, but you can also make a whole side for company. It is scrumptious and very Mediterranean in spirit.*

$\frac{1}{2}$ red bell pepper
$\frac{1}{2}$ yellow bell pepper
2 large shallots, thinly sliced
$1\frac{1}{2}$ tablespoons olive oil
1 anchovy filet
6 tablespoons dry white wine
14-ounce thick salmon fillet with skin
2 teaspoons fresh thyme leaves

Preheat the oven to 450°F. Cut the peppers into long, $\frac{1}{4}$-inch-wide strips. Heat the oil in a large skillet. Add the peppers and shallots and cook over high heat 8 minutes until the shallots are dark and peppers soft. Mash in the anchovy and stir in 2 tablespoons of the wine. Cook until it evaporates.

Place the salmon in the center of a very large piece of foil on a rimmed baking sheet. Spoon the pepper mixture atop the fish. Sprinkle with 1 teaspoon of the thyme. Pour the remaining 4 tablespoons wine over the fish. Bring the edges of the foil together to make a large, tight package and crimp to seal. Bake 15 minutes. Garnish with the remaining thyme. SERVES 2

"GOLDEN ROBE" SALMON WITH SNOW PEAS & RED CABBAGE

Who doesn't need a recipe for a gorgeous fish dish full of good nutrition that can be made in 10 minutes?

> $1/4$ cup white miso (also known as shiro miso)
> 1 teaspoon minced fresh rosemary
> 2 large garlic cloves
> 4 thick salmon fillets with skin, 6 ounces each
> 2 teaspoons turmeric
> 3 tablespoons olive oil
> 5 ounces shredded red cabbage
> 4 ounces snow peas, trimmed
> 2 tablespoons toasted sesame seeds

Preheat the broiler. Mix together the miso, rosemary, 1 garlic clove pushed through a press, and 2 tablespoons water. Rub the paste onto the salmon fillets, then rub in the turmeric until golden. Place on a rimmed baking sheet and drizzle with 1 tablespoon of the oil. Broil 5 inches from the heat for 2 minutes. Turn off the broiler and heat the oven to 500°F. Roast the salmon 5 minutes, until just firm.

Meanwhile, heat the remaining 2 tablespoons oil in a wok until hot. Add the cabbage and snow peas and cook over high heat, stirring, 2 minutes. Push the remaining garlic clove through a press into the wok. Cook the vegetables until crisp-tender, 3 minutes longer. Transfer to 4 plates. Top with the fish and sesame seeds. SERVES 4

KOREAN-STYLE SALMON "BULGOGI," BOK CHOY & SHIITAKES

Bulgogi refers to a Korean preparation for short ribs. Here it refers to an amazingly delicious way to make fish that's radically simple to prepare, despite its long list of ingredients.

1/4 cup soy sauce
1/2-inch piece peeled fresh ginger, chopped
1 scallion, chopped, white and green parts
1 tablespoon rice wine
2 teaspoons sugar
1 teaspoon Asian sesame oil
1/2 teaspoon Chinese chili paste
2 large garlic cloves
4 thick salmon fillets, 6 ounces each, skin removed
1 tablespoon olive oil
1 large bok choy, about 1 pound
3 1/2 ounces fresh shiitake mushrooms, stemmed and sliced

Preheat the broiler. Combine the soy sauce, ginger, scallion, wine, sugar, sesame oil, chili paste, and 1 garlic clove in a food processor; process until smooth. Place the salmon in a large, deep dish and cover with the marinade. Turn to coat; let sit 10 minutes. Remove the fish from the marinade and place on a rimmed baking sheet. Broil 8 inches from the heat for 8 minutes, until just firm.

Meanwhile, pour the marinade into a small saucepan and boil for 1 minute. Set aside. Heat the olive oil in a wok. Thinly slice the bok choy crosswise. Add to the wok with the mushrooms and remaining garlic clove pushed through a press. Stir-fry for 2 minutes; add salt. Transfer to plates. Glaze the fish with the marinade and set atop the vegetables. SERVES 4

Sautéed Cod with Chorizo, Orange & Wild Arugula, Sherry Vinaigrette

The better the chorizo (dried Spanish sausage), the more earthy this becomes; but Goya chorizo, available in most supermarkets, will suffice.

2 oranges
8 tablespoons olive oil
3 ounces dried chorizo, sliced ¼ inch thick
2 tablespoons sherry vinegar
3 ounces mixed wild arugula and mesclun
4 thick cod fillets, 6 ounces each

Cut the rind and pith from the oranges. Cut between membranes to release segments; save 2 tablespoons of the juice. Heat 1 tablespoon of the oil in a very large skillet. Add the chorizo and cook over high heat 2 minutes until crispy but not blackened.

Whisk together 6 tablespoons of the oil, 1 tablespoon of the vinegar, and salt and pepper. Toss the greens with the dressing and divide among 4 large plates. Top with the orange segments, chorizo, and pan drippings.

Add the remaining 1 tablespoon oil to the skillet. Season the fish with salt and pepper and cook over high heat until firm, 3 minutes each side. Add the remaining 1 tablespoon vinegar and orange juice and cook 30 seconds. Place the fish on the greens and drizzle with pan juices. SERVES 4

CRUNCHY CRUMBED COD WITH FROZEN PEAS

Yep, you use frozen peas straight from the freezer; just slam the package on the counter a few times to break them up. They provide moisture as the thick pieces of cod, topped with garlicky bread crumbs, are roasted at a high temperature. The peas also get roasted and take on a comforting starchy texture.

> 10-ounce package frozen peas
> 4 scallions
> 2 tablespoons fresh thyme leaves
> 4 tablespoons olive oil
> 1 cup panko
> 1 large garlic clove
> 4 thick cod fillets, 6 ounces each

Preheat the oven to 475°F. Put the frozen peas in a large bowl. Slice the scallions thinly on the bias and mix with the peas. Add the thyme, 2 tablespoons of the oil, and salt and pepper. Spread on a small rimmed baking sheet.

Mix the panko with the remaining oil, garlic pushed through a press, and salt. Season the fish with salt and pepper. Top each piece with a thick covering of panko and press down firmly. Place the fish atop the peas. Roast for 12 minutes, until the crumbs are golden and the fish is just firm. Serve the fish on the peas. SERVES 4

BRAISED COD WITH "SLICED TOMATO" SAUCE & FRESH OREGANO

Thick cod fillets steam upon a bed of sliced tomatoes—an idea inspired by cookbook author Arthur Schwartz, whose school Cook at Seliano in southern Italy is much sought-after. The clean, fresh, exuberant flavors of this radically simple preparation are a hallmark of his cuisine. Throw two handfuls of mussels in the pan, too, if you like.

> 4 cod fillets, 6 ounces each
> 2 or 3 very large very ripe tomatoes, about 1½ pounds
> 3 large garlic cloves, finely minced
> ⅓ cup fresh oregano leaves, plus sprigs for garnish
> Pinch hot-pepper flakes
> ⅓ cup olive oil

Season the fish with salt and pepper. Slice the tomatoes ¼ inch thick; place, overlapping, in a very large skillet. Scatter the garlic, oregano leaves, and pepper flakes over the tomatoes. Arrange the fish on the tomatoes and pour the olive oil over the fish. Heat over high heat until the oil sizzles. Cover the pan, reduce the heat, and cook 10 minutes, until just firm. Transfer the fish to 4 plates. Cook the sauce over high heat for 1 minute. Pour over the fish and garnish with oregano sprigs. SERVES 4

500-DEGREE COD WITH MACADAMIA BUTTER & RADICCHIO

This dish comes together in 6 or 7 minutes. The idea of roasting cod at such a high temperature was inspired by Shirley Corriher, scientist, chef, and author of the encyclopedic books, BakeWise and CookWise. I've added her felicitous pairing of buttery macadamia nuts and my wilted radicchio caressed with lemon. The combo is also great on sautéed chicken breasts.

4 thick cod fillets, 7 ounces each
1 cup unsalted macadamia nuts, about 3 ounces
1 medium head radicchio, about 8 ounces
7 tablespoons unsalted butter
1 lemon
⅓ cup coarsely chopped fresh flat-leaf parsley

Preheat the oven to 500°F. Season the fish with salt and pepper; place on a rimmed baking sheet. Roast for 6 to 7 minutes, until just firm. Meanwhile, finely chop the nuts. Shred the radicchio. Melt the butter in a large skillet. Add the nuts and cook over high heat, stirring constantly, until browned, 2 minutes. Add the radicchio and cook until soft, 2 minutes. Add salt and pepper. Transfer the fish to 4 plates. Spoon the nut mixture on top. Top with grated lemon zest, a little lemon juice, and parsley. SERVES 4

Sole Provençal with Petit Ratatouille

You may add a few tablespoons of pastis or Pernod to the ratatouille during the last few minutes of cooking. Folding the fish fillets to a double thickness prevents them from cooking too quickly.

5 tablespoons extra-virgin olive oil, plus more for drizzling
1 cup roughly chopped scallions, white and green parts
1$^1/_2$ teaspoons finely minced jalapeño pepper
2 ounces sun-dried tomatoes (not in oil), 10 small halves
1 medium red bell pepper
2 medium zucchini
1 tablespoon sherry vinegar
1 tablespoon honey
1 tablespoon fresh thyme leaves, plus sprigs for garnish
4 sole fillets, 7 ounces each

Heat 3 tablespoons of the oil in a large pan. Add the scallions and jalapeño and cook 2 minutes. Finely chop the dried tomatoes, bell pepper, and zucchini. Add to the pan and cook over high heat, stirring, until soft, 10 minutes. Add the vinegar, honey, thyme leaves, and $^1/_4$ cup water. Cook 1 minute and add salt and pepper. Place the fillets, folded in half, on top. Drizzle with the remaining 2 tablespoons oil and sprinkle with salt. Cover the pan and cook over medium-high heat for 6 minutes, until the fillets are cooked through. Drizzle with additional oil and garnish with thyme sprigs. SERVES 4

"Silver Packet" Flounder with Miso Mayo

Silver foil packets balloon as they steam in a hot oven, enveloping the fish with dreamy vapors. A bit of addictive miso mayo, inspired by Latin chef Maricel Prescilla, holds it together.

$^1/_2$ cup mayonnaise
2 tablespoons white miso (also known as shiro miso)
2 tablespoons mirin (sweet rice wine)
$^1/_4$ teaspoon ground cumin
4 thick flounder fillets, 7 ounces each
4 ounces baby spinach
4 ounces sun-dried tomatoes (not in oil), 20 small halves
4 large ramps or scallions, thinly sliced
$^1/_2$ cup slivered fresh basil
$^1/_4$ cup olive oil
Pinch hot-pepper flakes

Preheat the oven to 500°F. Stir together the mayonnaise, miso, mirin, and cumin. Set aside. Tear off four 15-inch pieces of foil. Season the fish with salt and pepper. For each: Put 1 ounce spinach in the center of the foil. Top with a fillet, 5 dried tomatoes to cover, one-fourth of the ramps, 2 tablespoons of the basil, 1 tablespoon of the oil, pepper flakes, and salt. Bring the edges of the foil together and crimp tightly to form a packet. Place on a rimmed baking sheet. Bake for 10 minutes, until the fish is just cooked through. Carefully open the packets. Transfer the fish and juices to 4 shallow bowls and dab with miso mayo. SERVES 4

RED SNAPPER WITH POP-POP TOMATOES

This dish was inspired by my chess tutor, Ben Resnick, who is also a credible cook. Pop-pop is what the tomatoes do in your mouth. Serve with a pile of blue potato chips.

1 tablespoon unsalted butter
3 tablespoons olive oil
1 pint grape tomatoes
1/3 cup finely minced shallots
1 large garlic clove, minced
1/4 cup dry white wine
1 teaspoon honey
Large pinch saffron threads
4 red snappers fillets without skin, 7 ounces each
Flour for dredging
Grated zest and juice of 1 lime
3 tablespoons chopped fresh chives

Heat the butter and 1 tablespoon of the oil in a 12-inch skillet. Add the tomatoes and cook 2 minutes over high heat. Add the shallots and garlic and cook, stirring, for 3 minutes. Add the wine, honey, and saffron. Cook until the tomatoes soften, 8 minutes.

Meanwhile, season the fish with salt; dredge lightly in flour. Heat the remaining 2 tablespoons oil in another skillet. Cook the fish over high heat until just firm, 3 minutes on each side. Bring the tomato mixture just to a boil and add the lime zest and juice. Simmer 1 minute and add the chives and salt and pepper. Transfer the fish to plates and top with the tomato mixture. SERVES 4

OVEN-STEAMED HALIBUT WITH CARROTS, LEMON & THYME

In this unorthodox procedure, the fish is oven-steamed in a packet, then vinaigrette is poured into the packet so that the fish marinates overnight. Served in smaller portions, it's a terrific alternative to gefilte fish for the beginning of a Seder dinner. Otherwise, it is a lovely chilled fish dish to serve in warmer weather.

1 large fennel bulb, fronds removed
1 large lemon, very thinly sliced
8 halibut fillets, 4 ounces each
2 large carrots, peeled and thinly sliced
12 ounces small cherry tomatoes, halved
$^3/_4$ cup plus 3 tablespoons olive oil
1 large bunch fresh thyme
2 medium garlic cloves
Lemon wedges

Preheat the oven to 450°F. Line a rimmed baking sheet with foil twice as long as the sheet. Slice the fennel paper-thin and scatter in the center. Scatter the lemon slices over the fennel. Season the fish with salt and pepper and place on top. Scatter the carrots and tomatoes on and around the fish. Drizzle with the 3 tablespoons oil. Top with 16 thyme sprigs. Fold over the overhanging foil and crimp the edges to make a tight packet. Bake 12 minutes, until the fish is just firm.

Process the $^3/_4$ cup oil, garlic, and salt and pepper in a blender until smooth. Carefully open the packet and pour the sauce over the warm fish. Reseal; let cool for 1 hour. Refrigerate overnight. Discard the thyme. Serve with lemon wedges and fresh thyme. SERVES 8

ROASTED HALIBUT WITH TOMATOES & SAFFRON VINAIGRETTE

This elaborate-looking and complex-tasting main course is great for a crowd. Its most alluring quality is that it is equally delicious warm or at room temperature.

3 pounds assorted heirloom tomatoes
1 pint each red and yellow cherry tomatoes
8 thick halibut steaks, 8 ounces each
$\frac{1}{2}$ cup olive oil
3 tablespoons white balsamic vinegar
2 tablespoons finely minced scallions, white part only
2 tablespoons finely chopped fresh basil
2 tablespoons finely chopped fresh cilantro
$\frac{1}{4}$ teaspoon saffron threads

Preheat the oven to 450°F. Cut the heirloom tomatoes into 1-inch chunks. Place on a large rimmed baking sheet in one layer. Cut the cherry tomatoes in half lengthwise and add to the baking sheet. Sprinkle with salt and pepper. Season the fish with salt and arrange atop the tomatoes. In a small bowl, whisk together the oil, vinegar, and scallions. Add the basil, cilantro, saffron, and salt and pepper. Spoon over the fish and let sit 10 minutes. Roast 10 minutes, until the fish is just firm. Serve hot or at room temperature with the pan juices. SERVES 8

HALIBUT IN PROSCIUTTO WRAPPERS, RED ONIONS & CRISPY BASIL

When in doubt about dinner, make this. Period.

5 tablespoons olive oil
1 large garlic clove
4 halibut fillets without skin, 7 ounces each
8 thin slices prosciutto
1 large red onion, sliced very thin
16 large basil leaves

Preheat the oven to 450°F. Stir together 2 tablespoons of the oil and garlic pushed through a press. Wrap each halibut fillet tightly with 2 slices of prosciutto to cover. Brush the prosciutto with the garlic oil. Scatter the onions on a rimmed baking sheet. Arrange the fish on top, separated a few inches apart. Roast for 10 minutes, until just firm.

Meanwhile, heat the remaining 3 tablespoons oil in a large skillet until very hot. Add the basil and cook until crispy, 2 minutes. Transfer to paper towels and sprinkle with salt. Serve the fish and onions topped with the crispy basil. SERVES 4

FENNEL-ROASTED STRIPED BASS, TINY TOMATOES & CRISPY CAPERS

A whole center-cut fish fillet is a sophisticated way to feed a crowd. And for a quick, delicious sauce, whisk together some caper brine and olive oil to drizzle on the warm fish. A spring shower of finely chopped fennel fronds is a great counterpoint to all the flavors.

1 medium fennel bulb with fronds
1 medium red onion
2$\frac{1}{2}$-pound-thick fillet of striped bass or halibut
20 grape tomatoes, halved lengthwise
$\frac{3}{4}$ cup olive oil
3 tablespoons capers plus 3 tablespoons brine
1 large garlic clove

Preheat the oven to 450°F. Remove the fronds from the fennel and chop coarsely to get 2 tablespoons. Cut the fennel bulb in half lengthwise, then crosswise into paper-thin slices; scatter down the center of a rimmed baking sheet. Cut the onion in half and slice paper-thin. Scatter over the fennel. Season the fish with salt and pepper and place on the vegetables. Arrange the tomatoes around the fish. Pour $\frac{1}{4}$ cup of the oil over the fish and tomatoes. Scatter the capers on top. Roast for 20 minutes, until just firm.

Whisk together the remaining $\frac{1}{2}$ cup oil and the caper brine. Push the garlic through a press and add to the dressing. Stir in the chopped fennel fronds. Drizzle each portion of fish with some dressing; scatter any extra fronds on top. SERVES 6

CHILEAN SEA BASS WITH PISTACHIO-PESTO CRUST & GREEN BEAN "FRIES"

This is also great made with fresh salmon. Make your own pesto (page 85) or use store-bought.

4 thick Chilean sea bass fillets, 7 ounces each
1/2 cup best-quality basil pesto
1/2 cup finely ground pistachios
12 ounces green beans, trimmed
2 tablespoons olive oil
1 lemon

Preheat the oven to 450°F. Season the fish with salt and pepper and arrange on a rimmed baking sheet. Spread each fillet with 2 tablespoons pesto to cover completely. Distribute the pistachios equally among the fillets, patting to form a crust. Drizzle the green beans with the oil and sprinkle with salt. Place around the fish. Roast for 16 minutes, until the fish is firm. Grate lemon zest on the fish. Cut the lemon into wedges and serve with the fish and beans. SERVES 4

BRAISED BLACK SEA BASS ON PANCETTA-STUDDED CABBAGE

A drizzle of Beet Vinaigrette (page 67), though not necessary, is gorgeous and dramatic for company.

4 ounces pancetta in one piece
1 large head Napa cabbage
$1/2$ cup dry white wine or dry vermouth
2 tablespoons unsalted butter
2 teaspoons sweet or smoked paprika
2 teaspoons ground cumin
4 black sea bass fillets without skin, 7 ounces each
$1/4$ cup fresh chervil sprigs

Dice the pancetta into $1/4$-inch pieces. Cook in a 12-inch skillet over high heat until the fat is rendered, about 5 minutes. Finely chop the cabbage. Add the cabbage, wine, and butter to the skillet and cook over high heat until the cabbage softens, 10 minutes. Add salt and pepper. In a small bowl, stir together the paprika, cumin, and $1/2$ teaspoon salt. Rub into the fillets and place them atop the cabbage. Cover the pan and cook over medium heat for 8 minutes, until the fish is cooked through. Serve the fish on a bed of cabbage and garnish with chervil. SERVES 4

HOLY MACKEREL

Mackerel should be given more respect. Prepared this way, it is radically delicious and terribly good for you, thanks to an abundance of healthy omega-3 fatty acids.

3 tablespoons olive oil, plus more for drizzling
$1\frac{1}{2}$ cups finely chopped onions
6 thick slices bacon, finely diced
1 cup very finely chopped fresh tomato
2 tablespoons chopped capers
4 thick mackerel fillets, 8 ounces each
1 lemon, cut in wedges

Preheat the broiler. Heat the oil in a large skillet. Add the onions and bacon. Cook over high heat for 2 minutes. Add the tomato and cook until soft and lightly browned, 10 minutes. Stir in the capers and salt and pepper. Meanwhile, lightly oil the mackerel fillets and sprinkle with salt and pepper. Place on a rimmed baking sheet and broil several inches from the heat for 5 minutes, until just firm. Spoon the vegetables over the fish, drizzle with oil, and serve with lemon wedges. SERVES 4

holy mackerel

BLUEFISH SALMORIGLIO WITH RED PEPPER JULIENNE

Salmoriglio refers to a classic Italian preparation in which fish gets doused with a mixture of lemon juice, olive oil, and dried oregano. Using fresh oregano and julienned sweet bell peppers makes it taste brand new. Try this with swordfish if you like.

4 bluefish fillets with skin, 7 ounces each
½ large red bell pepper
¼ cup olive oil
⅓ cup packed fresh flat-leaf parsley
2 tablespoons fresh oregano leaves
1 tablespoon lemon juice
1 small garlic clove

Preheat the broiler. Season the fish with salt and pepper. Cut the pepper into long, very thin strips, about ⅛ inch wide. Place the fish and bell pepper strips on a rimmed baking sheet. Puree the oil, parsley, oregano, lemon juice, and garlic in a food processor until smooth; add salt and pepper. Pour half of the mixture over the fish. Broil several inches from the heat for 5 minutes, until the fish is cooked through but still moist; the peppers will blacken a bit. Serve the fish topped with the peppers and some of the remaining dressing drizzled over all. SERVES 4

SEARED TUNA WITH FRESH CORN & WASABI "CREAM"

This recipe was featured in Oprah's magazine as well as in her first cookbook. The "cream" sauce is dairy-free, made with the "milk" of fresh corn and thickened with wasabi.

3 large ears corn
1 teaspoon prepared wasabi paste
4 thick tuna steaks, 8 ounces each
1 tablespoon olive oil

Shuck the corn; discard the silk. Cut the kernels from the cobs to get 2 cups. Combine 1½ cups kernels in a small saucepan with 1¾ cups water. Bring to a boil, reduce the heat, and cook until very soft, 15 minutes. Transfer to a blender with 3 tablespoons water and puree until very smooth. Strain through a sieve into a bowl. Stir in the wasabi and salt. Place the remaining $^1/_2$ cup of corn in a saucepan with water to cover. Boil 10 minutes. Drain.

Season the tuna with salt. Heat the oil in a large skillet. Sear the tuna 2 minutes on each side. Reheat the sauce and pour over the fish. Garnish with the corn. SERVES 4

Black & Blue Tuna with Garlic Asparagus & Yogurt-Caper Sauce

So rich and compelling, you would never know it was healthy. I enjoyed a version of this at a trendy underground dining club in Brooklyn that sadly no longer exists.

> 5 tablespoons extra-virgin olive oil
> 1 large garlic clove
> 2 pounds thin asparagus, bottoms trimmed
> 1 cup plain Greek yogurt
> 2 tablespoons drained capers, chopped, plus 2 tablespoons brine
> Grated zest of 1 lemon
> 1 tablespoon sweet paprika
> 2 teaspoons smoked paprika
> 4 tuna steaks, 6 ounces each

Preheat the oven to 400°F. Mix together 1 tablespoon of the oil, the garlic pushed through a press, and $^1/_2$ teaspoon salt. Toss with the asparagus on a rimmed baking sheet. Roast 10 minutes. In a small bowl, combine the yogurt, 3 tablespoons of the oil, capers and brine, and zest. Set aside.

Mix together both paprikas and $^1/_2$ teaspoon salt. Press onto both sides of the tuna steaks. Heat the remaining 1 tablespoon oil in a large skillet over high heat. Sear the tuna 2 minutes on one side; turn and sear $1^1/_2$ minutes on the second side. Keep the fish very rare. Cut each steak on the bias into 4 thick slices. Place puddles of yogurt sauce in the centers of 4 large plates. Add a mound of asparagus; top with overlapping tuna slices. SERVES 4

CHARRED TUNA, MIZUNA & PEAR WITH BLACK VINAIGRETTE

This alluring vinaigrette is made with Chinese black vinegar, available in most Asian food stores, and further darkened with soy sauce. A slice of fresh sweet pear, warming slightly under the fish, is a radical jolt of pleasure.

$^1/_2$ cup Chinese black vinegar
$^1/_2$ cup soy sauce
2 tablespoons honey
2 tablespoons extra-virgin olive oil, plus more for the tuna
2 teaspoons Asian sesame oil
1-inch piece peeled fresh ginger
1 large garlic clove
2 thick tuna steaks, 10 to 12 ounces each
3 cups Asian greens, including mizuna
1 ripe Bartlett pear or Asian pear, thinly sliced
2 tablespoons toasted sesame seeds

Mix the vinegar, soy sauce, honey, olive oil, and sesame oil in a bowl; stir until the honey dissolves. Grate the ginger and garlic on a Microplane grater; add to the dressing. Halve the tuna steaks (you want 4 thick pieces) and coat lightly with olive oil and salt. Heat a large skillet until hot. Sear the tuna 2 minutes on each side. Keep the tuna very rare.

Divide the greens among 4 shallow bowls and top each portion with 2 pear slices. Drizzle with some of the dressing. Cut the tuna into thick slices; arrange atop the salads. Drizzle dressing on and around the tuna and sprinkle with sesame seeds. SERVES 4

Grilled Tuna with Lemony Tahina, Greens & Pomegranate Seeds

This dish is made with both cilantro, also called fresh coriander, and ground coriander seed. The first perfumes the fragrant tahina sauce; the latter contributes its aroma to the fish.

$^1\!/_2$ cup tahina
$^1\!/_3$ cup fresh lemon juice
1 medium garlic clove
$^1\!/_2$ cup chopped cilantro
5 tablespoons olive oil
4 thick tuna steaks, 6 ounces each
2 tablespoons ground coriander
$1^1\!/_2$ teaspoons ground cumin
4 ounces mesclun
$^1\!/_3$ cup pomegranate seeds

Combine the tahina, lemon juice, garlic, and cilantro in a food processor. Process, slowly adding $^1\!/_2$ to $^2\!/_3$ cup cold water, until smooth and thick. Add salt and pepper.

Drizzle 3 tablespoons of the oil all over the tuna steaks and season with salt. Mix the coriander and cumin on a plate; rub into the fish. Heat a ridged cast-iron grill pan over high heat. Sear the tuna 2 minutes on each side. Keep the tuna very rare.

Toss the mesclun with the remaining 2 tablespoons oil. Add salt and divide among 4 plates. Place the tuna on the greens. Pour the tahina sauce over the fish and scatter with the pomegranate seeds. SERVES 4

"sushi-rare" tuna

Swordfish Steaks with Sardine "Bolognese"

Canned sardines and tomatoes, with some deft spicing, become a riff on Bolognese—a scrumptious Italian sauce more commonly made with bits of beef simmered in a tomato-y puree. It's great on pasta, too.

28-ounce can tomatoes in puree
2 (4$\frac{1}{2}$-ounce) cans skinless, boneless sardines in oil
$\frac{1}{2}$ cup milk
3 tablespoons dry red wine
2 tablespoons tomato paste
1 teaspoon fennel seeds
Pinch ground cinnamon
3 large garlic cloves
2 celery stalks with leaves
4 swordfish steaks, 7 ounces each, skin removed
2 tablespoons extra-virgin olive oil

Combine the tomatoes, sardines, and oil from one sardine can in a food processor. Process coarsely until it resembles ground meat. Transfer to a large saucepan. Add the milk, wine, tomato paste, fennel seeds, cinnamon, and garlic pushed through a press. Reserve the celery leaves and chop the stalks to get $\frac{1}{2}$ cup. Add the chopped celery to the saucepan. Bring to a boil, reduce the heat, and simmer 15 minutes.

Rub the swordfish with the olive oil. Season with salt and pepper. Heat a very large skillet over high heat. Sear the fish 2 minutes on each side until golden. Cover and cook 2 minutes, until the fish is just cooked through. Top with the sauce; garnish with celery leaves. SERVES 4

Green Curry Swordfish with Shiitakes & Basil

This takes your palate in an unusual direction. Green curry paste is available in most supermarkets and all Asian markets.

4 teaspoons green curry paste
4 (1-inch-thick) swordfish steaks, 7 ounces each
3 tablespoons olive oil
8 ounces shiitake mushrooms, stemmed and sliced
1 medium garlic clove
2 tablespoons slivered fresh Thai basil, plus sprigs for garnish

Rub the curry paste into both sides of the swordfish steaks; let sit 10 minutes. Sprinkle with salt. Heat 1 tablespoon of the oil in a large pan until hot. Sear the fish for 3 minutes on each side, until just cooked through. Remove the fish from the pan and keep warm. Add the remaining 2 tablespoons oil to the pan. Add the mushrooms and garlic pushed through a press. Cook over high heat for 2 minutes. Stir in the slivered basil and cook 1 minute longer. Serve the fish topped with the mushrooms and garnish with basil sprigs. SERVES 4

ROASTED SWORDFISH WITH TOMATOES-ON-THE-VINE & ROSEMARY TARTARE SAUCE

The idea here is to cook the fish at a very high temperature and have the tomatoes wither on the vine.

1 large red onion, thinly sliced
7 tablespoons olive oil
4 (1-inch-thick) swordfish steaks, 8 ounces each
12 ounces cherry tomatoes on the vine
$\frac{1}{2}$ cup mayonnaise
$1\frac{1}{2}$ teaspoons finely minced fresh rosemary
Grated zest and juice of 1 lemon
$\frac{1}{4}$ cup finely chopped Kosher dill pickles with 1 teaspoon brine
$\frac{1}{2}$ small garlic clove
1 teaspoon Dijon mustard
1 teaspoon Thai fish sauce

Preheat the oven to 500°F. Spread the onion slices in one layer in the center of a rimmed baking sheet. Drizzle with 1 tablespoon of the oil. Coat the swordfish steaks with 2 tablespoons of the oil. Season the fish with salt and pepper and place atop the onions. Place the tomatoes alongside, still affixed to the branches. Roast 12 minutes.

Stir together the mayonnaise, rosemary, grated lemon zest, chopped pickles and brine, and garlic pushed through a press. In another bowl, stir together the mustard, fish sauce, and 1 tablespoon lemon juice. Whisk in the remaining 4 tablespoons oil until blended.

Divide the fish, onions, and tomatoes among 4 plates. Drizzle with the dressing and dollop with rosemary tartare sauce. SERVES 4

SHEET-PAN MUSSELS WITH RED CURRY–GARLIC ➤ BROTH

What a great way to handle lots of mussels! Four pounds fit on a rimmed baking sheet nicely. Blast them in a 500°F oven until they open wide. Serve with Basil-Scrubbed Toasts (page 102).

4 pounds large mussels, scrubbed, beards removed
2 cups dry white wine
6 tablespoons unsalted butter
1 large garlic clove
$^{1}/_{2}$ teaspoon red curry paste

Preheat the oven to 500°F. Spread the mussels on a rimmed baking sheet. Pour the wine over the mussels. Roast for 10 minutes, until the mussels open. Melt the butter in a small skillet. Add the garlic pushed through a press and cook for 1 minute but do not brown. Pour $^{1}/_{2}$ cup of the pan juices into the melted butter along with the curry paste. Boil for 30 seconds. Transfer the mussels to bowls; discard any that do not open. Pour the butter sauce over the mussels. SERVES 6

STEAMED CLAMS WITH SAKE & CHILIES

This serves four as a main course and is also a lovely starter for six. Bread, for sopping, is a must.

5 tablespoons unsalted butter
1$^{1}/_{2}$ cups thinly sliced scallions, white and green parts
2 cups sake or dry vermouth
1 cup packed chopped cilantro
4 large garlic cloves, finely minced
6 little bird chilies, split lengthwise
1 teaspoon Worcestershire sauce
4 dozen littleneck clams, scrubbed

Melt 4 tablespoons of the butter in a large pot. Add the scallions and cook over medium heat until soft, 3 minutes. Add the sake, cilantro, garlic, chilies, Worcestershire, and 1 teaspoon salt. Bring to a boil. Add the clams and cover. Cook 8 minutes, shaking the pot occasionally, until the clams open.

Use a slotted spoon to distribute the clams among bowls. Discard any that do not open. Boil the sauce for 1 minute. Whisk in the remaining 1 tablespoon butter and pour over the clams. SERVES 4 OR 6

SHRIMP ESCABECHE WITH BLOOD ORANGE MOJO

Served chilled, this becomes a desirable summer dinner served with a stack of warm tortillas, a platter of "Green" Corn (page 264), and your favorite tomato or potato salad.

7 tablespoons olive oil, plus more for drizzling
2 pounds peeled large shrimp
5 large garlic cloves, finely minced
2 cups fresh blood orange juice or navel orange juice
1 cup fresh lemon juice
2 large red bell peppers, finely diced
1½ cups finely chopped celery
1 cup finely chopped red onion, plus slivered onion for garnish
½ cup finely chopped cilantro, plus more for garnish
½ scotch bonnet pepper, seeded and finely minced

Heat the oil in a very large skillet. Add the shrimp and half the garlic. Cook over high heat until the shrimp are opaque, 1 to 2 minutes. Transfer the shrimp and pan juices to a large bowl.

Return the skillet to the heat. Add the orange juice, lemon juice, and the remaining garlic. Bring to a boil; cook over high heat until reduced to 1 cup, about 15 minutes. Cool. Add the bell peppers, celery, onion, cilantro, and scotch bonnet pepper. Pour over the shrimp and add salt. Cover and refrigerate until cold.

Divide the shrimp among 4 plates. Garnish with slivered red onion, chopped cilantro, and more oil, if desired. SERVES 4

RISO IN BIANCO WITH SHRIMP SCAMPI

Riso in bianco *uses the same ingredients as risotto, but without the fuss. Instead of the slow incorporation of boiling stock, Arborio rice is fast-boiled and tossed with the other ingredients at the last moment. Garlicky shrimp, simply broiled, taste like the scampi of my youth.*

1 pound large shrimp, peeled and deveined
$\frac{1}{3}$ cup extra-virgin olive oil
2 large garlic cloves
1$\frac{3}{4}$ cups Arborio rice
1 cup finely diced red onion
3 tablespoons unsalted butter
$\frac{1}{2}$ cup finely chopped fresh flat-leaf parsley
$\frac{1}{2}$ cup finely chopped fresh basil
$\frac{2}{3}$ cup freshly grated Parmigiano-Reggiano

Preheat the broiler. Bring 3$\frac{1}{2}$ quarts salted water to a boil. Toss the shrimp with the oil and garlic pushed through a press. Add $\frac{1}{4}$ teaspoon salt and black pepper. Add the rice and onion to the boiling water and boil until the rice is tender, 16 minutes. Drain well, saving $\frac{1}{2}$ cup cooking liquid. Return the rice to the pot. Add the butter, parsley, basil, and reserved cooking liquid. Stir in the cheese; cover to keep warm.

Place the shrimp on a broiler pan fitted with a rack. Broil 5 inches from the heat for 3 minutes, until just opaque. Arrange the shrimp atop the rice and drizzle with the pan juices. SERVES 4

SEARED SCALLOPS ON SWEET PEA PUREE

This is one of the most beloved recipes from my original Recipes 1-2-3, *but I've updated it with dry vermouth and a garnish of trendy pea shoots. It is a dish for any time of the year because* frozen petits pois, *always available, provide the base of the lovely buttery puree.*

10 ounces frozen petits pois, thawed
4 tablespoons unsalted butter
20 medium-large sea scallops
3 tablespoons dry vermouth
Handful of pea shoots, mâche, or microgreens

Put the peas in a saucepan with water to just cover. Boil 2 minutes. Drain well and save 6 tablespoons cooking water. Put the peas, 2 tablespoons of the butter, and the cooking water in a blender. Puree until very smooth and thick. Add salt and pepper. Return to the saucepan. Keep warm.

Melt 1 tablespoon of the butter in a large skillet. Season the scallops and sear over high heat 2 minutes per side until golden and just cooked through. Spread the warm pea puree in the centers of 4 large warm plates. Arrange the scallops on the puree. Add the vermouth and the remaining butter to the skillet. Cook over high heat until syrupy, 30 seconds. Pour over the scallops and top with pea shoots. **SERVES 4**

SALT-WATER LOBSTERS, HEALTHY DRAWN BUTTER

Calling the drawn butter "healthy" is a bit of an exaggeration, but it is better for you and lower in saturated fats than the unadulterated stuff. The secret is to mix olive oil with a small amount of melted salted butter and spices.

> 3 live lobsters, 1³⁄₄ pounds each
> ¹⁄₂ cup olive oil
> ¹⁄₄ teaspoon smoked paprika
> ¹⁄₄ teaspoon ground cayenne
> 4 tablespoons salted butter

Fill a very large pot two-thirds full with *very salty* water. Bring to a rapid boil. Plunge the lobsters into the pot, head first. Cover and quickly return to a boil. Once boiling, cook the lobster for 12 minutes over high heat. Transfer to a platter and let cool for 5 minutes. Split the lobsters in half through the undersides.

Mix together the olive oil, paprika, and cayenne. Melt the butter and skim off the white foam. Stir the butter into the oil and serve alongside hot lobsters. SERVES 3 OR 6

POULTRY

Kitchen life, not to mention food shopping, is radically streamlined when recipes have six or fewer ingredients. You'll find 10 such recipes in this chapter. Simple, too, is when you can put a chicken dinner on the table in 20 minutes time, and there are a dozen lip-smacking ways to do that here as well.

But nothing highlights the essence of radically simple cooking better than the recipe I've affectionately named An Opinionated Way to Roast a Chicken: A naked supermarket bird, without a smidgen of seasoning, goes into a hot oven and roasts upside-down, then right-side up—to perfection. Only at the end is a lovely foaming chive-and-garlic butter sauce deployed. Living in an era when so very many things may "taste like chicken," I feel that chicken rarely does. That is, until now.

Many of my dishes re-create authentic taste-memories such as a Tandoori-style chicken, inspired by a trip to Jaipur; Chicken with Prosciutto, Tomatoes & White Wine, recalled from a vacation in northern Italy; Crisped Chicken with Chimichurri & Avocado, gleaned from a sojourn in Bogota; and Garlicky Cumin Chicken on a bread salad, a mind-sticker from a trip to Jerusalem.

Others strive for a new direction, where either the technique is fascinating—marinating chicken in Thai fish sauce with scallions, or bathing it in shiro miso and fresh ginger to transform the texture of the flesh—or where the combination of ingredients is new, such as stuffing a chicken under the skin with goat cheese, lavender, and basil, or adding decidedly Thai green curry paste to a Mexican-inspired layered chicken soup. New techniques inform many of these recipes, such as a healthier chicken "confit" made moist by slow heat rather than lots of fat; chicken "softened" in crème fraîche; a bird tenderized in a mixture of yogurt and grated onion; turkey massaged in a whirlpool of wine-and-brine; and a new one-pan approach to a stealth chicken Parmesan.

I'm fickle when it comes to buying chicken. Sometimes I buy supermarket chickens when they are irresistibly on sale, other times I trade up for an organic bird from a local producer. I tend to prefer birds that are air chilled rather than water cooled, which tends to make them waterlogged. I'm so fickle, in fact, that sometimes when shopping for a chicken, I buy a turkey instead. I offer you a handful of ways to consider the turkey, which normally gets star billing only once a year but really deserves more attention.

chicken breasts

Asian Chicken with Scallions **180**

A Radically Simple Chicken Parmigiana **180**

BLT Chicken with Cumin Seed & Lime Mayonnaise **181**

Crisped Chicken with Chimichurri & Avocado **182**

Cardamom Chicken with Chickpea & Orange Couscous **185**

Miso Chicken with Fresh Ginger **186**

Red Curry–Coconut Chicken **186**

Sautéed Chicken with Roasted Grapes & Grape Demi-Glace **187**

Manchego Chicken with Prosciutto, Arugula & Pumpkin Seeds **190**

Chicken "Nuggets" with Sherry Vinegar & a Handful of Herbs **191**

chicken thighs

"Almost Confit" Chicken with Melted Garlic **192**

Chicken Thighs with Rosemary & Two Paprikas **194**

Chicken Zahav with Blackened Onions & Turmeric **194**

Chicken with Chorizo, Peppadews & Fino Sherry **195**

Chicken Ras el Hanout with Tomato-Ginger Chutney **197**

cut-up chicken parts

Poulet au Crème Fraîche **198**

Blistered Chicken, Tandoori-Style **198**

Chicken with Prosciutto, Tomatoes & White Wine **199**

Chicken with Za'atar, Lemon & Garlic **200**

whole chicken

Chicken with Goat Cheese, Basil & Lavender **201**

Chicken with 40 Cloves of Garlic, Anisette & Greens **201**

Velvet Chicken with Warm Asian Vinaigrette **202**

An Opinionated Way to Roast a Chicken **203**

turkey

Bombay Turkey Sliders, Hurry-Curry Sauce **204**

Wined-and-Brined Turkey with Bay Leaves & Oregano **205**

Rolled-and-Tied Turkey Roast with Prosciutto, Prunes & Sage **206**

ASIAN CHICKEN WITH SCALLIONS

It may take a day of marinating, but there are few more interesting or radically delicious ways to make chicken than this. The secret ingredient is Asian fish sauce, which results in exquisitely flavored and textured flesh. Use the same preparation for chicken thighs and grill outdoors. It's good cold, too.

4 large bone-in chicken breast halves, with skin, about 10 ounces each
$\frac{1}{4}$ cup Asian fish sauce
4 scallions
1 large garlic clove

Cut each chicken breast in half crosswise. Place in a bowl and pour the fish sauce over. Discard the top 3 inches of the scallions. Cut the remainder into $\frac{1}{4}$-inch pieces. Add to the chicken with the garlic pushed through a press. Toss and cover; refrigerate 18 to 24 hours.

Preheat the oven to 500°F. Lift the chicken from the fish sauce, allowing some scallions to remain. Place on a rimmed baking sheet. Roast 12 minutes, until cooked through. Turn the oven to broil. Broil the chicken 2 minutes, until golden. SERVES 4

A RADICALLY SIMPLE CHICKEN PARMIGIANA

My juicy rendition of Chicken Parm goes like this: The chicken is "breaded" with finely grated Parmesan cheese, covered with mozzarella cheese (which oozes wonderfully when cooked), and topped with roasted grape tomatoes. It all happens on one sheet pan in the oven.

$\frac{1}{4}$ cup olive oil
1 large garlic clove
12 ounces grape tomatoes
$1\frac{1}{2}$ teaspoons dried oregano
Large pinch hot-pepper flakes
4 skinless boneless chicken breasts, 8 ounces each
$1\frac{1}{4}$ cups freshly grated Parmigiano-Reggiano
5 ounces fresh mozzarella cheese, thinly sliced
Handful of torn fresh flat-leaf parsley or small basil leaves

Preheat the oven to 500°F. Combine the oil, garlic pushed through a press, and $\frac{1}{2}$ teaspoon salt in a small bowl. Transfer 2 tablespoons to another bowl and add the tomatoes, oregano, and pepper flakes. Lightly pound the chicken breasts and coat with the remaining garlic oil. Spread 1 cup Parmesan on a large plate. Dredge one side of each breast in the Parmesan. Place, cheese side up, on one side of a rimmed baking sheet. Place the tomatoes on the other side. Bake 10 minutes.

Place overlapping slices of mozzarella on the chicken and pop back into the oven until cheese melts. Serve the chicken topped with the tomatoes. Sprinkle with the remaining Parmesan and parsley. SERVES 4

BLT Chicken with Cumin Seed & Lime Mayonnaise

Think of this as total ease for dinner. It's not bad for lunch, either. To add a bit of sophistication, I omit the lime zest and juice from the mayonnaise and add 1 teaspoon white truffle oil.

$^1/_3$ cup mayonnaise
Grated zest and juice of 1 large lime
4 large boneless chicken breasts, skin-on
2 tablespoons olive oil
2 large garlic cloves
5 ounces thick-cut bacon
2 large ripe tomatoes, cut in $^1/_2$-inch pieces
1 teaspoon cumin seeds
6 ounces baby romaine, cut into $1^1/_2$-inch pieces
1 tablespoon red wine vinegar

Preheat the broiler. Stir together the mayonnaise, lime zest, 1 teaspoon lime juice, and pepper. Set aside. Toss the chicken with the olive oil, 2 tablespoons lime juice, and garlic pushed through a press. Add salt and pepper and broil, skin side down, several inches from the heat, for 3 minutes. Turn and broil 5 minutes longer, until the skin is crispy.

Meanwhile, cut the bacon into $^1/_2$-inch pieces. Cook in a large skillet over medium heat until the fat is rendered, 5 minutes. Add the tomatoes and cumin and cook 3 minutes over high heat. Add the romaine and vinegar and cook until wilted. Add salt and pepper. Serve the chicken topped with the lettuce mixture and a dollop of lime mayonnaise. SERVES 4

CRISPED CHICKEN WITH CHIMICHURRI & AVOCADO

A quick combo to light up your tastebuds. The classic chimichurri sauce from Argentina traditionally uses parsley, but is made here instead with the more pungent cilantro.

1 cup finely minced cilantro

3 large garlic cloves, finely minced

Juice of 1 lime

1 teaspoon cider vinegar

1 tablespoon good-quality dried oregano

$1/_8$ teaspoon red-pepper flakes

7 tablespoons olive oil

4 skinless boneless chicken breasts, 8 ounces each

2 tablespoons unsalted butter

2 cups panko

1 large ripe avocado, peeled, quartered, and sliced lengthwise

Stir together the cilantro, garlic, lime juice, cider vinegar, oregano, and pepper flakes in a medium bowl. Add 5 tablespoons of the oil, 2 tablespoons water, and salt to taste. Put the chicken in a shallow dish with $2/_3$ cup of the chimichurri sauce, turning to coat. Marinate 10 minutes.

Heat the butter and the remaining 2 tablespoons oil in a large skillet until hot. Dredge the chicken in the panko to coat on both sides. Cook the chicken 3 minutes on each side until golden brown and crispy on the bottom. Transfer to 4 plates. Top with the avocado and remaining chimichurri. SERVES 4

chimichurri

CARDAMOM CHICKEN WITH CHICKPEA & ORANGE COUSCOUS

I like this best when the chicken is charred in a grill pan, but it is also delicious broiled.

6 tablespoons extra-virgin olive oil
1 tablespoon ground cardamom
2 garlic cloves
4 large skinless boneless chicken breasts, 8 ounces each
1 1/2 cups couscous
3/4 cup cooked chickpeas
1/4 cup golden raisins
1 scallion, finely chopped
Grated zest and juice of 1 orange
2 teaspoons ground cumin
8 ounces plain Greek yogurt, room temperature

Combine 2 tablespoons of the oil, cardamom, and 1 garlic clove pushed through a press in a small cup. Rub onto the chicken. Heat a stovetop grill pan. Cook the chicken over high heat until cooked through, 4 minutes on each side.

Meanwhile, bring 1 3/4 cups salted water to a boil in a large saucepan. Stir in the couscous, chickpeas, raisins, and scallion. Cover, remove from the heat, and steam 5 minutes. Fluff with a fork. Stir in the orange zest, orange juice, 1 teaspoon of the cumin, 1 tablespoon of the oil, and salt. Cover the pan. In a small bowl, stir together the yogurt, the remaining garlic clove pushed through a press, the remaining 3 tablespoons oil, the remaining 1 teaspoon cumin, 1 tablespoon water, and salt.

Serve the chicken on the warm couscous, topped with the yogurt sauce. SERVES 4

MISO CHICKEN WITH FRESH GINGER

Allow 18 hours for the chicken to marinate so that the miso can perform its magic. Miso is a great carrier of flavors and helps tenderize the flesh.

$\frac{1}{2}$ cup white miso (also known as shiro miso)
2 large garlic cloves
5-inch piece peeled fresh ginger
4 very large bone-in chicken breasts, skin on
Handful of mizuna for garnish

In a large bowl, combine the miso, $\frac{1}{3}$ cup water, and the garlic pushed through a press. Grate the ginger on the large holes of a box grater. Put the ginger in a paper towel and squeeze to get 2 tablespoons juice. Add the juice to the bowl with the finely chopped pulp. Cut the chicken breasts in half across the width. Add to the marinade and toss. Cover and refrigerate 18 to 24 hours.

Preheat the oven to 500°F. Transfer the chicken to a rimmed baking sheet. Sprinkle with salt. Roast 10 minutes, then turn on the broiler. Broil skin side up about 6 inches from heat for several minutes, until golden. Garnish with mizuna. SERVES 4

RED CURRY–COCONUT CHICKEN

You can find incendiary curry paste and creamy coconut milk, two staples of Thai cooking, in the Asian section of most supermarkets. Serve with steamed basmati rice.

4 very large bone-in chicken breasts, skin on
2 tablespoons red curry paste
1$\frac{1}{2}$ cups light coconut milk
$\frac{1}{3}$ cup crushed roasted peanuts
1 scallion, slivered, green part only

Make 3 deep slashes across the width of each chicken breast. Rub the curry paste into the slits and skin of the breasts. Place the chicken in a shallow dish. Pour $\frac{1}{2}$ cup of the coconut milk on top. Sprinkle with salt. Cover and refrigerate for 4 hours.

Preheat the oven to 475°F. Put the chicken on a rimmed baking sheet. Roast for 20 minutes, until the chicken is cooked through. Meanwhile, combine the remaining 1 cup coconut milk and any remaining marinade in a saucepan. Boil for 1 minute, then reduce the heat and simmer 5 minutes. Add salt to taste. Transfer the chicken to plates and pour the sauce on top. Top with peanuts and slivered scallion. SERVES 4

SAUTÉED CHICKEN WITH ROASTED GRAPES ➤ & GRAPE DEMI-GLACE

Looking like a professional chef-made demi-glace, the remarkable sauce here is actually made from freshly made grape juice. In addition, whole grapes are roasted until they shrivel, creating tiny explosions of intense flavor in your mouth.

³/₄ pound small seedless red or black grapes
³/₄ pound small seedless green grapes
4 tablespoons unsalted butter, chilled
4 skinless boneless chicken breasts, 8 ounces each
¹/₄ cup minced fresh chives

Preheat the oven to 375°F. Remove the grapes from their stems. Put half of the grapes on a rimmed baking sheet. Roast 1 hour, turning after 30 minutes. Puree the uncooked grapes in a blender until very smooth. Strain through a sieve, pressing down hard on the skins.

Melt 2 tablespoons of the butter in a large skillet over high heat. Season the chicken with salt and pepper and cook 4 minutes on each side. Add the grape juice and cook until the chicken is cooked through and the juice becomes syrupy, 5 minutes. Transfer the chicken to a platter. Add the remaining butter to the pan and cook, stirring over high heat, 1 minute. Add the roasted grapes and cook 1 minute longer. Pour the sauce over the chicken. Sprinkle with chives. SERVES 4

Manchego Chicken with Prosciutto, Arugula & Pumpkin Seeds

Pretty sophisticated but radically simple, chicken cutlets are the "bread" for a sandwich of prosciutto and nutty Manchego cheese. Pop the "sandwiches" onto a sheet pan and they're ready in 8 minutes.

8 large chicken cutlets, 3 ounces each
8 thin slices prosciutto
6 ounces Manchego cheese, thinly sliced
5 tablespoons extra-virgin olive oil
4 ounces wild arugula
Grated zest and juice of 1 lemon
$1/3$ cup toasted salted pumpkin seeds

Preheat the oven to 450°F. Pound the cutlets until $1/4$ inch thick if necessary. Season the chicken with salt and pepper. Place 4 cutlets on a rimmed baking sheet. Top each with 2 slices of prosciutto and cover with the cheese slices. Top with another cutlet and press down. Drizzle the "sandwiches" with 2 tablespoons of the oil and sprinkle with salt. Bake 8 minutes, until the chicken is cooked through.

Meanwhile, toss the arugula with the remaining 3 tablespoons oil and a little grated lemon zest. Add lemon juice and salt to taste. Top the chicken with the arugula and sprinkle with pumpkin seeds. SERVES 4

CHICKEN "NUGGETS" WITH SHERRY VINEGAR & A HANDFUL OF HERBS

This is a terrific emergency dinner—it can be prepared in less than 15 minutes yet tastes quite luxurious. The first time I made it was with a package of cut-up chicken labeled "chicken stew." That can be tricky to find, and so now I use chicken breasts that I hack up.

3 pounds bone-in chicken breasts, skin on
6 tablespoons olive oil
$^1/_3$ cup sherry vinegar, plus more for sprinkling
2 large garlic cloves, finely chopped
$^3/_4$ cup mixed fresh herbs: parsley, basil, cilantro, tarragon, thyme
1 tablespoon Dijon mustard
$^1/_4$ cup dry vermouth
2 tablespoons unsalted butter, chilled

Preheat the broiler. Cut (or hack) the chicken breasts crosswise into 2-inch pieces and place in a large bowl. Add the oil, vinegar, garlic, $^1/_2$ cup of the herbs, the mustard, 1 teaspoon salt, and pepper. Mix well. Put the chicken skin side down on a rimmed baking sheet. Broil 4 minutes. Turn the chicken over and broil 6 minutes longer, until cooked through. Transfer the chicken to a warm platter and cover.

Scrape the pan juices and any browned bits from the baking sheet into a small skillet. Add the vermouth and butter and cook 1 minute. Pour the sauce over the chicken. Sprinkle with additional vinegar and the remaining herbs. SERVES 4

"ALMOST CONFIT" CHICKEN WITH MELTED GARLIC

Confit is a preparation in which a protein is cooked in its own fat or in copious amounts of oil, after which it usually is crisped. Here is a much healthier approach in which no additional oil or fat is added, but that nonetheless yields exceedingly succulent results.

8 large bone-in chicken thighs, 8 ounces each
14 large garlic cloves
$1\frac{1}{2}$ tablespoons fresh thyme leaves, plus sprigs for garnish
6 fresh bay leaves
$\frac{1}{2}$ teaspoon ground allspice
$\frac{1}{4}$ teaspoon freshly ground white pepper
Freshly grated nutmeg

Preheat the oven to 300°F. Put the chicken in a large bowl. Press 2 garlic cloves through a press and rub into the chicken. Add the thyme leaves, bay leaves, allspice, white pepper, and $1\frac{1}{2}$ teaspoons salt. Grate some nutmeg over the chicken and toss.

Place the chicken in a roasting pan, skin side down. (I use an enamel paella pan.) Cover the pan tightly with foil and bake 45 minutes. Turn the chicken skin side up and scatter the remaining garlic cloves around. Re-cover and bake 1 hour longer. Turn on the broiler. Uncover the chicken and broil several inches from the heat for 5 to 10 minutes, until the skin is crispy. Discard the bay leaves. Garnish with thyme sprigs. SERVES 4

"Almost

Confit"

Chicken Thighs with Rosemary & Two Paprikas

This is among my family's favorite emergency meals. It was inspired by our friend, cooking maestro Arthur Schwartz. Nice with garlicky broccoli rabe.

8 large bone-in chicken thighs, skin-on
2 large garlic cloves
4 teaspoons sweet paprika
2 teaspoons sweet smoked paprika
16 large sprigs fresh rosemary

Preheat the oven to 450°F. Make 2 deep slits across the width of each thigh. Push the garlic through a press and rub into the chicken. Season with salt and pepper. Mix the paprikas with $1/2$ teaspoon salt. Sprinkle the mixture into the slits, then place a rosemary sprig in each slit. Arrange the chicken on a rimmed baking sheet. Roast on the top oven rack for 40 to 45 minutes, until firm and cooked through but still juicy. SERVES 4

Chicken Zahav with Blackened Onions & Turmeric

Some alchemy occurs when you marinate protein in a mixture of grated onion and yogurt, a technique popular in the Middle East. The flesh becomes very juicy and tender. The turmeric turns the chicken golden; zahav *means "gold" in Hebrew.*

8 large bone-in chicken thighs, skin-on
1 tablespoon turmeric
2 large yellow onions
$1^1/_2$ cups plain yogurt
2 tablespoons extra-virgin olive oil, plus more for drizzling

Place the chicken in a large bowl and toss with the turmeric, 1 teaspoon salt, and pepper. Cut 1 onion in half and grate on the large holes of a box grater. Add the onion pulp and juice to the bowl. Finely chop the second onion. Add chopped onions and yogurt to the bowl. Mix well, cover and refrigerate 8 hours.

Preheat the oven to 400°F. Put the chicken on a rimmed baking sheet with the chopped onions on top. Drizzle with the oil. Roast for 35 minutes, then turn on the broiler. Broil the chicken 5 inches from the heat for 2 minutes, until some of the onions are blackened. Drizzle with more oil and sprinkle with salt. SERVES 4

CHICKEN WITH CHORIZO, PEPPADEWS & FINO SHERRY

An invention based on a trip to Catalonia where our company created a tapas bar for Hotel Arts Barcelona. It is a dish replete with the requisite flavor cues of the region: spicy chorizo, fino sherry, lemon, and capers. Peppadew peppers can be found in jars in good food shops—they are both sweet and spicy. If you don't have a paella pan, use a large ovenproof skillet. You will need a paella pan or a very large ovenproof casserole.

3 large garlic cloves
8 large bone-in chicken thighs, skin on
1 large lemon
5 ounces chorizo, sliced $\frac{1}{4}$ inch thick
12 small sun-dried tomato halves, about 2 ounces
12 small Peppadew peppers
2 tablespoons drained capers
2 tablespoons dark brown sugar
$\frac{1}{4}$ cup fino sherry
$\frac{1}{2}$ teaspoon ground cumin
$\frac{1}{2}$ cup torn fresh basil leaves

Preheat the oven to 350°F. Push 2 garlic cloves through a press and rub into the chicken. Grate the lemon zest into a bowl and add the chorizo, dried tomatoes, Peppadews, capers, sugar, and 2 teaspoons salt. Add the chicken and toss. Arrange in a large paella pan in one layer. Cut off the remaining rind and pith from the lemon. Cut the flesh into segments; scatter over the chicken. Bake 50 minutes.

Turn on the broiler. Transfer the chicken to a rimmed baking sheet and broil 5 minutes. Transfer the paella pan to the stovetop; bring the pan juices to a boil. Add the sherry, cumin, and remaining garlic pushed through a press. Boil 5 minutes. Pour the sauce over the chicken; garnish with basil. SERVES 4

CHICKEN RAS EL HANOUT WITH TOMATO-GINGER CHUTNEY

Juicy and aromatic, this cooks up in no time. Ras el hanout is a complex, burnt umber-colored spice mixture from Morocco; you may substitute garam masala.

4 large skinless boneless chicken thighs
2 tablespoons extra-virgin olive oil
1½ tablespoons ras el hanout
3 ripe tomatoes, about 1 pound
1½ tablespoons dark brown sugar
2 large garlic cloves
1-inch piece peeled fresh ginger
½ scotch bonnet pepper
1 teaspoon ground cumin

Preheat the broiler or a ridged stovetop grill pan. Pound the chicken slightly to flatten so that each thigh lies flat. Place in a large bowl and add the oil, ras el hanout, and 1 teaspoon salt. Toss to coat. Broil or grill the chicken for 4 minutes on each side, until cooked through.

Cut the tomatoes in chunks and put in a food processor with the brown sugar, garlic, ginger, scotch bonnet, and cumin. Pulse until coarsely chopped. Add salt to taste and serve the chicken topped with the chutney. SERVES 4

POULET AU CRÈME FRAÎCHE

*Super succulent! My favorite accompaniments are steamed basmati rice to sop up the juices and
a simple salad of watercress and orange dressed with walnut oil.*

1 cup crème fraîche
¼ cup strong French Dijon mustard
1 tablespoon fresh thyme leaves, plus more for garnish
1 large garlic clove
3½-pound chicken, cut into 8 pieces

Stir together the crème fraîche and mustard in a large bowl. Add the thyme, garlic
pushed through a press, and 1 teaspoon salt. Add the chicken and mix well. Set aside at
room temperature for 2 hours or up to 6 hours in the refrigerator.

Preheat the oven to 400°F. Transfer the chicken, with some of the marinade still
clinging, to a rimmed baking sheet. Roast for 45 minutes, until golden and cooked
through. Serve sprinkled with fresh thyme. SERVES 4

BLISTERED CHICKEN, TANDOORI-STYLE

*The deep flavor and moist flesh of this Indian-inspired chicken come from long marinating in
yogurt, pulpy onion juice, and aromatic spices. It's fabulous hot or cold.*

8 very large bone-in chicken thighs
8 large bone-in chicken breast halves
2½ tablespoons turmeric
2½ tablespoons ground cumin
2½ tablespoons garam masala
2½ teaspoons cayenne pepper
2½ teaspoons ground cardamom
2½ tablespoons sweet paprika
4 cups plain yogurt
2 very large yellow onions, halved

Remove the skin from the chicken. Combine the turmeric, cumin, garam masala, cayenne, cardamom, paprika, and 2½ tablespoons salt. Make 3 long, deep slashes in each piece of chicken. Divide the chicken between two large bowls. Rub the spices thoroughly into the chicken and pour 2 cups yogurt into each bowl. Grate 2 onion halves into each bowl using the large holes of a box grater, adding the juice and pulp. Toss well. Cover and refrigerate 18 to 24 hours.

Preheat the oven to 550°F. Place a baking rack on each of 2 heavy rimmed baking sheets lined with foil. Transfer the chicken onto the racks, making sure the pieces are separated and covered with yogurt. Roast for 35 minutes, until firm and golden. SERVES 8 OR MORE

CHICKEN WITH PROSCIUTTO, TOMATOES & WHITE WINE

This is my adaptation of a simple dish from northern Italy. The chicken parts are sautéed briefly, then the whole dish goes into the oven to finish cooking.

4 large split bone-in chicken breasts, skin on
2 large chicken leg quarters, skin on
2 tablespoons extra-virgin olive oil
6 large garlic cloves, thinly sliced
4-ounce slice prosciutto, cut into ¼-inch cubes
1¼ cups dry white wine
3 tablespoons minced fresh rosemary
1 cup imported canned crushed tomatoes
Large pinch of sugar

Preheat the oven to 325°F. Cut the chicken breasts in half crosswise. Separate the legs and thighs. Heat the oil in a very large ovenproof skillet. In 2 batches, cook the chicken skin side down over high heat for 8 minutes, until golden. Transfer to a platter.

Add the garlic, prosciutto, wine, and 2 tablespoons rosemary to the pan. Cook over high heat, stirring, for 3 minutes. Add the tomatoes and ½ teaspoon salt. Boil for 1 minute. Return the chicken to the pan. Bake 40 minutes. Transfer the chicken and solids to a platter; keep warm. Add the sugar and remaining 1 tablespoon rosemary to the pan juices. Boil on the stovetop until reduced to 1 cup, 5 minutes. Add salt and pepper and pour the sauce over the chicken. SERVES 6

CHICKEN WITH ZA'ATAR, LEMON & GARLIC

You will find za'atar, a heady spice blend of hyssop, sumac, and sesame seeds, in Middle Eastern markets. The best, in my opinion, comes from Lebanon, but you can also find varieties from Israel and Syria. I keep some in my fridge at all times.

$1/2$ cup za'atar
4 large chicken leg quarters, skin on
6 large plum tomatoes
12 large garlic cloves
$1/3$ cup extra-virgin olive oil
Grated zest and juice of 2 large lemons

Preheat the oven to 400°F. Rub the za'atar all over the chicken. Sprinkle generously with salt. Place skin side up on a rimmed baking sheet. Cut the tomatoes in half lengthwise and arrange around the chicken, cut side up. Scatter the garlic around the chicken. Drizzle all with the oil. Roast 30 minutes; turn the tomatoes over and baste the chicken with the pan juices. Roast 10 minutes longer. Turn the oven to broil. Slide the pan under the broiler for 1 minute to crisp the chicken. Transfer the chicken, tomatoes, and garlic to a platter. Sprinkle all with the lemon zest and juice. Spoon pan juices over the chicken. SERVES 4

CHICKEN WITH GOAT CHEESE, BASIL & LAVENDER

Invented by my husband, the globe-trotting international food and restaurant consultant.

5-pound roasting chicken
8 ounces firm fresh goat cheese
3 packed cups fresh basil leaves
1 tablespoon fresh lavender
Olive oil for drizzling

Preheat the oven to 350°F. Wash the chicken; discard the giblets. Dry well. Put the cheese, basil, and lavender in a food processor; process until smooth. Starting at the neck of the chicken, slip your fingers under the breast skin, carefully separating the skin from the flesh. Continue downward and, with your index finger, separate the skin around the thighs. Push all the cheese mixture under the skin to create a ¼-inch layer. Truss the chicken; rub salt and pepper into the skin. Place in a shallow roasting pan; drizzle with oil. Roast, basting several times, for 1½ hours, until cooked through. Let rest 10 minutes before separating the chicken into its constituent parts. Cut each breast across its width, if you wish. SERVES 6

CHICKEN WITH 40 CLOVES OF GARLIC, ANISETTE & GREENS

You must use a pot just a tad bit larger than the chicken. A 4-quart will do the trick. Forty cloves of garlic melt into an amazingly sweet sauce that moistens both chicken and greens.

3½-pound chicken
40 large garlic cloves, peeled
2 large sprigs fresh rosemary
¼ cup extra-virgin olive oil
2 tablespoons anisette or amontillado sherry
4 large handfuls mesclun

Preheat the oven to 350°F. Wash the chicken; discard the giblets. Dry well. Rub the chicken with salt and pepper. Place in a 4-quart pot. Scatter the garlic and rosemary around the chicken; pour the oil and anisette over the chicken. Cover and bake 1 hour. Uncover; raise the oven temperature to 500°F. Bake for 20 minutes longer, until the chicken is golden and cooked through. Transfer the chicken to a cutting board; cut into pieces. Put the mesclun on a platter. Top with the chicken. In the pot, smash the garlic with a potato masher until it emulsifies into a smooth sauce; heat the sauce and pour over the chicken. SERVES 4

VELVET CHICKEN WITH WARM ASIAN VINAIGRETTE

The simplest way to cook a whole chicken is to deploy an ancient Chinese method that was meant to save fuel, but results in the most succulent, tender meat imaginable.

4-pound chicken
$^2/_3$ cup rice vinegar
$^1/_4$ cup soy sauce
$^1/_4$ cup mirin (sweet rice wine)
$^1/_4$ cup dark brown sugar
2 tablespoons dark Asian sesame oil
2 tablespoons finely minced scallion, dark green part only
1 teaspoon slivered fresh peeled ginger

Wash the chicken; discard the giblets. Tie the legs together with string. Put the chicken in an 8-quart pot. Add cold water to cover, about 5 quarts. Add 2 tablespoons salt. Cover the pot. Cook over high heat for 20 to 25 minutes, or until you can hear the water boiling rapidly. Do not lift the cover. Remove the pot from the heat; let sit for 3 hours, with no peeking! Remove the chicken from the broth. Save the broth for another use. Remove the chicken from the bones.

In a small saucepan, stir together the vinegar, soy sauce, mirin, sugar, and oil. Heat until hot. Stir in the scallion and ginger. Cut up the chicken. Serve the chicken with the warm vinaigrette and scatter watercress on top. SERVES 4

An Opinionated Way to Roast a Chicken

Even though people lament that "chicken has no taste," I have on occasion been inclined to leave it alone and cook it stark naked (the bird, that is). No salt, even. The result is something that tastes surprisingly like, well . . . chicken; golden and moist. Only at the end, after carving, do I simply add salt and pepper to the pan juices, or give it a keen sheen of water-enriched garlic-chive butter, whisk until frothy. A small roasting pan, just large enough to hold the chicken is key: I use a small paella pan, but a metal-handled skillet will do.

4-pound roasting chicken

Preheat the oven to 475°F. Wash the chicken; discard the giblets. Dry well. Place breast side down in a small roasting pan. Roast for 30 minutes. Turn the chicken over and baste. Roast for 40 minutes longer, until cooked through. Remove from the oven and sprinkle with salt. Let rest for 5 minutes. Add salt and pepper to the pan juices and boil 2 minutes. Carve the chicken and serve with pan juices or butter sauce. SERVES 4

Garlic-Chive Butter Sauce

4 tablespoons unsalted butter
2 teaspoons finely minced fresh chives
1 small garlic clove, very finely minced

Melt the butter in a saucepan. Add the chives, garlic, 3 tablespoons water, and salt. Bring to a boil, whisking constantly, 1 minute. Pour over chicken.

BOMBAY TURKEY SLIDERS, HURRY-CURRY SAUCE

Sliders are all the rage nowadays; these, made with ground turkey, are especially terrific served with a garlicky curry sauce. You may pile them up with thinly sliced cucumber, tomato, and red onion, or you can make the burgers larger.

$^3/_4$ cup mayonnaise
2 tablespoons curry powder
1 tablespoon ketchup
1 tablespoon plain yogurt
1 small garlic clove, very finely minced
2 pounds ground turkey
6 tablespoons finely chopped cilantro
$^1/_4$ cup finely minced scallions, white part only
2 teaspoons ground cumin
$^3/_4$ teaspoon hot chili powder
2-inch piece peeled fresh ginger
12 small dinner rolls

Preheat the broiler. Stir together $^1/_2$ cup of the mayo, $^1/_2$ tablespoon of the curry powder, ketchup, yogurt, and garlic; set aside.

Put the turkey in a large bowl. Add the remaining $^1/_4$ cup mayonnaise, the remaining $1^1/_2$ tablespoons curry powder, cilantro, scallions, cumin, and chili powder. Grate the ginger on the large holes of a box grater onto a paper towel. Gather the towel and squeeze the juice into the bowl. Finely chop the ginger pulp and add to the turkey with 1 teaspoon salt. Mix well and form into 12 flat patties. Put the burgers on a lightly oiled broiler pan and broil 2 minutes on each side. Serve on rolls with the curry sauce. SERVES 4

WINED-AND-BRINED TURKEY WITH BAY LEAVES & OREGANO

This is radical: A deconstructed holiday turkey featuring white and dark meat that cooks in just 1¼ hours! The flesh stays ultra-moist and flavorful because of its overnight immersion in wine and brine. Smaller, flatter pieces allow faster browning and less cooking time.

2 cups dry white wine
2 large turkey breast halves, about 2½ pounds each
2 large turkey thighs, about 1½ pounds each
16 fresh or dried bay leaves
6 tablespoons olive oil
1 large garlic clove
2 tablespoons best-quality dried oregano

Combine the wine, 6 cups water, and ⅓ cup kosher salt in a very large pot. Submerge the turkey pieces. Cover and refrigerate overnight.

Preheat the oven to 400°F. Position a rack in the middle of the oven. Remove the turkey from the brine; pat dry. Scatter the bay leaves in a large roasting pan. Place the turkey on top. Combine the oil and garlic pushed through a press in a cup. Rub the garlic oil into the turkey. Sprinkle with the oregano, salt, and pepper. Roast the turkey, skin side up, for 45 minutes. Turn the pieces over and roast 35 minutes longer, until cooked through. Transfer the turkey, skin side up, to a cutting board. Pour 1 cup boiling water into the pan, scraping up the browned bits; strain through a sieve. Carve the turkey and serve with the pan juices. SERVES 8

ROLLED-AND-TIED TURKEY ROAST WITH PROSCIUTTO, PRUNES & SAGE

I love preparing a "turkey roast," which is nothing more than a boned breast half with the skin on. Here it is filled with prosciutto, sage leaves, and prunes, then rolled and tied.

2$\frac{1}{4}$-pound turkey roast (boned half breast, skin on)
4 ounces thinly sliced prosciutto
10 large pitted prunes
$\frac{1}{4}$ cup pine nuts
12 large fresh sage leaves
12 medium shallots, peeled
3 tablespoons extra-virgin olive oil
1 cup chicken broth
$\frac{1}{2}$ cup dry white wine
1 tablespoon unsalted butter

Preheat the oven to 400°F. Using a mallet, flatten the turkey (skin side down) to 1-inch thickness. Cover evenly with the prosciutto. Arrange the prunes in a tight row down the center. Top with pine nuts and 6 sage leaves. Roll up tightly. Season with salt and pepper. Tie with string at 1-inch intervals and tuck 6 sage leaves under the string.

Place the turkey and shallots in a small roasting pan. Drizzle with the oil. Roast 45 minutes, until cooked through. Transfer the turkey and shallots to a board.

Pour the broth and wine into the pan. Place on the stovetop and boil, scraping up browned bits, until syrupy, 3 minutes. Strain into a saucepan. Whisk in the butter and cook 1 minute. Remove the string from the turkey; thickly slice. Serve with the shallots and pan sauce. SERVES 6

a large
"turkey roast"
for six

MEAT

The essence of meat cookery is applying the proper technique to the right cut of meat and then serving it at the right temperature. I like flash-in-the-pan methods such as grilling a pork chop or searing a steak, each of which chars and caramelizes the surface, leaving a slightly chewy interior: These are great for getting dinner on the table quickly. With a plop of my Magic Green Sauce (page 235), dinner becomes an instant winner. Equally simple, though less quick, are recipes using moist, unattended heat that transform hefty pork shoulders, sinewy beef, and gelatinous roasts into spoon-tender meat bathed in lip-sticking natural juices. This chapter contains both.

Just as you wouldn't pan-sear a thick short rib or stew a porterhouse steak, you shouldn't leave it to the kitchen gods to signal when your roast is ready. Professional chefs, and smart home cooks, keep an instant-read thermometer within easy reach. Use it to tell when your very expensive filet mignon or prime rib of beef is rare (an internal temperature of 125°F) or medium-rare (135°F). Keep in mind that a large piece of hot meat continues to cook as it rests on the cutting board, so resist any temptation to leave it longer in the oven.

By nature I cook meat simply. I grew up on the world's most delicious pot roast, made with a handful of ingredients. The alchemy of almost-burnt onions, seared beef, plus a few glugs of dry vermouth turned a hunk of rump into something worthy of a dinner party. Today, I've added kimchee and use sake instead of vermouth.

I also grew up eating juicy steaks with butter poured over the top at Peter Luger's in New York. (This last detail was performed out of one's sight line but was the magical step in the delicious outcome.) And in Italy, I've enjoyed delectable *bistecca alla fiorentina*, steak grilled and anointed with first-pressed extra-virgin olive oil and sea salt. Sometimes there was a splash of *balsamico* or a sprig of rosemary nearby. Along the way, I've made discoveries, the most recent being a favorite new way to make a steak at home: rubbing in copious amounts of sumac and searing it in a hot pan upon the thinnest layer of salt until only blood rare. It even makes the flap meat from Costco taste swell.

In this chapter you'll find the simplest filet mignon served with a "new world" wasabi-garlic cream; Pork Chops & Apples with Madeira–Bay Butter Sauce; a leg of lamb cooked in a bottle of Chardonnay; lowly lamb riblets elevated to stardom in a sticky sauce with Asian flavors. There is a sublime veal roast in a honey-mustard jus and Veal Chops with Sage Butter, Sunflower Seeds & Beet Drizzle. And my Flanken with Pomegranate Molasses, Ginger & Prunes has become a new holiday favorite in some households. The point? Cooking meat doesn't need lots of handwork to be sensational.

juicy pork

Pork Chops with Radicchio Snippets & Cornichon Vinaigrette **212**

Garlic-Miso Pork Chops, Orange Peppers & Arugula **212**

Sticky Country Ribs with Orange, Molasses & Vinegar **213**

Pork Chops & Apples, Madeira–Bay Butter Sauce **214**

18-Hour Pork Shoulder with Fennel, Garlic & Lemon **216**

"Peking" Pork with Scotch & Scallions **217**

Fennel Sausages with Wrinkled Grapes & Grape Extract **218**

Pork Loin in Cream with Tomatoes, Sage & Gin **219**

luscious lamb

Lamb Riblets with Sweet Asian Flavors **222**

Roast Rack of Lamb, Madeira-Peppercorn Reduction **222**

Lamb Shoulder with Figs, Lemon & Chartreuse **223**

Lamb Chops with Smoked Paprika Oil, Cumin & Arugula **225**

Double Lamb Chops with Mint & Ginger Crust **225**

Butterflied Lamb with Garam Masala, Yogurt & Lime **226**

A Leg of Lamb & a Bottle of Chardonnay **228**

Lamb Shanks Provençal with Cabernet & Dried Mushrooms **229**

tender veal

Veal Chops with Sage Butter, Sunflower Seeds & Beet Drizzle **230**

Grilled Veal Chops with Prosciutto & Basil-Lemon Oil **232**

Veal Roast with Fresh Thyme & Honey Mustard Jus **232**

Veal Steaks "Stroganoff" with Shiitakes & Portobellos **233**

the best beef

Big Juicy Sun-Dried Tomato Burgers **234**

Flap, Hanger, or Skirt Steaks with Sumac **234**

Sirloin Steaks with Magic Green Sauce **235**

Sizzling Skirts with Lime, Basil & Sriracha **237**

Reddened Rib Eye with Pimiento Cheese **238**

New Asia Steak **240**

Tournedos Balsamico with Rosemary & Gorgonzola Dolce **240**

A Prime Rib of Beef **241**

Filet of Beef with Wasabi-Garlic Cream **242**

Tri-Tip Filet in Soy & Red Wine with Chinese Mustard **244**

Rib Roast in the Style of Gravlax **245**

Mahogany Short Ribs **246**

Beef Rendang **246**

Pot Roast with Burnt Onions & Kimchee **247**

PORK CHOPS WITH RADICCHIO SNIPPETS & CORNICHON VINAIGRETTE

This is super easy and elegant when strewn with snippets of radicchio and cilantro.

5 tablespoons olive oil
2 tablespoons finely minced cornichons, plus 1 tablespoon brine
1 small garlic clove, finely minced
4 large thick rib pork chops, about 9 ounces each
2 tablespoons ground coriander
$1/3$ cup finely shredded radicchio
$1/3$ cup torn cilantro leaves

Put 4 tablespoons of the oil in a medium bowl. Add the cornichons, brine, and garlic. Add salt to balance flavors; set aside.

Rub the chops on both sides with the coriander and season with salt and pepper. Heat the remaining 1 tablespoon oil in a large frying pan or grill pan. Sear the chops over high heat until browned about 3 minutes per side. Let rest for 5 minutes. Spoon the vinaigrette over the chops and sprinkle with the radicchio and cilantro. SERVES 4

GARLIC-MISO PORK CHOPS, ORANGE PEPPERS & ARUGULA

This is a good time to try one of those great heritage pork breeds out there. They cost more but put factory-farmed pork to shame.

4 large thick pork chops, about 8 ounces each
$1/3$ cup white miso (also known as shiro miso)
2 large garlic cloves
3 tablespoons fino sherry
3 tablespoons extra-virgin olive oil, plus more for drizzling
2 cups baby arugula
1 small orange bell pepper
1 tablespoon rice vinegar

Put the pork chops in a large shallow dish and rub the miso all over. Push the garlic through a press and rub into the chops. Sprinkle with the sherry. Cover and refrigerate 2 to 8 hours.

Heat 1 tablespoon of the oil in a skillet large enough to hold the chops in one layer. Sear the chops over high heat until cooked through but still pink inside, about 3 minutes per side.

Put the arugula in a large bowl. Cut the bell pepper into thin julienne; add to the bowl with the remaining 2 tablespoons olive oil and the vinegar. Add salt and toss. Place a chop on each of 4 large plates. Top with arugula; drizzle with any pan juices and more olive oil. SERVES 4

STICKY COUNTRY RIBS WITH ORANGE, MOLASSES & VINEGAR

These extra-meaty ribs marinate a day before being baked in your oven or slowly grilled and smoked in your barbecue. The luscious marinade is cooked down until syrupy and used as a spicy barbecue sauce. Nice with my Two-Cabbage Slaw (page 62).

2$^1/_2$ cups orange juice
1 cup molasses
$^1/_4$ cup rice vinegar
1 tablespoon hot-pepper sauce
2 teaspoons ground cumin
1 teaspoon ground allspice
1 large shallot
24 country spare ribs, about 6 pounds

Mix together the orange juice, molasses, vinegar, hot-pepper sauce, cumin, and allspice. Grate the shallot on the large holes of a box grater; stir into the mixture with 2 teaspoons salt. Add the ribs; toss well. Cover and refrigerate 12 to 24 hours.

Preheat the oven to 350°F. Arrange the ribs on a broiler pan fitted with a rack. Cover tightly with foil and bake 1 hour. Pour the marinade into a saucepan. Boil the marinade until reduced and syrupy, 10 minutes. Remove the foil from the ribs and carefully pour off any liquid and discard. Baste the ribs with the reduced marinade. Bake the ribs, uncovered, for 30 to 40 minutes longer, until glazed. SERVES 8

PORK CHOPS & APPLES, MADEIRA–BAY BUTTER SAUCE

Butterscotch-y and delicious, a credible beurre blanc elevates a humble stack of cooked apples and pork to a four-star dish. You will feel very accomplished serving it.

2 cups chicken broth
$1/2$ cup Madeira
1 large garlic clove, finely minced
2 bay leaves
2 tablespoons unsalted butter
2 large thick rib pork chops
1 large apple
1 tablespoon olive oil
2 teaspoons finely minced fresh tarragon

Combine the broth, Madeira, garlic, and bay leaves in a skillet. Bring to a boil over high heat and continue to boil until reduced to 3 tablespoons, 15 minutes. Remove the bay leaves and stir in the butter. Add salt and pepper. Keep warm.

Preheat the broiler. Season the pork with salt and pepper. Place on a rimmed baking sheet. Slice through the entire apple to make six $1/4$-inch slices through the stem end; remove the core and seeds. Arrange the apple around the chops. Drizzle with the oil. Broil as close to the heat as possible for 5 minutes, until just soft and golden. Stack the apple on the chops; drizzle with the warm butter sauce. Sprinkle with the tarragon.

SERVES 2

18-HOUR PORK SHOULDER WITH FENNEL, GARLIC & LEMON

If you put this in the oven before you go to bed, it will be ready for dinner the next day—all crackly, succulent, and irresistible.

10-pound whole pork shoulder, skin on
2 large heads garlic, cloves separated and peeled
3 tablespoons fennel seeds
3 tablespoons cumin seeds
$\frac{1}{2}$ teaspoon hot-pepper flakes
2 lemons

Preheat the oven to 450°F. Make deep slits in the pork skin, about 1 inch apart, going through to the flesh. Combine the garlic, fennel, cumin, pepper flakes, and 2 teaspoons kosher salt in a food processor; process until coarsely ground. Spread the mixture all over the pork, making sure to pack some into the slits. Place the pork in a roasting pan. Roast for 30 minutes.

Squeeze the juice of 1 lemon over the pork and reduce the temperature to 250°F. Bake for 18 hours. Squeeze the juice of the second lemon over the pork during the last hour of cooking. When done, the skin will crackle and the flesh will be soft. Carve into thick slices. SERVES 8

"PEKING" PORK WITH SCOTCH & SCALLIONS

Lip-smacking and luscious, this meltingly tender pork roast, emboldened with Chinese hoisin sauce and scallions (like its namesake Peking Duck), can be made a day in advance and reheated.

6-pound boned pork shoulder
1 tablespoon olive oil
$^2/_3$ cup hoisin sauce
3 bunches scallions, trimmed
4 star anise
$^1/_4$ cup Scotch whisky

Preheat the oven to 300°F. Use a sharp knife to remove the skin from the pork but leave a thin layer of fat. Tie the roast at 2-inch intervals with kitchen string. Heat the oil in a Dutch oven. Add the pork, fat-side down, and brown on all sides, about 10 minutes. Remove from the heat; spread the hoisin over the pork. Cut the scallions into 2-inch lengths; scatter over and around the pork with the star anise. Cover and bake $3^1/_2$ hours, until the pork is very tender.

Transfer the pork to a cutting board. Using a large spoon, remove as much fat as possible from the pan juices. Add the whisky; cook over high heat several minutes, until syrupy. Cut the pork into thick slices. Serve with the scallions and pan sauce. SERVES 8

FENNEL SAUSAGES WITH WRINKLED GRAPES & GRAPE EXTRACT

This is a classic Italian recipe gussied up with juice extracted from fresh grapes, which adds acidity, depth, and great color to the sauce. Toasted pine nuts and parsley are additional adornments. Serve with a bowl of steaming lentils anointed with extra-virgin olive oil.

1 pound seedless red grapes
8 large sweet Italian sausages with fennel
1 tablespoon olive oil
⅓ cup pine nuts, lightly toasted
Torn leaves of flat-leaf parsley for garnish

Wash the grapes; pat dry. Put 1 heaping cup grapes in a blender and process until very smooth. Press through a strainer to get ½ cup juice. Discard the pulp.

Prick the sausages all over with a fork. Heat the oil in a 10-inch skillet. Add the sausages and brown over high heat, turning often, about 8 minutes. Add the grape juice and remaining grapes; cook over high heat until the sausages are cooked through, about 5 minutes. Transfer the sausages to a platter. Reduce the sauce over high heat for 1 minute. Pour the grapes and sauce over the sausages. Garnish with the pine nuts and parsley. SERVES 4

PORK LOIN IN CREAM WITH TOMATOES, ➤
SAGE & GIN

This is a riff on an Italian classic dish in which pork is cooked in milk flavored with juniper. My version is much simpler but equally divine. You can augment the sauce by adding some dry white wine in addition to the gin. It's lovely with a platter of sautéed broccoli rabe. I like to make this in a medium paella pan.

12 fresh sage leaves
4 large garlic cloves
2 tablespoons extra-virgin olive oil
$1\frac{1}{2}$ teaspoons dried Greek oregano
$2\frac{1}{2}$-pound center-cut pork loin, tied and lightly scored
1 pint grape tomatoes
$\frac{1}{2}$ cup heavy cream
$\frac{1}{4}$ cup gin, or more to taste

Process 6 sage leaves, the garlic, oil, oregano, and $\frac{1}{2}$ teaspoon salt in a mini processor to a fine paste. Rub all over the pork. Cover; let sit at room temperature 30 minutes or refrigerate up to 4 hours.

Preheat the oven to 425°F. Heat a very large ovenproof skillet until very hot. Brown the pork on all sides, 5 minutes. Scatter the tomatoes around the pork; cook 1 minute. Pour $\frac{1}{4}$ cup cream over the pork. Roast 40 minutes. Add the 6 remaining sage leaves, the remaining $\frac{1}{4}$ cup cream, and the gin. Roast 15 to 20 minutes longer, until tender. Transfer the pork to a cutting board. Place the pan on the stovetop and boil the sauce, adding more gin, salt, and pepper, until slightly reduced, 1 minute. Slice the pork and serve with the sauce. SERVES 6

LAMB RIBLETS WITH SWEET ASIAN FLAVORS

Once upon a time, lamb ribs were never served in good restaurants; they were considered cheap and fatty. I consider them sensuous. Mâche, also known as lamb's lettuce, is the perfect garnish.

1 cup orange juice
$^2/_3$ cup hoisin sauce
$^1/_4$ cup soy sauce
3 tablespoons honey
1 tablespoon Dijon mustard
4 large garlic cloves, finely chopped
$^1/_4$ cup minced peeled fresh ginger
3 pounds lamb riblets, cut into individual ribs by butcher
Mâche or watercress for garnish

Combine the orange juice, hoisin, soy sauce, honey, mustard, garlic, and ginger in a large bowl. Add the ribs and toss to coat. Cover and refrigerate 4 to 8 hours.

Preheat the oven to 325°F. Remove the ribs from the marinade and arrange on a broiler pan fitted with a rack. Cover tightly with foil; bake 45 minutes. Meanwhile, transfer the marinade to a saucepan. Bring to a boil and boil 2 minutes. Set aside $^1/_2$ cup for serving.

Uncover the ribs. Continue to bake, uncovered and basting with the marinade, for 45 minutes, until very tender. Serve the ribs with the reserved marinade. Garnish with mâche. SERVES 4

ROAST RACK OF LAMB, MADEIRA-PEPPERCORN REDUCTION

Have your butcher trim the racks and remove the meat between the bones—a technique known as frenching. Serve with Creamy Potato Gratin (page 278).

6 large shallots
2 racks of lamb, $1^1/_4$ pounds each, frenched
4 tablespoons unsalted butter, chilled
$1^1/_4$ cups Madeira
2 large sprigs fresh rosemary, plus more for garnish
1 tablespoon green peppercorns in brine, drained and chopped

Preheat the oven to 400°F. Cut one of the shallots in half; grate on the large holes of a box grater. Rub the lamb with the shallot pulp, salt, and pepper. Roast on a rimmed baking sheet 25 minutes. Increase the heat to 500°F; roast 5 minutes longer, until an instant-read thermometer registers 125°F for rare. Let rest 5 minutes.

Finely chop the 5 remaining shallots. Melt 1 tablespoon of the butter in a saucepan. Cook the shallots until soft, 3 minutes. Add the Madeira, rosemary sprigs, and peppercorns. Boil until reduced to ²/₃ cup, 12 minutes. Reduce the heat and whisk in the remaining butter, salt, and pepper. Cut the lamb between the ribs. Serve with the sauce and garnish with rosemary. SERVES 4

LAMB SHOULDER WITH FIGS, LEMON & CHARTREUSE

This is a lovely—and unusual—stew made with walnut-stuffed figs and herbal-tasting green (not yellow) Chartreuse liqueur. Serve with Olive Oil–Mashed Potatoes (page 278).

16 moist, large dried Turkish figs
16 walnut halves
1¹/₂ pounds lamb shoulder, cut into 1¹/₂-inch cubes
3 tablespoons olive oil
5 large garlic cloves, smashed
Grated zest and juice of 1 large lemon
¹/₄ cup Chartreuse liqueur
Fresh chervil or tarragon sprigs for garnish

Cut a small slit in each fig; insert a walnut half. Season the lamb with salt and pepper. Heat the oil in a deep medium pot. Brown the lamb on all sides over high heat. Add 1 cup water, the garlic, and figs. Bring just to a boil. Cover, reduce the heat, and simmer 1 hour, until soft. With a slotted spoon, transfer the lamb and figs to a platter.

Add 2 tablespoons lemon juice and the Chartreuse to the pot. Cook over high heat until syrupy, about 10 minutes. Return the lamb to the pot; add salt and pepper. Continue cooking over low heat until the lamb is very tender, 20 to 30 minutes. Stir in the lemon zest. Garnish with chervil or tarragon. SERVES 4

shoulder chop

◄ LAMB CHOPS WITH SMOKED PAPRIKA OIL, CUMIN & ARUGULA

A very elegant way to gussy up an inexpensive cut of lamb.

1/2 cup olive oil
1 teaspoon sweet smoked paprika
1 small garlic clove
4 thick shoulder lamb chops, about 10 ounces each
4 teaspoons ground cumin
2 ounces wild arugula
2 tablespoons freshly squeezed lemon juice
Shards of Manchego cheese

Preheat the broiler. Stir together 1/4 cup of the olive oil, the smoked paprika, and the garlic pushed through a press. Add salt to balance flavors. Season the chops with the cumin, salt and pepper. Place on a broiler pan; broil 3 minutes on each side, until rare.

Put the arugula in a bowl. Drizzle with the remaining 1/4 cup olive oil and the lemon juice. Add salt and pepper to taste. Mound some arugula on each of 4 plates; top with a lamb chop. Drizzle with the paprika oil and top with more arugula and cheese. SERVES 4

DOUBLE LAMB CHOPS WITH MINT & GINGER CRUST

These sophisticated chops require no browning (so no spatter or smoke) and no carving.

2 cups diced day-old baguette, about 4 ounces
1/4 cup chopped fresh mint
1/4 cup chopped fresh basil
1/4 cup minced peeled fresh ginger
7 tablespoons unsalted butter, room temperature
8 double-rib lamb chops, about 1 3/4 inches thick and 5 ounces each

Preheat the oven to 450°F. Combine the bread, mint, basil, ginger, and 3/4 teaspoon salt in a food processor. Process until finely chopped. Cut the butter into pieces; add to the processor and process until a paste forms. Season the lamb with salt and pepper. Pack the bread crumb mixture onto the outer surface of the lamb (not the cut side) so that it adheres. Roast 18 to 20 minutes, until an instant-read thermometer registers 125°F for rare. Let stand 5 minutes; serve 2 chops per person. SERVES 4

BUTTERFLIED LAMB WITH GARAM MASALA, YOGURT & LIME

Yogurt and fresh lime juice act as tenderizing agents in this sublime method of preparing leg of lamb. The flavoring agent is garam masala, an aromatic spice blend from India. The lamb is great cooked on an outdoor grill but also delicious broiled.

3-pound butterflied leg of lamb
2 large garlic cloves
1 tablespoon garam masala
Grated zest and juice of 2 limes
1$\frac{1}{4}$ cups plain yogurt
$\frac{1}{3}$ cup pine nuts, lightly toasted
1 tablespoon chopped flat-leaf parsley

Put the lamb in a large bowl. Push the garlic through a press and rub into the lamb. Rub in the garam masala. Add the lime zest, lime juice, and 1 cup of yogurt. Toss the lamb well, cover, and refrigerate 8 to 12 hours, turning several times.

Preheat the broiler or charcoal grill. Remove the lamb from the marinade; pat dry. Place the lamb on a broiler pan and broil or grill 6 to 8 minutes on each side, until an instant-read thermometer registers 130°F for rare. Transfer to a cutting board and let rest 10 minutes. Sprinkle the lamb generously with salt and slice. Drizzle the remaining $\frac{1}{4}$ cup of yogurt on top and sprinkle with the pine nuts and parsley. SERVES 4

yogurt & lime

A Leg of Lamb & a Bottle of Chardonnay

This recipe of mine made its way around the world, winding up in an issue of House Beautiful *in South Africa. Unexpectedly, the lamb is cooked with a full-bodied white wine instead of the more predictable red and is unusually simple because it needs no browning.*

5$\frac{1}{2}$-pound leg of lamb, trimmed
3 very large heads garlic plus 4 cloves, about 9 ounces
1 large bunch fresh thyme
1 bottle chardonnay
2 tablespoons unsalted butter

Preheat the oven to 475°F. Place the lamb in a large, roasting pan with a cover. Push 2 of the garlic cloves through a press, and rub into the lamb.

Cut the garlic heads in half through the equators; arrange around the lamb. Scatter the thyme branches over the lamb. Roast 20 minutes. Reduce the temperature to 350°F. Pour the wine around the lamb. Cover; roast 2 hours and 40 minutes, until very tender. Transfer the lamb and garlic to a platter; tent with foil.

Place the roasting pan on burners and bring the pan juices to a boil. Add the butter and the remaining 2 garlic cloves pushed through a press. Boil several minutes, until syrupy. Slice the lamb and serve with the sauce. SERVES 6

LAMB SHANKS PROVENÇAL WITH CABERNET & DRIED MUSHROOMS

Nice and easy for such a complicated-sounding dish. I simplify the process by quickly searing the shanks under the broiler. Dust with freshly grated orange zest for fun.

6 tablespoons olive oil
6 large lamb shanks, 12 to 14 ounces each
2¹/₂ cups chopped leeks, white and green parts
6 large garlic cloves, finely chopped
2²/₃ cups Cabernet Sauvignon
1 cup canned crushed tomatoes with puree
¹/₂ ounce dried porcini mushrooms
1¹/₂ tablespoons herbes de Provence
1 pound slender carrots, peeled and cut into ¹/₄-inch batons
1 tablespoon arrowroot

Preheat the broiler. Rub the lamb with 3 tablespoons oil and season with salt and pepper. Place on a broiler pan; brown several minutes on each side.

Wash leeks and pat dry. Heat the remaining 3 tablespoons oil in an 8-quart Dutch oven. Add the leeks and garlic; cook over high heat until softened, 5 minutes. Add the shanks, wine, tomatoes, mushrooms, and dried herbs. Stir to coat. Bring to a boil. Reduce the heat, cover, and simmer 1 hour. Add the carrots, cover, and cook 30 minutes. Uncover and simmer 15 minutes, until the lamb is tender. Spoon off the fat. Dissolve the arrowroot in 1 tablespoon water and stir into the sauce. Add salt and pepper and simmer several minutes, until the sauce thickens. SERVES 6

VEAL CHOPS WITH SAGE BUTTER, SUNFLOWER SEEDS & BEET DRIZZLE

Serve with Sautéed Peppers with Golden Raisins & Arugula (page 270).

³⁄₄ cup chopped canned beets
2 tablespoons white balsamic vinegar
4 tablespoons olive oil
4 thick loin veal chops, about 9 ounces each
3 tablespoons unsalted butter
12 large fresh sage leaves
¹⁄₄ cup toasted sunflower seeds

Place the beets, 1 tablespoon vinegar, 3 tablespoons of the oil and ¹⁄₄ cup water in a food processor. Process until very smooth. Set aside.

Season the chops with salt and pepper. Heat the butter and remaining 1 tablespoon oil in a skillet large enough to hold the chops in one layer. Sear the chops over high heat until browned on one side, about 4 minutes. Place 3 sage leaves on the uncooked side of each chop and turn over. Cook over high heat until browned on the second side, 3 to 4 minutes longer. Add the remaining 1 tablespoon vinegar to the pan and cook 15 seconds. Transfer the chops and pan juices to plates. Serve chops, sage side up, sprinkled with sunflower seeds and drizzled with beet dressing. SERVES 4

sage butter,
beet drizzle...

GRILLED VEAL CHOPS WITH PROSCIUTTO & BASIL-LEMON OIL

Thick, bright-green herb oil is a felicitous match for juicy veal chops. For drama, have the butcher french the chops, exposing the long rib bone.

2 large bunches fresh basil
1/2 cup olive oil
Grated zest and juice of 1 large lemon
1 medium garlic clove, chopped
4 large veal rib chops, 10 to 12 ounces each
2 large handfuls wild arugula
4 wide paper-thin slices prosciutto

Preheat the oven to 400°F. Wash the basil; remove the leaves. Boil a pot of salted water. Fill a large bowl with ice water. Boil the basil 1 minute, then plunge into the ice water. Drain; squeeze dry. Place in a blender with all but 1 tablespoon of the oil, the zest, garlic, and 1/3 cup water. Process until smooth; add lemon juice and salt to taste.

Rub the remaining 1 tablespoon oil into the chops; season with salt and pepper. Heat a very large skillet over high heat. Sear the chops 3 minutes on each side, until browned. Transfer to a rimmed baking sheet. Bake 10 minutes, until pink inside. Let rest 5 minutes. Mound arugula on 4 large plates and drizzle with some basil oil. Top with the chops, drizzle with more basil oil, and drape with prosciutto. SERVES 4

VEAL ROAST WITH FRESH THYME & HONEY MUSTARD JUS

A veal roast, from the shoulder and neck meat, yields the most succulent results. These comforting flavors are perfect for Sunday supper.

3 1/2-pound veal shoulder roast, tied
1/2 cup good-quality honey mustard
2 large bunches fresh thyme
2 tablespoons olive oil

Place the veal in a shallow baking dish. In a small bowl, stir together the honey mustard and 2 tablespoons thyme leaves. Rub the mixture all over the roast. Cover; refrigerate for 2 hours.

Preheat the oven to 325°F. Scrape the marinade from the roast and reserve. Season the roast with salt and pepper. Heat the oil in a Dutch oven. Add the roast and quickly brown on all sides. Add ½ cup water and the reserved marinade; bring to a boil. Scatter the thyme branches around. Cover; roast 2½ hours, until the veal is very tender. Check every 30 minutes to make sure there is some liquid in the pot; if not, add water. Let the roast rest 5 minutes; carve into thick slices and serve with the pan juices. SERVES 6

VEAL STEAKS "STROGANOFF" WITH SHIITAKES & PORTOBELLOS

Flavors of fino sherry, espresso, and lemon "lift" an old-fashioned dish, generally made with beef, to something lighter and special.

4 thick veal steaks, about 9 ounces each
1 tablespoon olive oil
2 teaspoons sweet paprika
1 cup heavy cream
6 tablespoons fino sherry
8 ounces baby portobello mushrooms, sliced
8 ounces shiitake mushrooms, stemmed and thinly sliced
2 teaspoons chopped fresh lemon thyme
¼ teaspoon espresso powder
2 tablespoons finely minced fresh chives

Preheat the broiler. Rub the veal with the olive oil. Season with the paprika and salt and pepper and arrange on a broiler pan. Heat the cream in a large skillet until bubbly. Add 3 tablespoons of the sherry and all the mushrooms. Cook over high heat, stirring, until the mushrooms soften, 4 minutes. Add the remaining 3 tablespoons sherry, thyme, espresso powder, and salt and pepper. Cook, stirring, until the mushrooms exude their liquid and then absorb much of the sauce, 3 minutes.

Meanwhile, broil the veal 6 inches from the heat for 3 to 4 minutes on each side, until just cooked through. Let rest 5 minutes; thickly slice on the bias. Top with the mushroom sauce and sprinkle with chives. SERVES 4

BIG JUICY SUN-DRIED TOMATO BURGERS

These days, hamburger meat has gone gourmet, so your market may offer upscale blends of ground chuck and brisket, or ground chuck and sirloin. Experiment if you wish.

3½ pounds ground beef
14 ounces sun-dried tomatoes in olive oil
1 large yellow onion
3 tablespoons dried basil leaves
2 teaspoons ground cumin
¼ cup balsamic vinegar
8 kaiser rolls or focaccia squares, toasted

Put the beef in a large bowl. Drain the sun-dried tomatoes, reserving 2 tablespoons oil. Chop the tomatoes into very small pieces to get 1⅓ cups; add to the bowl. Cut the onion in half; grate on the large holes of a box grater to get ½ cup grated onion pulp and juice. Add to the bowl with the reserved tomato oil, the basil, cumin, ½ teaspoon salt, and pepper. Mix well, and form into 8 thick patties. Grill or broil the burgers for 3 to 4 minutes on each side for medium-rare, or until desired doneness. Splash with balsamic vinegar and serve on the rolls. MAKES 8

FLAP, HANGER, OR SKIRT STEAKS WITH SUMAC

Rubbed heavily with ground sumac and put in a searingly hot pan on a thin layer of salt, flap, hanger, or skirt steaks are quite addictive when prepared this way. Ground sumac can be found in Middle Eastern food markets. Serve the steaks with a simple onion salad: Soak sliced onions in cold water for 30 minutes; drain. Mix with sumac, torn parsley leaves, and olive oil.

2 pounds flap steaks, skirt steaks, or hanger steaks
½ cup ground sumac
Olive oil, if broiling

If cooking on the stovetop, dredge the steaks in the sumac. If broiling, rub a little oil onto the steaks before dredging in the sumac. Heat a large pan with a thin layer of salt until searingly hot. Add the meat and cook over high heat for 4 minutes on each side for rare, or until desired doneness. Transfer to a cutting board. Sprinkle with salt and pepper and let rest 5 minutes. Cut the steak on the bias. SERVES 4

Sirloin Steaks with Magic Green Sauce

It takes only minutes, and four ingredients, to make a radically delicious sauce to accompany a great steak. That's magic enough, but the flavors coalesce so that even guests who don't think they like cilantro probably will. Serve the steaks cooked any way the spirit moves you: seared in a cast-iron pan, broiled, or grilled outdoors.

1 cup packed fresh cilantro leaves with a bit of their stems
$\frac{1}{4}$ cup capers plus 2 tablespoons brine
2 tablespoons chopped scallions, white parts only
6 tablespoons olive oil, plus more for the steaks
4 thick sirloin steaks

Combine the cilantro, capers, brine, and scallions in a food processor. Slowly add the oil and 2 tablespoons water; process until almost smooth. Add salt and pepper.

Brush the steaks with a little oil; season with salt and pepper. Heat a charcoal grill, broiler, or cast-iron pan until screaming hot (the way my friend Evan Chender describes it). Cook the steaks 4 to 5 minutes on one side, turn and cook 3 minutes on the other side for medium-rare. If using a grill, turn the steaks a quarter-turn halfway through cooking each side to create hatch-marked grill marks. Allow the meat to rest 10 minutes; sprinkle with salt. Serve the steaks whole or thickly sliced, topped with the green sauce. SERVES 4

Sizzling Skirts with Lime, Basil & Sriracha

It's fun to add more sizzle by splashing a little tequila into the pan at the end. Serve with a stack of warm flour tortillas.

2 pounds skirt steaks
4 large garlic cloves, finely chopped
1 large Spanish onion, halved and thinly sliced
1½ tablespoons ground cumin
2 limes
1½ tablespoons Sriracha
2 tablespoons olive oil
12 cherry tomatoes, cut in half
½ cup finely julienned fresh basil leaves

Cut the steaks into 4 equal pieces. Season with salt and pepper. Place in a shallow dish. Mash the garlic into the meat. Add the onion, cumin, grated zest and juice of 1 lime, and Sriracha to the steaks and toss to coat; let sit 15 minutes.

Heat the oil in a large skillet until hot. Add the steaks and onion; sear the steaks for 1 minute on each side. Add the tomatoes and basil; continue to cook the steaks over high heat for several minutes on each side until rare. Squeeze the juice of the second lime into the pan and cook 1 minute longer. Transfer the steaks to a board, sprinkle with salt, and let rest 5 minutes. Slice the steaks thickly on the bias and serve with the tomato mixture. SERVES 4

REDDENED RIB EYE WITH PIMIENTO CHEESE

I always have smoked paprika, sweet paprika, and ground sumac in my global pantry. One day I decided to use them together—with rather remarkable results. Mixed with a touch of salt and sugar, they formed a ruddy crust for rib eye steaks. Topping it with homemade pimiento cheese makes a sundae for a cowboy.

8 ounces very sharp yellow Cheddar
3 ounces pimientos from a jar, with 3 tablespoons brine
6 tablespoons mayonnaise
1 small garlic clove
1$\frac{1}{2}$ teaspoons sugar
1 teaspoon sweet smoked paprika
$\frac{1}{2}$ teaspoon sweet paprika
4 thick rib eye steaks, about 12 ounces each
$\frac{1}{4}$ cup ground sumac

Preheat the broiler. Chop the cheese and put in a food processor with the pimientos, brine, mayonnaise, and garlic. Process until smooth; add salt and pepper. Chill.

Mix together the sugar, both paprikas, and 1$\frac{1}{2}$ teaspoons salt. Rub the steaks thoroughly with the mixture and let sit 10 minutes.

Rub the sumac thickly on both sides of the steaks. Place on a rimmed baking sheet; broil as close to the heat as possible for 3 to 4 minutes on each side for medium-rare, or until desired doneness. Top each steak with a scoop of pimiento cheese. SERVES 4

NEW ASIA STEAK

I refer to this recipe affectionately as "cheapsteak," for it shows how Thai fish sauce can enhance the color, taste, and texture of less-expensive cuts of meat such as flank steak. Delicious as it is unlikely.

1$\frac{1}{2}$ pounds flank steak
$\frac{1}{4}$ cup Thai fish sauce
1 bunch scallions
Several tablespoons olive oil

Place the steak in a shallow baking dish. Pour the fish sauce over and turn the steak to coat thoroughly. Trim the scallions. Set aside 4 whole scallions. Finely mince the remaining scallions to get $\frac{1}{2}$ cup. Toss with the beef. Cover and refrigerate 4 to 6 hours.

Remove the steak from the marinade and pat dry. Brush a large skillet with a little oil and heat until hot. Cook the steak over high heat for 3 to 4 minutes on each side, until glazed outside and rare inside. Transfer to a cutting board and let rest 5 minutes. Toss the 4 whole scallions with a bit of oil and put in the skillet to soften. Cut the steak on the bias into thick slices, sprinkle with salt, and top with the whole scallions. SERVES 4

TOURNEDOS BALSAMICO WITH ROSEMARY & GORGONZOLA DOLCE

Tournedos are thick round slices taken from a filet of beef and taste divine under a blanket of Gorgonzola dolce.

4 thick beef tenderloin filets, about 10 ounces each
$\frac{1}{3}$ cup extra-virgin olive oil
6 tablespoons balsamic vinegar
1 tablespoon minced fresh rosemary, plus sprigs for garnish
4 ounces creamy gorgonzola cheese, cut into 4 slices

Place the filets in a shallow baking dish. Season with salt and pepper. Pour the oil and 2 tablespoons of the vinegar over the beef. Rub the rosemary into the meat.

Heat a cast-iron skillet or grill pan until very hot. Add the filets; cook 3 to 4 minutes on each side for medium-rare. Transfer to a platter and let rest 5 minutes.

Cook the remaining 4 tablespoons vinegar in a small skillet over high heat until reduced by half. Drizzle the steaks with the reduced vinegar; top with a thin slice of cheese. Garnish with rosemary sprigs. SERVES 4

A PRIME RIB OF BEEF

The method for cooking this fabulous cut of meat is borrowed from Patricia Wells; I have found it fool-proof. It is a single, thick beef rib roasted at a high temperature. An instant sauce: Stir together $^1/_2$ cup crème fraiche, 2 tablespoons grated horseradish, and $^1/_2$ teaspoon dry sherry, or simply dribble with a few drops of truffle oil.

    $1^1/_2$ cups kosher salt
    1 prime rib of beef, about 2 pounds

Preheat the oven to 500°F. Mound the salt in the center of a rimmed baking sheet. Season beef with salt and pepper. Place the beef, fat side up, so that the bone is sitting upright in the salt, using it to "anchor" the beef. Roast 22 minutes, until the fat is crackling and brown and an instant-read thermometer registers 125°F for rare. Transfer the beef to a platter and cover loosely with foil. Let rest 10 minutes.

Cut the meat away from the bone; slice on the bias into thick slices. Sprinkle with salt. Serve with any juices from the platter. SERVES 2

FILET OF BEEF WITH WASABI-GARLIC CREAM

Radical elegance for your favorite guests.

2 tablespoons olive oil
2³/₄-pound filet of beef, tied
1 tablespoon sugar
1¹/₂ cups heavy cream
2 very large garlic cloves, peeled and smashed
1 tablespoon prepared wasabi

Preheat the oven to 425°F. Drizzle the oil on a rimmed baking sheet; roll the filet in the oil. Combine the sugar and 1 tablespoon kosher salt. Rub into the top and sides of the filet, but not the bottom or it will burn. Roast the beef 25 minutes, until an instant-read thermometer registers 125°F for rare.

Meanwhile, bring the cream and garlic to a boil in a saucepan. Reduce the heat and cook, stirring, until reduced to 1 cup, 15 minutes. Push the softened garlic through a press; whisk back into the sauce. Add the wasabi, cook 1 minute, and remove from the heat. Add salt.

Transfer the beef to a cutting board. Let rest 10 minutes. Gently reheat the sauce. Remove the strings from the beef and thickly slice. Serve with the sauce. SERVES 6

radical

elegance

Tri-Tip Filet in Soy & Red Wine with Chinese Mustard

The triangles found at the bottom of the sirloin are commonly called tri-tip beef roasts; they run from 1½ to 2½ pounds and are about 2 inches thick. It is a flavorful but lean cut of meat, so it is best to cook it rare. If you don't want to make your own Chinese mustard, gather those little takeout packets lurking in your fridge.

2½ tablespoons dry mustard
2 tablespoons honey
2-pound beef tri-tip filet
⅓ cup dry red wine
2 tablespoons soy sauce
3 large garlic cloves, very finely minced
2 tablespoons peanut or olive oil
8 ounces baby portobello mushrooms, trimmed and halved
2 bunches scallions, trimmed

In a small bowl, stir together 2 tablespoons of the dry mustard, honey, 2 tablespoons water, and ¼ teaspoon salt until smooth.

Preheat the oven to 450°F. Put the filet in a large bowl with the wine, soy sauce, garlic, and remaining ½ tablespoon mustard. Let sit 20 minutes, turning twice.

Remove the filet from the marinade; pat dry. Place the meat in the center of a broiler pan and arrange the mushrooms and scallions around. Drizzle with oil. Roast 12 minutes. Turn the meat and vegetables and roast 10 minutes longer, until an instant-read thermometer registers 125°F for rare. Transfer the meat to a cutting board; let rest 5 minutes. Cut in ¼-inch-thick slices. Serve with the scallions, mushrooms, and any pan juices. Drizzle with the Chinese mustard. SERVES 4

RIB ROAST IN THE STYLE OF GRAVLAX

The editors at Gourmet *magazine once said that my simple roast was one of the best they had ever tasted. It is "cured" in the same way that fresh salmon is for gravlax, literally buried in a mixture of coarse salt, sugar, dill, and cracked black pepper.*

$\frac{1}{4}$ cup kosher salt
3 tablespoons sugar
1$\frac{1}{2}$ teaspoons coarsely cracked black pepper
3$\frac{1}{2}$-pound boneless rib roast, rolled and tied
1 cup chopped fresh dill

Stir together the salt, sugar, and pepper in a small bowl; rub all over the beef. Pat the dill over the salt mixture. Wrap the beef tightly in plastic wrap. Make a small hole in the bottom of the plastic so that any liquid around the beef can drain. Place in a small roasting pan and weight down with a baking sheet topped with a few large heavy cans. Refrigerate 24 hours.

Unwrap the beef; let sit at room temperature 30 minutes. Preheat the oven to 400°F. Scrape the coating off the beef and pat dry with paper towels. Place in a roasting pan. Roast in the middle of the oven 1$\frac{1}{4}$ hours, until an instant-read thermometer registers 130°F for medium-rare. Transfer to a cutting board and tent with foil; let rest 15 minutes. Carve as desired. SERVES 8

MAHOGANY SHORT RIBS

This irreverent merger of foodstuffs results in a tantalizing dish that will amaze and amuse your guests. Buy short ribs that are cut between the bones. These are known as long cut, to differentiate them from flanken, which is cut across the bone.

4 whole short ribs, about 3 pounds
1 cup teriyaki sauce
1 cup prune juice
1 teaspoon whole black peppercorns

Combine the short ribs, teriyaki, and prune juice in a large bowl. Cover and refrigerate overnight.

Pour the marinade into a 4-quart pot. Add 1 cup water and the peppercorns. Bring to a boil. Lower the heat; add the short ribs. Cover and simmer for 2 hours, or until the meat is very tender. Transfer the ribs to a platter. Skim off as much fat as possible from the sauce; bring to a boil. Boil 5 minutes until thick and syrupy. Pour over the short ribs and serve. SERVES 4

BEEF RENDANG

In this exotic beef dish from Southeast Asia, cubes of beef are cooked in coconut milk and lovely aromatics until almost dry but intriguingly tender. Serve hot with jasmine rice, lettuce leaves, and pickled daikon.

1 medium onion, chopped
4 garlic cloves
2-inch piece ginger, peeled and coarsely chopped
1 teaspoon chopped scotch bonnet or Thai bird pepper
2 tablespoons tamarind paste
2 teaspoons ground coriander
1 teaspoon turmeric
2 pounds beef chuck, cut into 1$\frac{1}{2}$-inch cubes
4 stalks lemongrass
2$\frac{1}{2}$ cups unsweetened coconut milk
10 fresh or dried curry leaves, optional

Process the onion, garlic, ginger, hot pepper, tamarind, coriander, turmeric, and ½ cup water in a food processor until smooth. Transfer to a large bowl; add the beef and toss. Cover and marinate at room temperature 1 hour or refrigerate 4 hours.

Bruise the lemongrass stalks and tie each in a knot. Combine the lemongrass, coconut milk, and curry leaves in a 4-quart pot; set aside while the meat marinates.

Bring the coconut milk mixture to a boil. Add the meat and marinade; return just to a boil. Reduce the heat to low. Cook, stirring occasionally, until the liquid becomes a thick paste and the beef begins to sizzle, 1½ to 2 hours. Continue to cook, stirring more frequently, until the paste becomes sticky, about 25 minutes. Discard the lemongrass and curry leaves. SERVES 4

POT ROAST WITH BURNT ONIONS & KIMCHEE

Have the butcher leave a ¼-inch layer of fat on the brisket. Kimchee, a fermented Korean vegetable slaw, is available in the refrigerated section of most Asian food markets.

> 4-pound first-cut brisket
> 2 tablespoons olive oil
> 3 pounds onions, very thinly sliced
> 1¼ cups sake
> 1 cup kimchee
> 1 fresh bay leaf

Season the brisket with salt and pepper. Heat the oil in a Dutch oven; brown the meat all over. Remove from the pot. Add the onions to the pot and cook over high heat until soft and very dark, about 15 minutes. Stir in ½ cup of the sake, scraping up browned bits. Scatter the kimchee over the onions; place the meat on top. Add another ½ cup sake and the bay leaf; bring to a boil. Reduce the heat, cover, and simmer 2½ hours.

Transfer the meat to a cutting board. Bring the cooking liquid to a boil and boil 5 minutes, adding the remaining sake and salt and pepper. Slice the meat ¼ inch thick across the grain and return to the pot. Cover and simmer 30 minutes, until the meat is tender. Discard the bay leaf. SERVES 6

8

VEGETABLES & SIDE DISHES

've never met a vegetable that I didn't admire or enjoy. My favorite changes weekly, but I am currently enamored of parsnips that have been simply cut into 1-inch pieces and steamed for 8 minutes. That's it! Sometimes I drizzle olive oil on top, squirt on some fresh lemon juice, add sliced toasted almonds, or do all three, but even unadorned their texture and inherent sweetness are seductive.

In this chapter, you'll enjoy two dozen vegetables, from asparagus to zucchini—not quite one for each letter of the alphabet, but close. With nutritionists telling us to significantly increase our intake of vegetables, I offer some new techniques and flavor combinations that make that challenge a pleasure. You'll find a brand-new way to cook broccoli: first blanched and then broiled on a hot sheet pan so that it tastes grilled. String beans are blasted at a high temperature so that they caramelize and become deliciously wrinkled.

Some recipes leave you asking an interesting question: What is a vegetable's true taste, anyway? You can answer that for yourself after you try poaching, steaming, and roasting asparagus; and decide whether it is roasting or sautéing that brings out the essence of Brussels sprouts. Then there are two recipes for vegetables cooked in steam heat. One recipe brings out the extraordinary sweetness in carrots; the other plumps up three green vegetables with tenderness. Perhaps this method provides the truest taste of all.

When vegetables are fresh and in season, nature gives us permission to keep it simple. For that reason, you will find that most of these recipes use only a handful of ingredients. Many vegetables need no recipe at all: Add a trickle of melted chive butter to a platter of steamed baby carrots; splash warm roasted beets with walnut oil and grated lemon zest; add toasted hazelnuts to sautéed haricots verts.

The recipes have been divided into two sections: The 10- to 20-minute recipes vary from 10 minutes (Sheet-Pan Spinach) to just under 20 minutes ("Chipped Beets" & Beet Greens). Slow & Easy sides acknowledges that many root vegetables, including potatoes, take a while to cook yet can be radically simple to prepare.

We have witnessed a gradual greening of America over the last decade and have been enthralled with the quality and variety of vegetables available to us. A new age of produce has truly arrived. The movement to replant heirloom varieties, the growth of organic farms, the rise of better distribution systems, the boom in sustainable agriculture and its characteristic respect for the seasons, the markets' continued enthusiasm for the new and the exotic, and the passion of local farmers for hand-selecting and "small-batch" cultivation and their devotion to organics and good nutrition—all of this will provide us with many gratifying choices in the years ahead.

10 to 20 minutes

Roasted Asparagus with Bay Leaves & Crispy Capers 252

Poached Asparagus with Lemon-Mint Panko 252

Steamed Asparagus with Wasabi-Miso Butter 254

Steamed Broccoli with Blue Cheese, Red Onion & Mint 254

A New Way to Cook Broccoli: Charred & Tossed with Chilies & Garlic 256

"Chipped Beets" & Beet Greens 256

Jane Brody's Brussels Sprouts 257

Roasted Brussels Sprouts with Medjool Dates 259

Carrot "Nib" Orzo 259

Carrots-and-Onions in High Humidity 261

Milky Carrot & Parsnip Puree 261

Roasted Sliced Cauliflower with Cheddar & Rosemary 262

Whole Cauliflower, Ras el Hanout Crumble 262

Swiss Chard with Lemony Tahina & Cashews 264

"Green" Corn 264

Steamed Fennel & Red Peppers with Garlic Oil & Lemon Zest 265

Blasted Green Beans & Grape Tomatoes 265

Steamed Parsnips with Toasted Almonds 267

Peas & Couscous with Curry Oil 267

Roasted French Breakfast Radishes 268

Roasted Parsnip Fries 268

Sautéed Peppers with Golden Raisins & Arugula 270

Sheet-Pan Spinach 270

Spinach, Ricotta & Basil Puree 271

Sugar Snaps with Diced Bacon & Radishes 273

Three Green Vegetables in High Humidity 273

Stir-Fried Watercress with Garlic Chips 274

Pistachio-Coconut Rice 274

slow & easy

Braised Red Cabbage with Cranberries 275

Caramelized Cabbage & Noodles 275

Crispy Shredded Potato Cakes 276

Bay-Smoked Potatoes 276

Creamy Potato Gratin 278

Olive Oil–Mashed Potatoes 278

Wasabi-Mashed Potatoes 279

Rutabaga, Crème Fraîche & Havarti Torte 279

Roasted Sweet Potatoes with Whipped Butter & Maple "Honey" 282

Sweet Potato Puree with Fresh Ginger & Orange 282

White Beans with Spinach, Tomatoes & Rosemary 283

Tian of Eggplant, Tomato & Herbs 284

"Creola" Rice 285

ROASTED ASPARAGUS WITH BAY LEAVES & ➤ CRISPY CAPERS

An intense dose of heat keeps the spears green and snappy. Fried capers add a startling accent. More startling still: Fry up some large caperberries, still on their stems.

> 2 pounds medium asparagus
> 4 tablespoons olive oil
> 6 large fresh bay leaves
> ¼ cup large capers in brine

Preheat the oven to 500°F. Trim 2 inches from the bottoms of the asparagus spears. Drizzle 2 tablespoons of the oil on a rimmed baking sheet. Add the asparagus and toss in the oil to coat. Tuck in the bay leaves and sprinkle lightly with salt. Roast, shaking the pan once, 8 to 10 minutes, until browned and just tender. Transfer to a large platter.

Drain the capers and pat dry. Heat the remaining 2 tablespoons oil in a small skillet. Add the capers and fry until crispy, 1 minute. Pour the capers and oil over the asparagus; add salt and pepper. SERVES 6

POACHED ASPARAGUS WITH LEMON-MINT PANKO

Of the myriad ways to prepare asparagus, I think poaching produces the truest, freshest flavor. A shower of minty, lemony bread crumbs brightens the experience.

> 2 pounds thick fresh asparagus
> 1 tablespoon olive oil
> 2 tablespoons unsalted butter
> 1 cup panko
> Grated zest and juice of 1 lemon
> 2 tablespoons finely chopped fresh mint, plus sprigs for garnish

Trim 2 inches from the bottoms of the asparagus. Lightly peel the stalks. Fill a 12-inch skillet with 3 inches of salted water. Bring to a boil. Add the asparagus and cook until tender but still bright green, 10 minutes. Meanwhile, heat the oil and 1 tablespoon of the butter in a medium skillet. Add the panko; stir over medium heat until golden, 3 minutes. Stir the lemon zest and 1 teaspoon juice into the crumbs. Cook 30 seconds; add the chopped mint and salt and pepper. Drain the asparagus well and transfer to a platter. Dot with the remaining 1 tablespoon butter; scatter the crumbs on top. Garnish with mint sprigs. SERVES 6

STEAMED ASPARAGUS WITH WASABI-MISO BUTTER

This is a radically nice way to treat asparagus when it first makes its appearance at the market. Subject to availability, sometimes I use freshly grated white horseradish instead of wasabi and garnish the dish with gorgeous purple basil sprouts instead of the sesame seeds.

1½ pounds medium asparagus
4 tablespoons unsalted butter, very soft
2 teaspoons white miso (also known as shiro miso)
1½ teaspoons wasabi paste
Few drops freshly squeezed lemon juice
1 tablespoon black sesame seeds

Bring a pot of water fitted with a steamer basket to a rapid boil. Trim 2 inches from the bottoms of the asparagus spears. Peel the stalks lightly. Mash the butter in a bowl until smooth. Add the miso, wasabi, lemon juice, and salt. Stir until smooth.

Add the asparagus to the steamer basket, cover, and steam 10 minutes, until just tender. Transfer to a platter; sprinkle with salt and spoon the butter over the top. Sprinkle with sesame seeds. SERVES 4

STEAMED BROCCOLI WITH BLUE CHEESE, ➤ RED ONION & MINT

This is such a pleasure to make and then eat with a steak.

2 large heads broccoli
2 large red onions
¼ cup olive oil, plus more for drizzling
6 ounces blue cheese, crumbled
⅔ cup fresh mint leaves, coarsely chopped

Bring a pot of water fitted with a steamer basket to a rapid boil. Cut the broccoli into florets with 2 inches of stem. Add the broccoli to the steamer basket; cover and steam 10 minutes, until tender but still bright green.

Cut the onions in half through the root ends and thinly slice lengthwise. Heat the oil in a large skillet. Add the onions and cook over high heat until soft, dark brown, and crispy, 10 minutes. Transfer the broccoli to a large bowl. Add the onions, cheese, and mint. Toss, add salt and pepper, and drizzle with additional oil. SERVES 6

blue cheese

red onions

green broccoli

A New Way to Cook Broccoli: Charred & Tossed with Chilies & Garlic

Blanch long broccoli florets for 2 minutes, pat very dry, toss with oil, and broil on a sheet pan! The result is a lovely char. Garlic, chilies, and a splash of Thai fish sauce make it addictive. This recipe was inspired by the fabulous restaurant Ottolenghi in London.

2 large heads broccoli
6 tablespoons olive oil
3 large garlic cloves
2 red Thai bird chilies
1 teaspoon Thai fish sauce

Preheat the broiler. Bring a large pot of salted water to a boil. Cut the broccoli into florets with 2 inches of stem. Add the broccoli to the boiling water and cook 2 minutes. Drain immediately and refresh under very cold running water; pat dry. Heat a rimmed baking sheet under the broiler. Toss the broccoli with 2 tablespoons of the oil; carefully arrange on the hot pan. Broil 7 minutes, rotating the pan twice, until the broccoli is nicely charred.

Meanwhile, heat the remaining 4 tablespoons oil in a small skillet over medium heat. Thinly slice the garlic and chilies (remove seeds) and add to the skillet. Cook until the garlic is crispy and golden, 2 minutes. Add the hot oil and fish sauce to the broccoli and toss. Season with salt and pepper. SERVES 4

"Chipped Beets" & Beet Greens

If you use nature's "package" of beets' roots, stems, and greens, you can feed four lavishly with just one large bunch. The roots get "chipped" and cook quickly in this unusual melding of flavors.

1 large bunch beets (leafy greens plus 1 pound medium beets)
2 large garlic cloves
3 tablespoons extra-virgin olive oil
¼ cup orange juice
1 tablespoon balsamic vinegar
3-ounce piece feta cheese

Wash the beets and greens. Cut the stems and leaves into $1/2$-inch pieces. Peel the beets and cut into quarters. Pulse the beets and garlic in a food processor until coarsely ground ("chips"). In a very large pan, heat 2 tablespoons of the oil. Add the chipped beet mixture; cook 5 minutes over high heat. Add the stems and greens; cook 5 minutes. Add the orange juice, vinegar, and $1/4$ cup water. Cook 5 minutes over high heat; cover the pan and cook 5 minutes longer, until the beets, stems, and greens are tender. Add salt and pepper. Transfer to a platter and crumble the feta on top; sprinkle with the remaining 1 tablespoon oil. SERVES 4

JANE BRODY'S BRUSSELS SPROUTS

Jane Brody, the personal health columnist for the New York Times *since 1975, is my neighbor in Brooklyn. She is crazy about Brussels sprouts. This is her recipe; it is adapted from a dish at the Bear Cafe, one of her favorite restaurants in Woodstock, New York.*

$1/2$ cup pecan halves
$1^{1}/_{2}$ pounds Brussels sprouts, trimmed
2 tablespoons olive oil
2 tablespoons unsalted butter
1 small yellow onion, finely chopped
2 large garlic cloves, finely chopped

Bring a large pot of salted water to a boil. Toast the pecans in a nonstick skillet over medium-high heat until fragrant, 2 minutes. Set aside. Add the Brussels sprouts to the boiling water and blanch 5 minutes. Drain well; cut each in half through the stem end.

Heat the oil and butter in a large skillet. Add the onion and cook over high heat until golden, 5 minutes. Add the garlic and Brussels sprouts and cook until the sprouts are tender and browned in spots, 5 to 10 minutes. Transfer to a serving bowl. Break the toasted pecans halves in half and sprinkle over the sprouts. Season with salt and pepper.
SERVES 4

◄ ROASTED BRUSSELS SPROUTS WITH MEDJOOL DATES

This is a delicious merger of flavors. Use large, plump, moist Medjool dates. They come from Iran but now also from California. You can buy them in Middle Eastern markets.

1 pound Brussels sprouts, trimmed and halved
4 tablespoons olive oil, plus more if needed
6 large soft Medjool dates, pitted and diced
¼ cup freshly grated Parmigiano-Reggiano
2 teaspoons fresh thyme leaves

Preheat the oven to 400°F. Toss the Brussels sprouts with 2 tablespoons of the oil on a rimmed baking sheet. Sprinkle with salt and pepper. Turn the sprouts cut side down. Roast for 10 minutes. Add the dates to the pan and toss with the sprouts. Roast 10 minutes longer, until caramelized. Transfer the sprouts to a platter. Toss with the cheese, thyme, and remaining 2 tablespoons oil. Add salt and pepper and more oil if needed. **SERVES 4**

CARROT "NIB" ORZO

Baby carrots get pulverized to become little "nibs" that fleck golden orzo. The orzo is first sautéed, with liquid added later, much in the style of making risotto.

6 ounces baby carrots
2 tablespoons unsalted butter
8 ounces orzo
1¼ cups chicken broth
1 large garlic clove
¼ cup freshly grated Parmigiano-Reggiano
½ cup fresh chopped chives

Put the carrots in a food processor; pulse into pieces about twice as large as the orzo, 10 to 12 times. Melt the butter in a 6-cup saucepan. Add the orzo and carrots and cook, stirring constantly, until the orzo is golden, 5 minutes. Add the broth, garlic pushed through a press, and 1½ cups water. Cook over medium-high heat, stirring, until the liquid is absorbed and the orzo is tender, about 12 minutes. Add the cheese and ⅓ cup of the chives. Add salt and pepper. Garnish with the remaining chives. **SERVES 4**

◄ CARROTS-AND-ONIONS IN HIGH HUMIDITY

There is an exquisite elegance in this simple and inexpensive preparation. I serve it alongside roast chicken or with a piece of simply grilled fish perched on top, drizzled with a bit of my very best olive oil and sprinkled with coarse sea salt.

> 2 medium onions
> 1 pound long, slender carrots
> 8 long sprigs fresh thyme, plus leaves for garnish
> $\frac{1}{4}$ cup extra-virgin olive oil
> 1 tablespoon freshly squeezed lemon juice

Bring a large pot of water fitted with a steamer basket to a rapid boil. Slice the onions very thin. Place in the basket. Peel each carrot and cut in quarters through the width and length. Arrange on the onions with the thyme sprigs. Cover and steam until the vegetables are tender, 10 minutes. Whisk the olive oil with the lemon juice; add salt. Transfer the carrots and onions to a platter; sprinkle with salt and drizzle with the dressing. Scatter with thyme leaves. SERVES 4

MILKY CARROT & PARSNIP PUREE

When carrots and parsnips bubble in a milk bath with fresh sage and a clove of garlic, the resultant puree is the color of orange sherbet with a voluptuous texture and an alluring flavor. Nice with pork.

> 1 pound carrots
> 1 pound parsnips
> 2 cups whole milk
> 4 large fresh sage leaves
> 1 large garlic clove
> 2 tablespoons unsalted butter

Peel the carrots and parsnips and cut into $\frac{1}{2}$-inch pieces. Place in a large saucepan. Add the milk (it will not cover the vegetables), sage, garlic, and salt. Bring to a boil. Reduce the heat, place the cover askew, and simmer 20 minutes, until the vegetables are very soft. Drain, saving the liquid. Transfer the vegetables to a food processor and process until very smooth, adding cooking liquid as needed to make a thick and creamy puree. Add the butter and process; season with salt and pepper. SERVES 6

ROASTED SLICED CAULIFLOWER WITH CHEDDAR ➤ & ROSEMARY

Slicing cauliflower into shingles allows for quicker cooking and desirable browning. Tossed at the last minute with cheese, rosemary, and chives, it looks great spread out on a platter.

1 medium head cauliflower
4 tablespoons olive oil
4 ounces very sharp yellow Cheddar cheese, shredded
2 teaspoons very finely minced fresh rosemary
1/4 cup finely chopped fresh chives

Preheat the oven to 475°F. Core the cauliflower and cut in half through the stem end. Place flat side down on a cutting board and cut crosswise in 1/4-inch-thick slices (some will fall apart). Arrange on a rimmed baking sheet. Drizzle the cauliflower with 3 tablespoons of the oil and sprinkle with salt. Roast 10 minutes; turn the slices over and roast 10 minutes longer, until tender and golden brown. Transfer to a platter. Toss with the cheese, the remaining 1 tablespoon oil, and salt and pepper. Sprinkle with the rosemary and chives. SERVES 4

WHOLE CAULIFLOWER, RAS EL HANOUT CRUMBLE

A riff on the classic Cauliflower Polonaise, this tastes exotic and evocative. Substitute garam masala or curry for the ras el hanout if you must.

1 medium head cauliflower, about 1³/₄ pounds
1¹/₂ tablespoons unsalted butter
3 tablespoons olive oil
1 cup panko
1¹/₂ teaspoons ras el hanout

Core the cauliflower, keeping the head whole. Bring a pot of water fitted with a steamer basket to a rapid boil. Add the cauliflower, cover, and steam 15 minutes, until the cauliflower is soft.

Meanwhile, melt the butter and 1 tablespoon of the oil in a medium skillet. Add the panko and cook over medium heat until golden, 2 minutes. Stir in the ras el hanout and a large pinch of salt. Cook 15 seconds, then remove from the heat.

Transfer the hot cauliflower to a platter; drizzle with the remaining 2 tablespoons oil and sprinkle with salt. Scatter the crumbs all over. SERVES 4

cauliflower

cheddar

Swiss Chard with Lemony Tahina & Cashews

This is a great way to serve chard (in rainbow colors), collards, or kale. It contains a wealth of antioxidants, too.

$\frac{1}{2}$ cup tahina
Grated zest and juice of 2 large lemons
1 large garlic clove, peeled and smashed
2 pounds Swiss chard, collards, or kale
3 tablespoons extra-virgin olive oil
2 cups finely chopped onions
$\frac{1}{2}$ cup roasted cashews, broken in pieces

Put the tahina in a food processor. Add the lemon zest, $\frac{1}{4}$ cup juice, and the garlic. Process, adding $\frac{1}{3}$ to $\frac{1}{2}$ cup cold water, until smooth. Add salt and pepper.

Wash the greens and cut into $\frac{1}{2}$-inch pieces. Heat the oil in a very large nonstick skillet. Add the onions and cook over high heat, stirring constantly, 3 minutes. Add the greens (with some water clinging to them); cook over high heat 5 minutes. Add a large pinch of salt, cover, and cook the greens until tender but still bright green, 5 minutes longer. Transfer to a platter and drizzle with the tahina sauce and sprinkle with the cashews. SERVES 4

"Green" Corn

Rub steamy ears of fresh corn with fresh basil and you'll inhale a perfume that screams "Summer!"

6 large ears fresh sweet corn, shucked
Fistful of large fresh basil leaves
2 tablespoons unsalted butter, in small pieces
1 lime

Bring a large pot of salted water to a boil. Add the corn, return to a boil, and cook 3 minutes. Wash the basil and dry very well. Sprinkle with kosher salt. Transfer the corn to a platter. Rub each ear with salted basil leaves. Dot with butter; squeeze lime juice on top. SERVES 6

STEAMED FENNEL & RED PEPPERS WITH GARLIC OIL & LEMON ZEST

I could eat this every night. In summer, I grill a huge tranche of bluefish and place it simply on top. It's great hot or at room temperature.

> 1 large fennel bulb, about 1½ pounds
> 2 small red bell peppers, about 4 ounces each
> ¼ cup olive oil
> 1 small garlic clove
> Grated zest of 1 lemon

Bring a large pot of water fitted with a steamer basket to a rapid boil. Remove the stems and fronds from the fennel; chop the fronds to get 2 tablespoons and set aside. Cut the bulb in half lengthwise. Place cut side down on board; cut crosswise very thinly. Cut the bell peppers into very thin rings; remove the seeds. Put the fennel and peppers in the steamer and sprinkle with salt. Cover and steam for 12 minutes, until soft.

Combine the oil and garlic pushed through a press in a cup. Transfer the vegetables to a platter; toss with the garlic oil and salt and pepper. Sprinkle with lemon zest and chopped fennel fronds. SERVES 4

BLASTED GREEN BEANS & GRAPE TOMATOES

Roasting green beans at a high temperature, until they wrinkle and caramelize, is a radically simple way to maintain their vivid color while adding a layer of complexity.

> 1 pound green beans, ends trimmed
> 1½ tablespoons extra-virgin olive oil, plus more for drizzling
> 32 grape tomatoes, halved lengthwise
> 1 teaspoon crumbled dried oregano
> Pinch hot-pepper flakes

Preheat the oven to 450°F. Toss the beans with the oil on a rimmed baking sheet; arrange in a single layer. Sprinkle with salt. Roast, shaking the pan several times, 8 minutes, until they soften. Add the tomatoes and oregano and toss. Roast for 6 minutes longer, until the beans are browned in spots and the tomatoes have shriveled. Drizzle with more oil; sprinkle with salt and pepper flakes. SERVES 4

◄ STEAMED PARSNIPS WITH TOASTED ALMONDS

This could suffice as a one-ingredient recipe because steamed parsnips are divine with just a sprinkling of salt. However, they're also great when drizzled with a bit of olive oil and lemon juice and showered with sliced toasted almonds. It's up to you.

> 1 pound parsnips
> 3 tablespoons sliced almonds
> 2 tablespoons olive oil
> 2 teaspoons freshly squeezed lemon juice

Bring a large pot of water fitted with a steamer basket to a boil. Peel the parsnips and cut into ½-inch slices. Place the parsnips in the basket; cover and steam 8 minutes, until tender. Meanwhile, lightly toast the almonds in a small skillet over medium heat until fragrant, about 2 minutes. Transfer the parsnips to a bowl and drizzle with the oil and lemon juice. Add salt and pepper; scatter the toasted almonds on top. SERVES 4

PEAS & COUSCOUS WITH CURRY OIL

Here's an interesting technique for cooking frozen peas and couscous together. In 5 minutes, you have both vegetable and starch in one pot. It's a great way to give peas (even frozen ones) a chance.

> 1 cup couscous
> 1 cup frozen peas
> 3 tablespoons olive oil
> ¾ teaspoon curry powder
> 1 small bunch cilantro

Combine the couscous, peas, and 2 cups salted water in a large saucepan; bring to a boil. Reduce the heat; cook and stir 1 minute. Cover and cook 3 minutes, until the peas are just tender. Remove from the heat. Let stand, covered, for 5 minutes. Mix the oil, curry powder, and a pinch of salt in a small bowl. Sliver 3 tablespoons cilantro and add to the oil. Finely chop ½ cup cilantro leaves. Transfer the couscous to a warm bowl; fluff with a fork. Stir in the curry oil and salt and pepper. Top with the chopped cilantro. SERVES 4

ROASTED FRENCH BREAKFAST RADISHES ➤

1 bunch breakfast radishes
2 ounces Spanish Manchego or aged Pecorino Romano cheese

Preheat the oven to 425°F. Wash the radishes and halve lengthwise. Remove the tails but keep 1½ inches of stems with leaves. Put the radishes on a rimmed baking sheet and rub with 2 tablespoons olive oil. Bake 25 minutes, shaking twice during baking, until they wrinkle. Slice lengthwise, if desired. Sprinkle with coarse salt. Serve with thin slices of the Manchego or Pecorino Romano cheese. MAKES 4 TO 6

ROASTED PARSNIP FRIES

Cut the parsnips to look like french fries; you can even use a crinkle cutter.

1 pound parsnips
2 tablespoons olive oil
⅓ cup freshly grated Pecorino Romano
2 teaspoons fresh thyme leaves

Preheat the oven to 400°F. Peel the parsnips and cut into long thick strips to resemble french fries. Place on a rimmed baking sheet; toss with the oil and sprinkle with salt and pepper. Roast, turning once, 20 minutes, until golden brown and tender. Sprinkle with the cheese and thyme. SERVES 4

Sautéed Peppers with Golden Raisins & Arugula

This is a riot of colors and textures; the baby arugula is tossed in at the last moment and barely cooked. Serve hot, or add feta cheese, capers, or pine nuts and chill for a wonderful first course.

6 medium bell peppers of assorted colors
¼ cup extra-virgin olive oil
⅔ cup golden raisins
1 tablespoon fennel seeds
2 tablespoons balsamic vinegar, plus more if needed
5-ounce package baby arugula

Cut the peppers in half lengthwise and remove the ribs and seeds. Cut across the width into ¼-inch-wide strips. Heat the oil in a very large nonstick skillet. Add the peppers and cook over high heat for 5 minutes. Add the raisins, fennel seeds, and salt and pepper. Cook until the peppers are soft, 6 minutes longer. Stir in the vinegar. Immediately add the arugula and stir until barely cooked, about 2 minutes. Adjust seasonings, adding more vinegar, salt, or pepper as desired. SERVES 6

Sheet-Pan Spinach

As much as I love spinach, I never found an adequate way of dealing with a large amount. A bountiful pound shrinks to feed only 2 when it's boiled or steamed. But I discovered that when it's baked in a 500°F oven and spritzed with water a couple of times, a pound of spinach can actually feed 4. It takes less than 10 minutes and the "sauna" technique keeps the spinach vivid green.

1 pound prewashed curly spinach leaves
1½ tablespoons olive oil, plus more for drizzling

Preheat the oven to 500°F. Remove any large stems from the spinach and pat the leaves completely dry. Place on a large rimmed baking sheet; toss thoroughly with the oil. Sprinkle with kosher salt. Roast 5 minutes. Using a spritz bottle filled with water, spritz the spinach while still in the oven; roast 2 minutes. Spritz again and roast 3 minutes longer, until the spinach is wilted. Sprinkle with salt and drizzle on a bit more oil, if desired. SERVES 4

SPINACH, RICOTTA & BASIL PUREE

Here's a version of creamed spinach that can rival the very best. Its richness comes mostly from ricotta cheese; its spinach flavor is heightened by the addition of fresh basil. I like it with a bit of garlic stirred in at the end; my husband thinks it's better without. Try it both ways.

2 (10-ounce) bags fresh spinach leaves
³⁄₄ cup fresh basil leaves
³⁄₄ cup whole-milk ricotta cheese
¹⁄₄ cup heavy cream
2 tablespoons unsalted butter
¹⁄₂ small garlic clove, smashed and minced

Bring 2 cups salted water to a boil in a very large pot. Add the spinach and cover. Cook 3 minutes, stirring twice, until soft and bright green. Drain well; squeeze out excess water. Transfer to a food processor. Add the basil, ricotta, and cream; blend until smooth. Melt the butter in a 3-quart pot. Add the garlic and cook, stirring, 1 minute. Add the creamed spinach and stir until well-blended. Season with salt and pepper. SERVES 4

◄ SUGAR SNAPS WITH DICED BACON & RADISHES

This is one of my favorite side dishes with simple grilled fish. Cut the bacon and radishes into the same small size to mimic one another.

> 12 ounces sugar snap peas
> 6 large radishes
> 3 ounces slab bacon
> Splash white balsamic vinegar

Trim the sugar snaps; remove the strings that run down the length of the pods. Cut the radishes and bacon into $1/4$-inch cubes. Bring a pot of salted water to a boil; add the snap peas and radishes and cook 4 minutes, until tender. Drain in a colander.

In a large skillet, cook the bacon over high heat until the fat is rendered and the bacon crisps, 2 minutes. Add the snap peas and radishes; cook several minutes, until tender. Splash with vinegar and season with salt and pepper. SERVES 4

THREE GREEN VEGETABLES IN HIGH HUMIDITY

Here, three verdant vegetables are steamed together and become a delicious, buttery sauce the color of jade. It's surprisingly healthy.

> 3 medium zucchini, 1 pound
> 2 tablespoons unsalted butter, chilled
> 12 ounces snow peas
> 12 ounces haricots verts

Cut 1 zucchini into 1-inch pieces; place in a small saucepan. Cover with water and bring to a boil. Reduce the heat and cook until very soft, 10 minutes. Transfer the zucchini with a slotted spoon to a food processor and puree, adding enough cooking water to make a thick sauce. Cut the butter into pieces; add to the zucchini and process until creamy. Transfer to a saucepan.

Meanwhile, bring a large pot of water fitted with a steamer basket to a boil. Trim the snow peas and haricots verts. Thinly slice the remaining zucchini. Add the snow peas, haricots verts, and zucchini to the basket; cover and steam 7 minutes, until tender. Transfer to a bowl; stir in the warm zucchini sauce and salt and pepper. SERVES 6

STIR-FRIED WATERCRESS WITH GARLIC CHIPS

Good nestled next to a juicy grilled steak, better on a platter under a roast chicken, best atop a salad of buffalo mozzarella and tomatoes.

4 large bunches watercress
3 tablespoons olive oil
4 large garlic cloves, thinly sliced lengthwise
1 tablespoon extra-virgin olive oil

Remove most of the thick stems from the watercress. Heat the 3 tablespoons olive oil in a very large skillet until hot. Add the garlic and immediately remove the pan from the heat; the garlic will get crispy and brown. Add the watercress to the pan. Return to high heat and cook, stirring constantly, until the watercress barely wilts, 1 minute. Add salt; drizzle with the 1 tablespoon extra-virgin olive oil. SERVES 4

PISTACHIO-COCONUT RICE

Easy and exotic, and a great way to jazz up simple proteins like salmon, chicken, and lamb.

1 cup basmati rice
1 cup light coconut milk
$1/3$ cup finely chopped pistachios
1 tablespoon unsalted butter
$1/2$ teaspoon curry powder

Combine the rice, coconut milk, 1 cup water, and 1 teaspoon salt in a 3-quart saucepan. Bring to a boil and stir once. Reduce the heat and cover. Simmer, stirring once or twice, for 15 minutes, until the rice is tender and the liquid is absorbed. Meanwhile, lightly toast the pistachios in a small skillet over medium heat until fragrant, about 3 minutes.

Stir the toasted pistachios into the rice along with the butter, curry powder, and salt and pepper. SERVES 4

BRAISED RED CABBAGE WITH CRANBERRIES

You can buy a large red cabbage, core it, and shred it yourself, but it is radically simpler to buy cabbage already shredded. The result of braising the cabbage, then letting it steam in its own fragrant vapors, is intense. It cries out for roast duck.

4 tablespoons unsalted butter
2½ pounds shredded red cabbage
2 medium red bell peppers, diced
1 cup unsweetened dried cranberries
1½ teaspoons fennel seeds
2 to 3 tablespoons raspberry vinegar or raspberry balsamic vinegar

Melt the butter in a very large Dutch oven. Add the cabbage and bell peppers and cook over high heat, stirring, for 10 minutes. Add the cranberries, fennel seeds, and 1½ teaspoons salt. Cover and cook over low heat, stirring often to prevent sticking, for 35 minutes, until the cabbage is very soft. Add the vinegar and cook over high heat 1 minute; season with salt and pepper. SERVES 6

CARAMELIZED CABBAGE & NOODLES

This was my comfort food growing up with my gorgeous Hungarian mother. It was also my first three-ingredient recipe. A lovely first course for a winter meal; a great main course for a wistful day; a fabulous sidekick to a succulent pot roast or roast chicken.

1 large head green cabbage
½ cup (1 stick) unsalted butter
12 ounces home-style wide egg noodles

Core the cabbage, then halve and slice very thin. Place in a colander; sprinkle generously with coarse salt. Place a plate on the cabbage and top with a weight; let sit 1 hour. Rinse under water; squeeze very dry with your hands.

Melt the butter in a very large skillet. Add the cabbage and cook over medium-low heat, stirring often, until dark brown and very soft, 1 hour. Bring a large pot of salted water to a boil. Add the noodles and cook 10 minutes, until tender. Drain and shake dry. Add the noodles to the cabbage; stir and add salt and lots of black pepper. SERVES 4

CRISPY SHREDDED POTATO CAKES ➤

This recipe makes two large potato cakes that are cut into small wedges for serving. Our family makes this on Hanukkah instead of the more expected individual latkos. Parboiling the potatoes helps them stick together and results in a creamy interior. Nice with any applesauce or crème fraiche and caviar!

2 pounds large boiling potatoes
3 tablespoons coarsely grated onion
4 tablespoons olive oil

Boil the potatoes in a large pot of salted water 20 minutes, until just tender. Rinse under cold water; peel. Let cool. Preheat the oven to 300°F. Into a bowl, shred the potatoes lengthwise on the large holes of a box grater. Add the onion, 1 teaspoon salt, and pepper.

Heat 1 tablespoon of the oil in a 10-inch skillet over high heat. Add half the potatoes; spread to form an even layer. Reduce the heat and cook until the bottom is golden, 12 minutes. Invert a large plate over the skillet and invert the potato cake onto the plate. Add another 1 tablespoon oil to the pan; slide the cake back in. Cook until crispy, 10 minutes. Keep warm in the oven. Repeat with the remaining potatoes and oil. Cut into wedges. SERVES 6

BAY-SMOKED POTATOES

This technique will bathe your house in Mediterranean warmth and make the potatoes taste very good, too.

1½ pounds very small white new potatoes
3 tablespoons extra-virgin olive oil
12 dried California bay leaves

Preheat the oven to 400°F. Wash and scrub the potatoes; dry well. Do not peel. Toss with the oil and 2 teaspoons kosher salt. Distribute the bay leaves in a heavy ovenproof covered sauté pan. Arrange the potatoes on top of the bay leaves in a single layer. Cover tightly with foil or a cover. Bake for 55 minutes to 1 hour, until the potatoes are soft and wrinkled. Transfer the potatoes and bay leaves to a platter. SERVES 4

röesti

latke

CREAMY POTATO GRATIN

A gratin refers to the golden, epicurean crust that forms on the surface of savory baked dishes. Here, pungent Gruyère cheese acts as a protective layer, preventing potatoes from drying out. The classic recipe is made with heavy cream. Mine is a bit lighter.

2$\frac{1}{2}$ pounds Yukon gold or all-purpose potatoes
3 cups half-and-half
4 ounces Gruyère cheese, in one piece
2 teaspoons fresh thyme leaves

Preheat the oven to 350°F. Peel the potatoes and slice paper-thin. Put the potatoes in a 4-quart pot with the half-and-half, 2 teaspoons salt, and pepper. Stir well and bring to a boil. Reduce the heat and simmer until the potatoes begin to soften, 15 minutes. Meanwhile, shred the cheese on the large holes of a box grater.

Transfer the potatoes and cream to a shallow ovenproof baking dish (the cream will not cover the potatoes). Press down with a spatula; sprinkle with 1 teaspoon of the thyme and cover with the cheese. Bake 40 minutes, until golden brown. Sprinkle with the remaining 1 teaspoon thyme. SERVES 8

OLIVE OIL–MASHED POTATOES

When boiling potatoes, I leave them whole so that they don't get waterlogged and fall apart. Use your best-tasting extra-virgin olive oil.

2 pounds Yukon gold potatoes, peeled
12 large garlic cloves, peeled
6 tablespoons extra-virgin olive oil
2 teaspoons fresh thyme leaves

Bring a large pot of salted water to a boil. Add the potatoes and 10 garlic cloves. Cook until the potatoes are tender, 40 minutes. Meanwhile, thinly slice the remaining 2 garlic cloves. Heat 2 tablespoons of the oil in a small skillet. Add the sliced garlic and cook over medium heat until soft but not brown, 5 minutes.

Drain the potatoes, reserving 1 cup cooking liquid. Cut the potatoes into chunks. Mash the potatoes and garlic with a potato masher. Add the sautéed garlic with its oil; pour in the remaining 4 tablespoons oil. Add enough cooking liquid to make a smooth puree. Add salt and pepper; sprinkle with thyme. SERVES 6

WASABI-MASHED POTATOES

I prefer baking potatoes for their crumbly texture when I want to mash them with butter.

> 2 pounds small baking potatoes
> 2 tablespoons wasabi powder
> $\frac{1}{2}$ cup (1 stick) unsalted butter
> $\frac{1}{4}$ to $\frac{1}{2}$ cup milk for thinning

Bring a large pot of water to a boil. Scrub the potatoes and place in the boiling water. Cover, reduce the heat, and cook until very tender, 40 minutes. Drain in a colander, saving $\frac{1}{4}$ cup cooking liquid. Peel the potatoes; place in a large bowl. Mash the potatoes until smooth.

Dissolve the wasabi in the reserved cooking liquid; stir until smooth. Add to the mashed potatoes. Cut the butter into small pieces and stir into the potatoes. Add milk to thin. Add salt to taste. Whip with an electric mixer until creamy. SERVES 6

RUTABAGA, CRÈME FRAÎCHE & HAVARTI TORTE ➤

I've made this oddball dish with turnips for years, modifying it slightly as I go along. Now I make it with rutabagas, which are much larger and require less handling. It is a refined accompaniment that looks surprisingly like a cake. It is even better reheated the next day.

> 2 very large rutabagas
> 2 tablespoons unsalted butter, room temperature
> $\frac{1}{2}$ cup crème fraîche
> 16 ounces sliced Havarti cheese with caraway

Trim the rutabagas and peel. Place in a large pot of salted boiling water. Boil 60 minutes, until just tender. Drain. When cool enough to handle, slice $\frac{1}{4}$ inch thick. Pat dry with paper towels.

Preheat the oven to 400°F. Grease a 9-inch springform pan with the butter. Arrange a layer of overlapping rutabaga slices to cover the bottom of the pan. Top with one-third of the crème fraîche. Sprinkle with salt and pepper and add a layer of cheese. Make 2 more layers, ending with a layer of crème fraîche spread evenly on top, and then cheese. Place the pan on a rimmed baking sheet. Bake 45 minutes, until the cheese is golden brown. Let rest 10 minutes before releasing the side of the pan and cutting into wedges. SERVES 10 TO 12

ROASTED SWEET POTATOES WITH WHIPPED BUTTER & MAPLE "HONEY"

Maple "honey" is nothing more than reduced maple syrup perfumed with cinnamon and lemon. It can be made in advance and reheated when the potatoes are freshly roasted.

8 medium sweet potatoes
1½ cups pure maple syrup
1 large cinnamon stick
Grated zest and juice of 1 lemon
½ cup whipped sweet butter
¼ cup minced fresh chives

Preheat the oven to 400°F. Scrub the potatoes; do not peel. Pierce several times with the tines of a fork. Place directly on oven racks and bake 50 to 60 minutes, until soft.

Put the syrup and cinnamon stick in a large saucepan. Bring to a boil and reduce the heat. Simmer until reduced to 1 cup, about 25 minutes. Carefully stir in the lemon zest and 1 tablespoon juice; the syrup will be very hot and bubble up. Remove from the heat.

Cut the potatoes in half lengthwise and place on a platter. Gently reheat the maple "honey." Dollop the potatoes with butter and drizzle with the hot syrup. Sprinkle with salt and chives. SERVES 8

SWEET POTATO PUREE WITH FRESH GINGER & ORANGE

Simplicity itself. It's fat-free but tastes very rich all the same. For a bit more intrigue, add a bit of ground cumin, ground coriander, or ground cardamom—or all three.

4 large sweet potatoes, about 3 pounds
2 juice oranges
3-inch piece peeled fresh ginger

Scrub the potatoes but do not peel. Place in a large pot with cold water to cover. Bring to a rapid boil, then reduce the heat to medium. Cook 50 minutes, until very soft. Meanwhile, grate the zest of the oranges to get 1 teaspoon. Squeeze the oranges to get ⅔ cup juice.

Drain the sweet potatoes and peel when cool enough to handle. Cut into large chunks and place in a food processor. Mince the ginger to get $1/4$ cup. Add to the processor with the orange zest and juice. Puree until very smooth. Transfer to a saucepan and reheat, stirring. Season with salt and pepper. SERVES 6

White Beans with Spinach, Tomatoes & Rosemary

A streamlined bean dish that is perfect for lamb and roast chicken.

10-ounce bag fresh spinach leaves
3 tablespoons extra-virgin olive oil
6 shallots, minced
24 grape tomatoes
2 teaspoons minced fresh rosemary
1 cup chicken broth
3 (15-ounce) cans cannellini beans, rinsed and drained

Heat a large deep nonstick skillet over high heat. Add the spinach to the dry skillet and cook until just wilted, 3 minutes. Transfer to a strainer set over a bowl.

Heat 2 tablespoons of the oil in the same skillet. Add the shallots and cook 3 minutes over high heat. Add the tomatoes and rosemary; cook 2 minutes. Add the broth, cover, and cook 5 minutes, until the tomatoes soften. Crush the tomatoes with a potato masher. Stir in the beans and the remaining 1 tablespoon oil. Bring to a boil; then simmer, uncovered, 5 minutes, until the juices thicken. Add the spinach for the last minute of cooking. Season with salt and pepper. SERVES 6

TIAN OF EGGPLANT, TOMATO & HERBS

This gorgeous layered vegetable gratin requires 3 hours in a slow oven for its alchemy to work. A tian *is an earthenware baking dish, but you can use a small paella pan or any casserole with a 10-cup capacity. The delicious liquid that accumulates in the dish can be used to make a vinaigrette. Serve the* tian *hot or at room temperature.*

1 large eggplant, about 1½ pounds, peeled
4 medium onions, about 1¼ pounds
5 large ripe tomatoes, about 2 pounds
2 tablespoons fresh thyme leaves
2½ teaspoons dried oregano
10 tablespoons freshly grated Pecorino Romano
1 cup olive oil

Preheat the oven to 300°F. Slice eggplant into thin rounds. Toss with 1 tablespoon salt. Thinly slice the onions, keeping the slices intact. Thinly slice the tomatoes.

Arrange half the eggplant in the bottom of a *tian* or paella pan. Top with an overlapping layer of half the tomatoes, and then half the onions. Sprinkle with 1 tablespoon thyme, 1 teaspoon oregano, and ¼ cup of the cheese. Add another layer of eggplant and tomatoes. Sprinkle with the remaining thyme, 1 teaspoon oregano, and ¼ cup cheese. Top with the remaining onions and sprinkle with the remaining 2 tablespoons cheese and ½ teaspoon oregano.

Pour the oil evenly over the vegetables. Press down firmly with a spatula. Bake 2½ hours. Pour off half the liquid. Bake 30 minutes longer, until the *tian* is very soft and the onions have blackened. SERVES 8 TO 10

"CREOLA" RICE

Colorful as crayons but with Creole flavors: Creola! This becomes a main course with the addition of cooked shrimp and chorizo. Prep all the ingredients before you throw it together.

2 tablespoons olive oil, plus more for drizzling
1 cup finely chopped onions
²/₃ cup finely diced green bell pepper
1 cup basmati rice
2 cups canned crushed tomatoes in thick puree
1 large garlic clove, finely minced
2 teaspoons rice wine vinegar
1 tablespoon fresh thyme leaves, chopped
¹/₄ teaspoon ground chipotle chili powder
¹/₂ cup freshly grated Parmigiano-Reggiano

Heat the oil in a 3-quart saucepan. Add the onions, bell pepper, and a large pinch of salt. Cook over high heat, stirring, for 5 minutes. Add the rice and cook, stirring, until golden, 5 minutes. Add the tomatoes, garlic, vinegar, half the thyme, the chili powder, 1¹/₂ cups water, and salt to taste. Bring to a boil, then cover. Reduce the heat and simmer, stirring occasionally, until the liquid is absorbed and the rice is tender, 20 minutes. Remove from the heat and set aside to let steam, covered, for 10 minutes With a fork, mix in the remaining thyme. Stir in the cheese and drizzle with oil, if desired. SERVES 6

DESSERTS

The truth is you don't need your grandmother's instincts, or a pastry chef's skills, to make desserts or bake a cake. You also don't need a recipe to serve a perfectly ripe pear or to present a pint of Häagen-Dazs in wedges rather than scoops. For drop-in guests, there's always chilled Sauternes and Fig Newtons.

At home my family and I prefer to end a meal with fruit and cheese, or dispense with dessert altogether, opting instead for a rich cup of coffee and a few plump prunes! But it's lovely to have some newfangled ways to satisfy your family's sweet tooth. For example, we occasionally dig into an intensely flavored wobbly flan with the unexpected tang of pineapple juice, or I'll prepare an indulgent chocolate mousse formulated so that it can be made one hour before dinner.

This chapter contains fruit desserts and sundaes that can be put together in 10 minutes and cheese offerings that can be used as a "pre-dessert"—a bridge from savory to sweet. My favorite? The improbable combination of semisweet chocolate and Parmigiano-Reggiano cheese accompanied by sweet red grapes.

There are simple cakes made with olive oil, a cookie the size of a kitchen towel, tarts and tartlets, a streamlined recipe for beloved cheesecake, and a four-ingredient chocolate cake I call the "little black dress" because it can be baked in 18 minutes and accessorized as your mood dictates—with crème fraîche and candied violets or raspberries and powdered sugar.

But the most radical idea of all, inspired by a meal in a trendy Barcelona restaurant, is a wineglass full of just-pressed orange juice, simply served with a spoon.

10-minute desserts

Peaches in Peach Schnapps with Basil **290**

Blueberries with Hibiscus Spice, Sugar Syrup **290**

Orange Flower Strawberries & Mint Sugar **290**

Watermelon "Carpaccio" with White Chocolate **292**

Pineapple Shingles with Caramel & Pistachio Dust **292**

Fresh Ricotta with Lemon Curd & Blackberries **293**

"Ceviche" of Spring Fruit with Sesame Seeds **294**

Tahina & Date Syrup Swirl, Fresh Apple Slices **294**

Watermelon, Raspberry & Pomegranate Salad **295**

Chocolate-Coconut Fondue, Fresh Fruit **295**

Fresh Figs & Shaved Halvah, Warm Honey Syrup **297**

Little Chocolate-Tahina Cups **297**

Chocolate, Parmigiano-Reggiano & Red Grapes **298**

More Fruit & Cheese Pairings **299**

tarts & cakes

Pear, Cherry & Pine Nut Tartlets **308**

All-Chocolate Velvet Tart **309**

E.A.T. (Easy Apple Tart) **310**

Almond Galettes with a Glass of Sherry **310**

Dutch Butter Ginger Cake **311**

French Yogurt Cake with Nutella **312**

Maple-Walnut Espresso Torte, Espresso-Lemon Syrup **314**

Coconut "Macaroon" Cake **315**

The "Little Black Dress" Chocolate Cake **317**

A Radically Simple Cheesecake **318**

cooked fruit desserts

Apples to the 3rd Power **300**

Rhubarb & Candied Ginger Compote with Coconut Sorbet **302**

Absurdly Easy Coconut Sorbet **302**

Poached Pears with Marsala, Cinnamon & Vanilla **303**

Prunes & White Chocolate, Port Wine Reduction **303**

custards

Pineapple Flan **305**

Chocolate "Pousse" **305**

Coconut-Espresso Crème Caramel **306**

White Chocolate Mousse with Apricot Compote **307**

cookies & more

Hungarian Walnut Cookies **319**

A Giant Sugar Cookie **319**

Sesame Seed–Olive Oil Cookies **320**

Vietnamese Coffee **321**

Nutella Sandwich Cookies **323**

Cinnamon-Sugar Crisps **323**

sorbets & ice creams

Honeydew-Kiwi Sorbet with Chartreuse **324**

Chocolate-Chipotle Sorbet **327**

Double Raspberry Sorbet **327**

Leftover-Cranberry-Sauce Sorbet **328**

Grapefruit-Framboise Granita **328**

Lemon-Buttermilk Ice Cream **329**

Maple Ice Cream **329**

Peaches in Peach Schnapps with Basil

4 very ripe large peaches
$\frac{1}{2}$ cup peach schnapps, chilled
2 tablespoons wildflower honey
$\frac{1}{4}$ cup julienned fresh basil

Wash and dry the peaches. Cut into thin wedges and place in a bowl. Stir together the schnapps, honey, half the basil, and $\frac{1}{4}$ cup ice water. Pour over the peaches and stir. Transfer to 4 wineglasses. Scatter with the remaining basil. SERVES 4

Blueberries with Hibiscus Spice, Sugar Syrup

4 cups big plump juicy blueberries
Loose tea from 2 Red Zinger tea bags
2 tablespoons plus $\frac{1}{2}$ cup sugar
2 to 3 teaspoons brandy, optional

Put 1 cup of the berries in each of 4 tumblers or wineglasses. Mix 1 tablespoon Red Zinger tea with 2 tablespoons sugar. Set aside. Put $\frac{1}{2}$ cup sugar and 1 cup water in a saucepan. Bring to a boil and boil, stirring, until the sugar dissolves, 2 minutes. Add the brandy if using. Transfer to a small pitcher. Sprinkle the tea/sugar mixture over the blueberries. Pass the pitcher of hot sugar syrup at the table. SERVES 4

Orange Flower Strawberries & Mint Sugar

2 pints very ripe strawberries, hulled and halved
$\frac{1}{2}$ teaspoon orange flower water
6 tablespoons granulated sugar
$\frac{1}{4}$ cup coarsely chopped fresh well-dried mint leaves
$\frac{1}{2}$ cup crème fraîche
2 tablespoons confectioners' sugar

Toss the berries with the orange flower water and 1 tablespoon of the granulated sugar. Put the remaining 5 tablespoons granulated sugar and mint in a food processor and process until incorporated. Divide the berries among 4 glasses and sprinkle with the mint sugar. Combine the crème fraîche with the confectioners' sugar and dollop on top. SERVES 4

WATERMELON "CARPACCIO" WITH WHITE CHOCOLATE

This dessert whimsically mimics the famous carpaccio made with raw beef and Parmesan cheese. Watermelon, its color deepened by a splash of Chambord (or cassis), stands in for the beef, while shards of white chocolate look a lot like wafers of cheese.

> 1 large wedge ripe red watermelon, about 1 pound
> ¼ cup Chambord or crème de cassis
> 3-ounce chunk white chocolate, room temperature
> Grated zest of 1 lime

Remove the seeds and rind from the watermelon. Cut the flesh into very thin slices. Arrange, slightly overlapping, so that they lie as flat as possible to cover the interior of 4 large plates. Trim the perimeters to make neat circles. Drizzle each plate with 1 tablespoon crème de cassis. Use a vegetable peeler to shave chocolate over the watermelon. Sprinkle with lime zest. SERVES 4

PINEAPPLE SHINGLES WITH CARAMEL & PISTACHIO DUST

This is a great last-minute offering. It's lots of fun to eat because the sugar hardens into spider candy. Pistachios can be ground in a spice grinder or food processor.

> 1 very ripe medium pineapple
> ¼ cup shelled pistachios, finely ground
> ⅓ cup sugar
> Few sprigs fresh lemon balm, lemon verbena, or pineapple mint

Use a sharp knife to remove the rind from the pineapple. Quarter lengthwise and remove the core. Cut the wedges lengthwise into very thin slices to create "shingles." Arrange the slices, tightly overlapping, in the centers of 4 large plates.

Put the sugar in a small skillet and cook over high heat, stirring with a wooden spoon, until it becomes a dark liquid caramel. Drizzle the syrup over the pineapple; scatter the nuts around the perimeters. Garnish with herbs. Serve immediately. SERVES 4

FRESH RICOTTA WITH LEMON CURD & BLACKBERRIES

My sister-in-law, Gail, came up with this radically simple idea. She serves it with Japanese Pocky sticks (really cool cookies you can get in many supermarkets and Korean greengrocers). You can use raspberries or kiwi instead of the blackberries, or serve without any fruit at all.

1⅓ cups fresh ricotta cheese
½ cup best-quality lemon curd
1 pint fresh blackberries
Confectioners' sugar

Divide the ricotta among 4 dessert dishes. Top with the lemon curd. Toss the berries with sugar to taste and scatter over the lemon curd. SERVES 4

"Ceviche" of Spring Fruit with Sesame Seeds

Begin with chilled ingredients. Cut the fruit into small pieces, about the size of bay scallops, to enhance the ceviche illusion. Red bell pepper is unexpected, but adds great color and flavor.

2 cups diced fresh pineapple
1 heaping cup diced honeydew melon
1 heaping cup diced mango
2 tablespoons slivered fresh basil
1 tablespoon slivered cilantro or fresh mint
2 tablespoons freshly squeezed lime juice
2 tablespoons honey
2 tablespoons finely minced candied ginger
2 tablespoons finely minced red bell pepper
1 tablespoon toasted sesame seeds

Combine the pineapple, melon, and mango in a large bowl. Add the basil, cilantro, lime juice, and honey. Stir well. Stir in the candied ginger and bell pepper. Let sit 5 minutes. Spoon into chilled martini glasses. Sprinkle with sesame seeds. SERVES 4

Tahina & Date Syrup Swirl, Fresh Apple Slices

Decades ago, there was a small restaurant in Tel Aviv called Eucalyptus. It had a tree growing up out the center of the floor to the sky. Magical. As is this simple dessert. Silan, or date syrup, is available in Middle Eastern food stores. (Twenty years later, I returned to the restaurant, in a new location, and ate the same dessert.)

¾ cup tahina
⅓ cup date syrup
Variety of apples

Stir the tahina well. Make a puddle of tahina in the center of each of 4 dessert plates. Drizzle the date syrup, in concentric circles on top; drag a butter knife through it to make a pretty, swirled design. Cut the apples into thin wedges. Serve alongside for dipping. SERVES 4

WATERMELON, RASPBERRY & POMEGRANATE SALAD

Seldom combined, these three fruits make a great team with a background jolt of citrus and honey. I sometimes serve it with a splash of light rum.

2$\frac{1}{2}$-pound wedge ripe watermelon
2 pints raspberries
Grated zest and juice of 1 orange
Grated zest and juice of 1 lemon
$\frac{1}{4}$ cup honey
3 tablespoons light rum, optional
$\frac{1}{3}$ cup fresh pomegranate seeds

Remove the rind and seeds from the watermelon. Cut into 1-inch pieces. Place in a large bowl and add the raspberries, orange zest, and lemon zest. Toss gently.

In a small bowl, combine $\frac{1}{4}$ cup orange juice, 2 tablespoons lemon juice, and honey. Stir until the honey dissolves. Pour over the fruit and stir. Add the pomegranate seeds and rum, if using. SERVES 6

CHOCOLATE-COCONUT FONDUE, FRESH FRUIT

Great for dipping chunks of ripe, fresh fruit, but excellent also with ladyfingers and biscotti. Even sesame breadsticks taste good!

15-ounce can cream of coconut (such as Coco Lopez)
12 ounces bittersweet chocolate, chopped
$\frac{1}{4}$ cup heavy cream
$\frac{1}{4}$ teaspoon coconut extract
Assortment of fresh fruit: strawberries, bananas, cherries, pineapple
Savoiardi cookies (ladyfingers) or small biscotti

Combine the cream of coconut and chocolate in a large heavy saucepan. Stir over very low heat until the chocolate melts and the mixture is smooth. Stir in the heavy cream and coconut extract. Transfer to a fondue pot. Serve hot with the fruit and/or cookies for dipping. SERVES 6

luscious figs

◄ Fresh Figs & Shaved Halvah, Warm Honey Syrup

Here's an unorthodox but compelling combo of fleshy fresh figs and thin slices of earthy halvah, a dense confection that resembles shards of cheese. This dish offers a good opportunity to try an interesting variety of honey such as wild thyme or linden.

½ cup fragrant honey
12 ripe large fresh black or green figs, or a combination
6-ounce chunk pistachio halvah
Handful fresh red currants, if available

Combine the honey and 2 tablespoons water in a small saucepan; boil for 1 minute, stirring constantly. Remove from the heat and keep warm. Wash the figs; cut in half lengthwise. Arrange, cut side up, on 4 large plates. Cut the halvah into paper-thin slices. Drizzle the honey on the figs; scatter the halvah on and around the figs. Garnish with currants. SERVES 4

Little Chocolate-Tahina Cups

This tastes like a Chunky Bar and looks very elegant with its decorative swirl of tahina. You will need 18 1-inch candy papers; I use gold foil cups lined with paper.

½ cup dried currants
8 ounces semisweet chocolate, chopped
4 teaspoons tahina

Soak the currants in 1 cup hot water for 5 minutes. Drain; pat dry with paper towels. Melt chocolate with 3 tablespoons tahina in a metal bowl set over a saucepan of simmering water, stirring until smooth. Stir in currants. Spray paper liners lightly with cooking spray. Spoon chocolate mixture into cups; let cool 5 minutes.

Decorate candies by dipping tip of a skewer or toothpick into remaining tablespoon tahina and swirling over tops. Chill until set. MAKES 18

CHOCOLATE, PARMIGIANO-REGGIANO & RED GRAPES

I use this tasting plate as a "pre-dessert." It stimulates conversation as well as your brain. Use 62 percent semisweet chocolate. Tasted with the grapes, the chocolate takes on cherry overtones; with the cheese, it finds a soul mate, and the cheese brings out wine-y notes in the chocolate. I use Scharffen Berger chocolate.

> 4-ounce piece Parmigiano-Reggiano
> 4-ounce bar 62 percent top-quality semisweet chocolate
> 4 small clumps red seedless grapes

Arrange 1 ounce of cheese and chocolate on each of 4 plates; add grapes. SERVES 4

MORE FRUIT & CHEESE PAIRINGS

A thoughtful pairing of fruit and cheese can be a fabulous alternative to dessert that gives everyone an opportunity to finish their wine.

> Halved plump Medjool dates with small chunks of well-aged Gouda

> ½ of a very ripe cantaloupe, peeled and cut in very thin wedges, drizzled with wild thyme honey, sprinkled with pepper, and topped with slivers of Spanish Manchego cheese

> 2 very ripe large Bosc pears, cored and sliced crosswise, tossed with 1½ tablespoons melon liqueur (such as Midori) and served with shards of Parmigiano-Reggiano cheese

> Tart apples with Pont-l'Évêque and apple cider syrup

> Forelle pears with Taleggio and chestnut honey

> Fuji apples with sharp farmhouse Cheddar and toasted pecans

> Fresh cherries with young goat cheese and roasted hazelnuts

> Ribbons of melon with Manchego and roasted almonds

> Thinly sliced watermelon with sheep's milk feta and a drizzle of wildflower honey

> Comice pears with runny Brie and pink peppercorns

> Very sweet apricots with Cabrales and warm Brazil nuts

> Fresh red currants and very ripe pears with Pecorino Romano

> Grilled fresh figs with gorgonzola dolce and toasted pine nuts

> Roasted grapes with Cabrales and port wine reduction

> Muscat grapes and dried figs with Saint André cheese

APPLES TO THE 3RD POWER

I pronounce these baked apples "to the 3rd power" because fresh apples, apple butter, and apple cider are used. The best varieties here are Cameo or Winesap apples. Serve slightly warm with lightly sweetened crème fraiche or heavy cream.

4 large apples, 9 to 10 ounces each
3 tablespoons sugar
$1\frac{1}{2}$ teaspoons ground cardamom
$\frac{1}{2}$ cup apple butter
$1\frac{1}{2}$ tablespoons unsalted butter
1 cup apple cider

Preheat the oven to 425°F. Core the apples; remove a very thin slice from each top. Stir together the sugar and cardamom and put 1 teaspoon in the cavity of each apple. Fill to the top with apple butter. Top each apple with a slice of butter and the remaining cardamom sugar.

Arrange the apples in a pie tin and pour the cider around them. Bake 50 minutes, until soft. Use a slotted spoon to transfer the apples to 4 serving plates. Transfer the pan juices to a saucepan and boil until reduced slightly, 2 minutes. Pour around the apples. SERVES 4

$$apple^3 =$$

apples, apple butter,

apple cider

RHUBARB & CANDIED GINGER COMPOTE WITH COCONUT SORBET

This is a delicious combination of textures and intensities when paired with the Coconut Sorbet below or store-bought vanilla ice cream.

2 pounds fresh rhubarb
1/2 cup seedless currant jelly
1/2 cup sugar
1/4 cup minced crystallized ginger
Grated zest and juice of 1 lemon

Cut the rhubarb into 1-inch pieces. Combine the rhubarb, currant jelly, sugar, ginger, lemon zest, and 2 tablespoons lemon juice in a large heavy saucepan. Bring to a boil. Reduce the heat, cover, and simmer 10 minutes, until slightly thickened. Serve warm or chilled, topped with the sorbet. SERVES 6

ABSURDLY EASY COCONUT SORBET

15-ounce can sweetened cream of coconut (such as Coco Lopez)
1 1/2 cups whole milk
1/2 teaspoon rum extract, optional

Combine the cream of coconut, milk, and a pinch of salt in a food processor. Process until very smooth. Add extract. Cover and refrigerate until cold. Freeze in an ice cream maker according to the manufacturer's instructions. SERVES 8

POACHED PEARS WITH MARSALA, CINNAMON & VANILLA

The smell of these simmering ingredients will fill your kitchen with sweet anticipation. Use ripe Bartlett or Anjou pears and serve warm or very cold, with cookies.

6 large firm pears with long stems
2¹/₂ cups dry Marsala
³/₄ cup sugar
2 cinnamon sticks
2 vanilla beans, split lengthwise
2 long strips orange zest
¹/₂ cup mascarpone

Peel the pears, leaving the stems intact. Place in a 4-quart pot. Add 2 cups of the Marsala, sugar, cinnamon sticks, vanilla beans, and orange zest. Add 2 to 3 cups water to just cover the pears. Bring to a boil, reduce the heat, and cover. Simmer 1 hour, turning the pears several times, until tender. Cool in the cooking liquid then remove with a slotted spoon.

Bring the liquid to boil. Cook until reduced to 2 cups, about 10 minutes. Pour the syrup over the pears. Splash with the remaining ¹/₂ cup Marsala and dollop with mascarpone. SERVES 6

PRUNES & WHITE CHOCOLATE, PORT WINE REDUCTION

The best way that I know of to eat prunes.

24 large prunes with pits, about 1 pound
1¹/₂ cups tawny port
4 allspice berries
2 star anise
3-ounce chunk white chocolate, room temperature

Put the prunes, port, allspice, and star anise in a medium saucepan. Add water just to cover. Bring to a boil, reduce the heat, and simmer 15 minutes, until the prunes are soft but still retain their shape. Cool in the liquid, then refrigerate overnight.

Transfer the prunes and some of their liquid to 4 shallow bowls or wineglasses. Top with curls of white chocolate, shaved with a vegetable peeler. SERVES 4

*eggs, sugar,
pineapple juice*

◄ PINEAPPLE FLAN

Here, just three ingredients—eggs, sugar, and pineapple juice—form a luscious, creamy (but creamless) custard of tropical intensity.

1 cup sugar
4 extra-large eggs plus 4 extra-large yolks
2 cups unsweetened pineapple juice
Fresh mint sprigs or edible flowers for garnish

Preheat the oven to 375°F. Melt ½ cup of the sugar in a small nonstick skillet over medium-high heat, stirring constantly with a wooden spoon, 3 minutes, until a clear dark caramel forms. Carefully divide among 5 (5-ounce) custard cups. Place the cups in a deep baking dish.

Using an electric mixer, beat the whole eggs and yolks. Add the remaining ½ cup sugar and beat 1 minute; beat in the pineapple juice. Divide among the custard cups. Add 2 inches boiling water to the baking dish. Bake 40 to 45 minutes, until firm. Remove the cups from the pan and let cool. Cover and refrigerate until very cold. Unmold onto plates. Garnish with mint. SERVES 5

CHOCOLATE "POUSSE"

Somewhere between pudding and mousse, this can be made as little as an hour before serving.

6 ounces top-quality semisweet chocolate chips
3 tablespoons unsalted butter
2 tablespoons sour cream or crème fraîche
2 teaspoons dark rum
5 extra-large egg whites

Combine the chocolate and butter in a small heavy saucepan. Melt over very low heat, stirring constantly, until smooth. Cool slightly; then stir in the sour cream and rum. With an electric mixer, beat the egg whites with a pinch of salt until stiff, with the consistency of shaving cream, 4 minutes. Fold the chocolate mixture into the beaten whites. Mix until smooth and creamy. The mixture will deflate dramatically. Spoon into 4 wineglasses. Cover and refrigerate until ready to serve. SERVES 4

Coconut-Espresso Crème Caramel

In this special flan, I scald whole milk and coconut milk together before adding to beaten eggs to give the dessert a velvety texture. Infusing lemon peel in the warm coffee mixture adds a subtle and evocative flavor. These can be made up to 3 days in advance.

$^3/_4$ cup sugar
14-ounce can unsweetened coconut milk
1 cup milk
1 long strip lemon zest
2 teaspoons instant espresso powder
3 extra-large eggs plus 2 extra-large yolks
$^1/_4$ teaspoon coconut extract

Preheat the oven to 350°F. Melt $^1/_2$ cup of the sugar in a small skillet over medium-high heat, stirring constantly with a wooden spoon, 3 minutes, until a clear dark caramel forms. Carefully divide among six (5-ounce) custard cups. Place the cups in a deep baking dish.

Put the remaining $^1/_4$ cup sugar, the coconut milk, milk, zest, and espresso in a large saucepan. Boil, whisking constantly, 1 minute. Cool slightly and discard the zest.

Using an electric mixer, beat the whole eggs and yolks. Beat in the warm milk mixture and extract. Divide among the custard cups. Add 2 inches boiling water to the baking dish. Bake 40 minutes, until firm. Remove the cups from the pan and let cool. Cover and refrigerate until very cold. Unmold onto plates. MAKES 6

WHITE CHOCOLATE MOUSSE WITH APRICOT COMPOTE

It's unexpected to pair slightly acidic stone fruit with white chocolate, but it works! In fact, it's sublime. Peaches, plums, or nectarines may be substituted.

4 ounces white chocolate, finely chopped
1¼ cups heavy cream
1½ pounds fresh apricots, pitted and quartered
½ cup wildflower honey
⅓ cup crushed Jordan almonds or pistachios

Put the white chocolate in a medium bowl. Bring 1 cup of the cream to a boil in a small saucepan; immediately pour over the chocolate. Let sit 1 minute; whisk until smooth. Cool. Cover with plastic wrap and refrigerate 8 hours.

Put the apricots and honey in a large saucepan. Bring to a boil, lower heat, and cook, stirring, 5 minutes, until soft. Cool. Cover and refrigerate until cold.

Pour the chilled white chocolate mixture into a large bowl. Add the remaining ¼ cup cream. With an electric mixer, beat 3 minutes on high until soft peaks form. Cover and refrigerate until firm.

Spoon the apricots into 6 wineglasses. Top with the mousse and sprinkle with crushed nuts. SERVES 6

PEAR, CHERRY & PINE NUT TARTLETS

Great for a tea party; they can be made up to 8 hours ahead. Thaw the pastry in the refrigerator to keep it cold.

$^1/_2$ cup apricot jam
$^1/_2$ teaspoon almond extract
1 large ripe Bartlett pear
$^3/_4$ cup dried cherries, about 4 ounces
1 sheet frozen puff pastry, thawed
1 egg yolk, beaten
2 tablespoons pine nuts, toasted

Preheat the oven to 400°F. Line a baking sheet with parchment. In a small saucepan, stir together the jam and extract. Transfer 3 tablespoons to a medium bowl. Peel and core the pear; cut into $^1/_4$-inch cubes. Chop the cherries. Add both to the bowl; toss to coat.

Using a 3-inch cookie cutter, cut 9 rounds from the cold pastry; discard the trimmings. Arrange on the baking sheet. Prick the center of each pastry with a fork, leaving a $^1/_4$-inch border. Brush the edges with egg yolk. Mound the fruit mixture onto the centers, pressing to compact. Bake 25 minutes, until golden.

Bring the remaining jam mixture just to a boil, stirring. Brush the pastries with the melted jam; sprinkle with pine nuts. Let cool. MAKES 9

ALL-CHOCOLATE VELVET TART

This extremely elegant dessert can be assembled in less than 20 minutes. Let it sit in the fridge until just firm, and serve with crème fraîche.

> 5 ounces chocolate graham crackers
> 5 tablespoons unsalted butter, room temperature
> 1 cup heavy cream
> 12 ounces semisweet chocolate, chopped
> 2 tablespoons unsweetened cocoa powder
> 1 tablespoon crème de cassis or 1 teaspoon grated orange zest
> 1 cup crème fraîche

Preheat the oven to 350°F. Lightly butter a 9-inch fluted removable-bottom tart pan. Combine the graham crackers and 4 tablespoons of the butter in a food processor. Pulverize until finely ground. Pack the crumbs into the pan to form an even bottom crust. Bake 10 minutes.

Bring the cream just to a boil in a large saucepan. Reduce the heat and simmer 5 minutes. Add the chocolate and stir constantly over low heat until melted. Stir in the cocoa, cassis, and the remaining 1 tablespoon butter. Pour into the crumb crust; refrigerate 45 minutes or until just firm. Serve with crème fraîche. SERVES 10 TO 12

E.A.T. (Easy Apple Tart)

This is such a snap to make that you'll want to do it again and again.

1 sheet frozen puff pastry, thawed
3 large Golden Delicious apples, peeled
2 tablespoons unsalted butter, melted
3 tablespoons sugar mixed with $^1/_2$ teaspoon cinnamon
$^1/_3$ cup apple jelly

Preheat the oven to 400°F. Place the pastry on a baking sheet. With a fork, prick lines $^1/_4$ inch in from the edges, creating a bare border. Prick the pastry all over within the border.

Halve the apples lengthwise. Place cut side down on a cutting board; slice thinly lengthwise, about $^1/_8$ inch thick. Arrange the apples on the pastry within the border in three long, tightly overlapping rows. Brush the apples with the melted butter; sprinkle with the cinnamon sugar. Bake 30 minutes. Meanwhile, combine the jelly and 2 tablespoons water in a saucepan. Boil 30 seconds, stirring. Using a pastry brush, glaze the apples with the melted jelly. Bake 10 minutes longer, until golden. Glaze again and sprinkle with more cinnamon sugar. Cool. SERVES 6

Almond Galettes with a Glass of Sherry

This is a "no-bowl" cake: It's made in the food processor. It's elegant and simple as can be with a glass of olorosa sherry, which is rich, dark, and fragrant, or served with strawberries and sweetened whipped cream.

6 ounces sliced almonds with skins, about 2 cups
3 extra-large eggs
$^3/_4$ cup plus 6 tablespoons confectioners' sugar
Grated zest of 1 lemon or orange, plus 1 tablespoon juice
Bottle of oloroso sherry, chilled

Preheat the oven to 325°F. Spread the almonds on a baking sheet. Bake 6 minutes, or until golden brown. Cool completely; set aside 3 tablespoons for garnish. Place the remainder in a food processor and process until finely ground. Add the eggs, $^3/_4$ cup confectioners' sugar, citrus zest, and a pinch of salt. Process until thick and smooth.

Coat four 4¹⁄₂-inch removable-bottom tart pans with cooking spray. Pour the batter into the pans. Place the pans on a baking sheet. Bake 18 minutes, until just set. In a small bowl, stir together the remaining 6 tablespoons confectioners' sugar and 1 tablespoon juice until completely smooth. Spread on the warm cakes to form a thin layer. Scatter with the reserved almonds. Let cool. Serve with small glasses of sherry. SERVES 4

DUTCH BUTTER GINGER CAKE

This is one of my mother's recipes. Written in her delicate handwriting on a yellowing note card, it bears witness to our remarkable relationship and decades of taste memories. The cake is lovely with vanilla ice cream and a drizzle of chocolate sauce.

> 1 cup (2 sticks) unsalted butter, room temperature
> 2 cups flour
> 1 cup sugar
> 1 extra-large egg, beaten
> 6 tablespoons finely chopped candied ginger

Preheat the oven to 350°F. Use ¹⁄₂ tablespoon of the butter to grease an 8- or 9- inch pie tin. Put the flour in a bowl. Cut the remaining butter into small pieces; add to the flour. Stir in the sugar, half the beaten egg, and ¹⁄₂ teaspoon salt. Using a wooden spoon, and then your fingers, knead the mixture until smooth. Add the ginger and mix until incorporated.

Press the dough into the pie tin, making sure the top is smooth. Brush the entire top with the remaining beaten egg. Using the back of a butter knife, lightly score the top of the cake with criss-crossed lines, 1 inch apart. Bake 30 minutes, until golden. Cool on a rack. Cut into wedges. SERVES 10 TO 12

FRENCH YOGURT CAKE WITH NUTELLA

This is very moist thanks to the yogurt and butter, but it is especially delicious thanks to the Nutella! Serve with raspberries, cherries, or whipped cream or plain.

$^1/_2$ cup (1 stick) unsalted butter
1$^1/_2$ cups flour
1$^1/_2$ teaspoon baking powder
3 extra-large eggs
1 cup sugar
1 teaspoon pure vanilla extract
$^1/_2$ cup plain Greek yogurt
$^1/_4$ cup Nutella

Preheat the oven to 350°F. Lightly butter a 9-inch springform pan. Melt the butter in a saucepan; set aside to cool. Mix together the flour, baking powder, and a large pinch of salt. Using an electric mixer, beat the eggs, sugar, and vanilla until thick, 3 minutes. Add the flour mixture, yogurt, and melted butter; mix until smooth.

Pour two-thirds of the batter into the pan. Add the Nutella to the remaining batter and beat until smooth. Pour atop the plain batter. Run a rubber spatula through the batter to make a marbled pattern. Bake 40 to 45 minutes, until just firm. Cool on a rack. Release the side of pan and serve. SERVES 8

MAPLE-WALNUT ESPRESSO TORTE, ESPRESSO-LEMON SYRUP

This cake is perfect for Passover. The same ingredients that go into the cake are used to make the syrup. I like to serve the cake with diced fresh pineapple, with the syrup poured over both fruit and cake.

$^2/_3$ cup plus $^1/_4$ cup sugar
2 tablespoons plus $^1/_2$ cup real maple syrup
5 teaspoons instant espresso powder
$2^1/_4$ teaspoons ground cardamom
Grated zest and juice of 1 large lemon
8 ounces walnuts, about 2 cups
$^1/_3$ cup matzoh meal
4 extra-large eggs

Preheat the oven to 325°F. Oil an 8-inch springform pan. In a small saucepan, combine 1 cup water, $^2/_3$ cup sugar, 2 tablespoons maple syrup, 1 teaspoon of the espresso, and $^1/_4$ teaspoon of the cardamom. Add 2 tablespoons lemon juice. Bring to a boil, stirring until the sugar dissolves, then simmer 5 minutes until thickened. Cool.

Process the walnuts and matzoh meal in a food processor until finely ground. With an electric mixer, beat the eggs, the remaining $^1/_2$ cup maple syrup, the remaining $^1/_4$ cup sugar, and $^1/_4$ teaspoon salt on high 5 minutes. Add the remaining 4 teaspoons espresso, the remaining 2 teaspoons cardamom, and zest; beat 3 minutes. Stir in the walnut mixture. Pour into the pan. Bake 40 minutes, until firm. Pour $^1/_4$ cup syrup over the cake; let cool. Serve in wedges, drizzled with the remaining syrup. SERVES 8

COCONUT "MACAROON" CAKE

I adapted this recipe from a New Zealand winery called Gillan Estate. It's eggless, dense, and "fudgy" in a macaroon-y way.

15-ounce can sweetened cream of coconut (such as Coco Lopez)
1 cup unsweetened desiccated coconut
²⁄₃ cup plain yogurt
²⁄₃ cup olive oil
2 teaspoons grated zest and juice from 4 large lemons
4 cups flour
2¹⁄₄ cups sugar
2 tablespoons baking powder

Preheat the oven to 350°F. Oil and flour a 12-cup Bundt pan. Using an electric mixer, beat together the cream of coconut, dried coconut, yogurt, and oil. Add the lemon zest and ²⁄₃ cup juice. Mix well. In another bowl, stir together the flour, sugar, and baking powder until combined. Stir the flour mixture into the coconut batter, 1 cup at a time; the batter will be very thick. Pour the batter into the pan. Bake on the center rack for 1 hour and 20 minutes, until firm and dark brown. Cool in the pan on a wire rack. Turn out onto a large plate; cool completely. SERVES 16 OR MORE

THE "LITTLE BLACK DRESS" CHOCOLATE CAKE

Like the legendary little black dress, this dessert is something I can't live without, a mousse-y rich cake with a soft, oozing center (provided you don't overbake it). And like the L.B.D., you can accessorize it in myriad ways: with fresh raspberries placed side by side and glazed with melted currant jelly; with sweetened crème fraiche and fresh orange segments; or with my "crème anglaise" (below) or a scoop of Lemon–Buttermilk Ice Cream (page 330).

> 10½ tablespoons unsalted butter
> 5 extra-large eggs
> 16 ounces top-quality semisweet chocolate, chopped
> 1 teaspoon vanilla extract, espresso powder, or orange zest

Preheat the oven to 375°F. Line the bottom of a 9-inch springform pan with parchment. Butter the sides of the pan with ½ tablespoon of the butter. Using an electric mixer, beat the eggs with a pinch of salt until tripled in volume, about 8 minutes. Melt the chocolate and the remaining 10 tablespoons butter slowly over low heat in a heavy medium saucepan; stir until smooth. Fold the chocolate mixture into the egg mixture with a flexible rubber spatula until completely incorporated. Add the vanilla. Pour into the pan. Bake 18 minutes: The center will be quite soft. Cool 30 minutes. SERVES 8

ONE-INGREDIENT EGGNOG "CRÈME ANGLAISE"

> 3 cups commercial eggnog

Bring the eggnog just to a boil in a medium saucepan. Reduce the heat to medium and cook, stirring frequently, until reduced to 1½ cups, about 40 minutes. Cover and refrigerate until cold. MAKES 1½ CUPS

A RADICALLY SIMPLE CHEESECAKE

Anne Kabo, from Margate, New Jersey, is one of the best home bakers I know, and she has created one of the best cheesecakes I've ever had. The crust doesn't need to be prebaked and, compared to most recipes, it is radically simple. It also freezes beautifully. You can shave white chocolate on top to cover up the cracks or top with fresh berries.

6 tablespoons unsalted butter, room temperature
5 ounces honey graham crackers
$\frac{1}{2}$ cup walnuts or pecans
$1\frac{1}{4}$ cups sugar
3 extra-large eggs, room temperature
16 ounces cream cheese, broken into pieces
2 teaspoons pure vanilla extract
1 tablespoon cornstarch
24 ounces sour cream

Preheat the oven to 375°F. Butter a deep 10-inch springform pan with 2 tablespoons of the butter. Finely crush the graham crackers, nuts, and $\frac{1}{4}$ cup of the sugar in a food processor. Melt the remaining 4 tablespoons butter; stir into the crumbs until moistened. Pat the crumbs onto the bottom and $\frac{1}{2}$ inch up the side of the pan to form a crust.

Using a standing mixer, beat the eggs for 3 minutes. Add the cream cheese and mix until smooth, 2 minutes. Add the remaining 1 cup sugar, vanilla, cornstarch, and $\frac{1}{4}$ teaspoon salt. Beat on high for 2 minutes. Add the sour cream and beat for 1 minute longer. Pour into the crust. Bake 50 minutes, until firm. Cool on a rack. Cover and refrigerate until very cold. SERVES 16

HUNGARIAN WALNUT COOKIES

Few cookies are easier to make. They are dedicated to my beautiful Hungarian mother, Marion, a vivacious cook who was more Zsa Zsa than Julia in the kitchen.

> 8 ounces shelled walnuts, about 2 cups
> 2 extra-large egg whites
> 1 cup packed dark brown sugar

Preheat the oven to 350°F. Chop the nuts into $\frac{1}{4}$-inch pieces. Place on a rimmed baking sheet. Bake 10 minutes until toasted. Cool and set aside.

Using an electric mixer, beat the egg whites and a pinch of salt on high speed until they stiffen, about 3 minutes. Slowly add the brown sugar and continue to beat on high until stiff and glossy, about 6 minutes. Fold in the nuts. Line the baking sheet with parchment. Drop the batter by 2 heaping tablespoons into tall mounds to make 20 to 24 cookies. Bake 20 minutes, until dark beige and firm. Let cool. MAKES 20 TO 24

A GIANT SUGAR COOKIE

There's high drama here as you serve one huge cookie to your guests and have them break it up at the table. Communal, to say the least. Practical, too. Sometimes I use the cookie as the platter and heap fresh berries, scoops of ice cream, and some gooey dessert sauce upon it.

> 8 ounces mascarpone cheese, room temperature
> 1 cup flour
> 2 tablespoons confectioners' sugar
> $\frac{1}{2}$ teaspoon ground cardamom
> $\frac{1}{3}$ cup pearl sugar or turbinado sugar

Using an electric mixer, combine the mascarpone, flour, confectioners' sugar, cardamom, and a pinch of salt until a smooth dough forms. Turn the dough out onto a lightly floured surface. Knead several minutes until smooth; pat into a 6-inch square. Wrap in plastic; chill 1 hour.

Preheat the oven to 425°F. With a rolling pin, roll out the dough on a lightly floured surface to make a 14x16-inch rectangle. Wrap the dough around the rolling pin; unroll onto a large ungreased baking sheet. Sprinkle evenly with the pearl sugar. Bake 12 to 14 minutes, until golden. The cookie will crisp and get puffy in spots. Cool. SERVES 8

SESAME SEED–OLIVE OIL COOKIES

These taste like cookies you might expect to find at an old-world Italian pastry shop. The olive oil gives them an interesting texture and flavor. Serve with Vietnamese Coffee (opposite page).

> 2 cups self-rising flour
> ²/₃ cup sugar
> 2 extra-large eggs
> ¹/₂ cup olive oil
> 2 teaspoons almond extract
> ²/₃ cup toasted sesame seeds

Preheat the oven to 325°F. Line 2 rimmed baking sheets with parchment. Combine the flour and sugar in a large bowl. In a small bowl, whisk together the eggs, oil, and extract. Add the egg mixture to the flour mixture and stir with a wooden spoon until a smooth dough forms; it will be crumbly and slightly oily.

Form the dough into small ovals, about 1¹/₂ inches long and ³/₄ inch wide. Roll the top and sides of each cookie in the sesame seeds. Place 1 inch apart on the baking sheets. Bake 25 minutes, until golden and just firm. Cool. MAKES 24

Vietnamese Coffee

2 tablespoons sweetened condensed milk
$\frac{1}{2}$ cup brewed espresso

Put condensed milk in the bottom of a small
heat-resistant glass. Fill with hot espresso.
MAKES 1

milk
& cookies

◄ Nutella Sandwich Cookies

The chocolate-hazelnut spread both flavors the batter and serves as the filling for the sandwich.

13-ounce jar Nutella
2 tablespoons unsalted butter, room temperature
1 extra-large egg
1¼ cups self-rising cake flour

Preheat the oven to 375°F. Line a rimmed baking sheet with parchment. Beat together ¾ cup of the Nutella, the butter, and egg. Slowly add the flour until a wet dough forms. Turn the dough out onto a floured surface and knead gently, adding more flour if necessary; the dough will be sticky. Divide the dough into 18 pieces and roll each into a perfect ball, flouring your hands as you go. Place several inches apart on the baking sheet. Bake 12 minutes, until firm. Cool 10 minutes on the sheet.

Using a serrated knife, split each cookie in half horizontally. Spread each bottom half with 1 teaspoon Nutella. Replace the tops, pressing lightly. MAKES 18

Cinnamon-Sugar Crisps

These radically simple cookies, fragrant and crisp, are fashioned from wonton wrappers (available in the freezer case of most supermarkets). They are the perfect accompaniment to most fruit desserts and great with a cup of hot green tea. They can be made with olive oil instead of butter.

¼ cup sugar
¾ teaspoon ground cinnamon
½ teaspoon five-spice powder
24 square wonton wrappers
4 tablespoons unsalted butter, melted
⅓ cup sesame seeds

Preheat the oven to 400°F. In a small bowl, mix together the sugar, cinnamon, and five-spice powder. Place 12 wontons on each of 2 ungreased baking sheets. Using a pastry brush, brush each with melted butter. Sprinkle heavily with the sugar mixture and then with the sesame seeds. Press the seeds in lightly. Bake for 7 minutes, until golden and crispy; cool. MAKES 24

HONEYDEW-KIWI SORBET WITH CHARTREUSE

The color? Jade green with tiny black dots. The flavor? Intriguing and herbal from an unexpected jolt of green Chartreuse. If you can find a beautifully ripe Galia melon, then use that instead of the honeydew.

$\frac{1}{2}$ cup plus 3 tablespoons sugar
4 cups chopped ripe honeydew melon
1$\frac{1}{2}$ cups chopped peeled kiwis
2 tablespoons freshly squeezed lime juice
6 tablespoons green Chartreuse
Thin slices ripe watermelon
Handful edible flower petals

In a small saucepan, boil $\frac{1}{2}$ cup water with the $\frac{1}{2}$ cup sugar, stirring, until the sugar dissolves. Let cool. Combine the melon, kiwis, lime juice, and a pinch of salt in a food processor; process until smooth. Combine the fruit puree and sugar syrup in a large bowl, cover, and chill well. Freeze in an ice cream maker according to the manufacturer's instructions, adding 3 tablespoons of the Chartreuse halfway through freezing.

Serve scoops of sorbet on watermelon slices and sprinkle with flower petals. Drizzle with the remaining Chartreuse. SERVES 6

chocolate
chipotle

lemon
buttermilk

maple

double raspberry

◄ CHOCOLATE-CHIPOTLE SORBET

A bit of chipotle smolders behind a chocolate chill. It's very cool to serve a scoop of this sorbet in a glass with some milk poured around it. Taste the mixture before you churn it—you might want to add a bit more chipotle powder and salt to augment the smoky flavor.

$^3/_4$ cup sugar
$^1/_4$ cup dark corn syrup
$^1/_2$ cup unsweetened Dutch-process cocoa powder
4 ounces semisweet chocolate chips
$^1/_8$ teaspoon ground chipotle powder

Combine the sugar, corn syrup, cocoa powder, and $1^1/_2$ cups water in a large saucepan. Whisk until smooth and bring to a boil. Boil 1 minute, whisking. Remove from the heat. Stir in the chocolate, chipotle powder, $^1/_4$ cup water, and a large pinch of salt. Stir until the chocolate melts. Pour the mixture into a blender and process 1 minute, until smooth. Refrigerate the mixture until very cold. Stir briskly and freeze in an ice cream maker according to the manufacturer's instructions. SERVES 6

◄ DOUBLE RASPBERRY SORBET

Pure berry, pure pleasure. Garnish with more fresh raspberries and confectioners' sugar, or sprinkle with a few drops of raspberry liqueur.

$^2/_3$ cup sugar
12 ounces fresh raspberries, plus more for garnish
10 ounces frozen raspberries in syrup, thawed

Combine the sugar and 1 cup water in a small saucepan. Bring to a boil. Simmer 1 minute, stirring. Set the syrup aside to cool.

Puree the fresh raspberries in a food processor until smooth. Add the thawed raspberries and their juices and $^1/_4$ cup water; process until very smooth. Pass the contents through a coarse-mesh sieve over a large bowl, pressing down to extract all the liquid. Add the cooled sugar syrup. Chill until cold. Freeze in an ice cream maker according to the manufacturer's instructions. Garnish with additional berries. SERVES 4

LEFTOVER-CRANBERRY-SAUCE SORBET

After Thanksgiving, if you have a block or two of leftover jellied cranberry sauce, as I often do, then you will enjoy this creative way to use it. Garnish with raspberries or pomegranate seeds. If you don't have an ice cream maker, you can prepare this as a granita by freezing the mixture and stirring it with a fork until slushy.

Grated zest and juice of 3 large lemons
Grated zest and juice of 2 large oranges
²/₃ cup sugar
¼ teaspoon pure vanilla extract
16 ounces jellied cranberry sauce

Combine the lemon zest, ½ cup lemon juice, orange zest, and ½ cup orange juice in a medium saucepan. Add the sugar, vanilla, and 2½ cups water; bring to a boil. Spoon the cranberry sauce, in large pieces, into the saucepan. Bring to a boil and whisk until melted and smooth. Cool, then chill well. Freeze in an ice cream maker according to the manufacturer's instructions. SERVES 8

GRAPEFRUIT-FRAMBOISE GRANITA

If you're using this as an intermezzo for a fancy dinner party, then swap in Campari for the framboise—it's less sweet and adds some alluring bitter notes.

½ cup sugar
3 cups freshly squeezed grapefruit juice
3 tablespoons framboise, plus more for drizzling
Fresh mint sprigs for garnish

Combine the sugar with ½ cup water in a small saucepan. Bring to a boil, reduce the heat, and cook, stirring, until the sugar is dissolved, 2 minutes. Let cool. Combine the sugar syrup, grapefruit juice, and framboise. Pour into a 13 × 9-inch baking pan and freeze, scraping up with a fork every 30 minutes to break up the ice crystals, 4 hours. Divide the granita evenly among 4 wineglasses. Serve drizzled with additional framboise and garnished with mint. SERVES 4

LEMON-BUTTERMILK ICE CREAM

Technically, this is not ice cream because it isn't made with cream, but the rich and silky frozen treat makes every day feel like summer. Some version of this recipe has snuck into every one of my 12 cookbooks. Sometimes I swap limes for the lemons and add cracked black pepper.

    2 cups sugar
    4 large lemons
    1 quart buttermilk

Put the sugar in a large bowl. Grate the zest of the lemons. Squeeze the lemons to get $^2/_3$ cup juice. Add the zest and juice to the sugar; stir until it dissolves. Whisk in the buttermilk and a pinch of salt. Stir until smooth. Chill for several hours, then freeze in an ice cream maker according to the manufacturer's instructions. SERVES 8

MAPLE ICE CREAM

Nice with a splash of bourbon and a dusting of espresso powder. You could also boil some maple syrup until thick; drizzle on top and add a few granules of trendy flaked salt.

    1 cup milk
    $^2/_3$ cup pure maple syrup
    $1^1/_2$ cups heavy cream

Combine the milk, maple syrup, cream, and a pinch of salt in a large saucepan. Bring to a boil, then reduce the heat and cook for 1 minute, stirring constantly. Cool, then chill well. Freeze in an ice cream maker according to the manufacturer's directions. SERVES 6

acknowledgments

During the course of writing my last 11 cookbooks, I have thanked those I love and those who love me. I have also acknowledged the wit and wisdom of the agents and editors, the photographers and stylists, who professionally lent a hand in the creation and completion of those books.

But there are two who stand out among all others in influencing my mind and heart—two who have caressed and challenged me to become a better writer, a deeper thinker, and a better cook. Arthur Schwartz, the food writer and critic known for his extraordinary culinary expertise, has been one of my very best friends since 1978 when we met in the kitchen of Gracie Mansion. I had just become chef to New York's Mayor Ed Koch, and Arthur was the restaurant critic of the *New York Daily News*. We have spoken almost daily since then. Arthur's cooking style has influenced mine for decades. He is the master of simplicity and authenticity—specifically in Italian regional cuisine, but he also possesses great knowledge of the foodways of many other cultures. It is a joy to have him and his partner, Bob Harned, in my life.

And there is my husband, Michael Whiteman, who sharpens my mind daily. He is one of the unsung maestros in the restaurant industry who was the founding editor of *Nation's Restaurant News* and who, with his partner Joe Baum, created two of the world's most legendary restaurants, the Rainbow Room and Windows on the World, and five of New York's three-star restaurants. Michael continues to develop high-profile projects around the world and he lights up my imagination every day. Twenty-four hours simply aren't enough to absorb all he knows. I thank him for that and for 22 years of marriage filled with munificent taste-memories and taste-making. And love.

Best friends? Yes. Steve North, Amy Berkowitz, Dale Bellisfield, Barbara Cohen, Helen Kimmel, Audrey Appleby, Katherine Newell Smith, Diana Carulli, Anne Kabo, Barbara-Jo McIntosh, Robin Zucker, Joanne Rosen, Lili Feldmann, all who make my life full. Thanks to my brother Leon Gold and sister-in-law Gail who kindly shares her great food ideas with me. To Dr. Judy Nelson, Amy Chender, Beth Labush, Jane Brody—healers, mentors, and supporters.

And thanks to everyone on the front line who made *Radically Simple* radically meaningful to do. My friend and sounding board, Erica Marcus (ace food writer for *Newsday*); my brilliant agent, Lydia Wills; my editor, Pam Krauss, whose big reputation is outsized by her big heart and acumen. To Kara Plikaitis, the art director at Rodale who once baked a coffee cake so I'd have something to eat with the first of my dozen cups of coffee that day. To the incomparable photographer Quentin Bacon whose work I have admired for decades. He brought light and life, excitement, and energy to every shot he took. To the beautiful Mariana Velasquez, who is beyond her years in talent. To her assistant, Natalia Gaviria, who made working hard a joy; even cleaning up was fun. Special thanks, too, to Matthew Klein, Phil Mansfield, and Robert Geary. And to Karen Rinaldi, publisher of Rodale, who always had my back and believed in me.

But up, up, and away, I want to thank my daughter, Shayna Rose DePersia, now 14. She is a wellspring of love and laughter and of all things possible. And to our son, Jeremy Whiteman, wishing him a delicious life.

index

Underscored page references indicate boxed text. **Boldfaced** page references indicate photographs.

Almonds

Almond Galettes with a Glass of Sherry, 310
Caramelized Almond Toasts, 18, **19**
Couscous with Dates & Almonds, 63
Double-Rise Pancakes with Strawberries, Bananas & Almonds, 24
Linguine with Pesto Rosso, 109
Steamed Parsnips with Toasted Almonds, **266**, 267

Apple cider or juice

Apple-Ginger-Pear Martinis, 6
Onion Soup with Apple Cider & Thyme, 86

Apples

Apples to the 3rd Power, 300, **301**
E.A.T. (Easy Apple Tart), 310
Eggless Caesar Salad with Green Apple "Croutons," 59
Fresh Fruit Muffins: Blueberry, Cinnamon-Apple, or Pear, 28
Parsnip-Apple Soup with "Bacon Candy," 93
Pork Chops & Apples, Madeira–Bay Butter Sauce, 214, **215**
Tahina & Date Syrup Swirl, Fresh Apple Slices, 294

Apricots and apricot jam

Palacsintas with Apricot Jam & Powdered Sugar, 18, **19**
White Chocolate Mousse with Apricot Compote, 307

Arugula

Fig, Fennel & Endive Salad with Pistachio Vinaigrette, 58
Garlic-Miso Pork Chops, Orange Peppers & Arugula, 212–13
Grapefruit, Date & Arugula Salad with Parmesan Shards, 57, **57**
Lamb Chops with Smoked Paprika Oil, Cumin & Arugula, **224**, 225
Lemony Arugula & Sun-Dried Tomato Salad with Smoked Mozzarella, 55
Manchego Chicken with Prosciutto, Arugula & Pumpkin Seeds, 190
Sautéed Cod with Chorizo, Orange & Wild Arugula, Sherry Vinaigrette, 148, **149**
Sautéed Peppers with Golden Raisins & Arugula, 270

Asparagus

Asparagus, Bok Choy & Radicchio Salad, 48
Asparagus Bisque with a Touch of India, 84
Black & Blue Tuna with Garlic Asparagus & Yogurt-Caper Sauce, 163
Chilled Asparagus Tonnato with "Confetti," 46–47, **47**
Poached Asparagus with Lemon-Mint Panko, 252
Roasted Asparagus with Bay Leaves & Crispy Capers, 252, **253**
Steamed Asparagus with Wasabi-Miso Butter, 254
Truffled Asparagus Soup with Pineapple Reduction, 95

Avocados

Crisped Chicken with Chimichurri & Avocado, 182, **183**
Spooned Avocado, Lime & Smoked Paprika, 38

Bacon. *See also* Pancetta

BLT Chicken with Cumin Seed & Lime Mayonnaise, 181
Parsnip-Apple Soup with "Bacon Candy," 93
Perciatelli with French Breakfast Radishes, Bacon & Greens, **122**, 123
Runny Eggs on Creamy Scallion-Bacon Grits, 11, **11**
Smoked Trout on Frisée with Warm Bacon-Maple Vinaigrette, 13
Sugar Snaps with Diced Bacon & Radishes, **272**, 273

Bananas

Double-Rise Pancakes with Strawberries, Bananas & Almonds, 24

Basil

Basil-Scrubbed Toasts, 102
"Green" Corn, 264
Linguine with Pesto Rosso, 109
Peaches in Peach Schnapps with Basil, 290, **291**
Sizzling Skirts with Lime, Basil & Sriracha, **236**, 237
Smoked Salmon, Basil & Lemon Quesadillas, **14**, 15
Tortellini in Pesto Broth, 85

Beans. *See also* Chickpeas; Green beans

Italian White Bean Salad, 65
Russian Red Bean Salad, 65
Split Pea Soup with Soppressata & Fresh Oregano, 91
White Beans with Spinach, Tomatoes & Rosemary, 283

Beef. *See also* Veal

Beef Rendang, 246–47
Big Juicy Sun-Dried Tomato Burgers, 234
cooking, tip for, 210
Double-Strength Beef Broth, 98
Filet of Beef with Wasabi-Garlic Cream, 242, **243**
Flap, Hanger, or Skirt Steaks with Sumac, 234
Mahogany Short Ribs, 246
New Asia Steak, 240
Pot Roast with Burnt Onions & Kimchee, 247
A Prime Rib of Beef, 241
Reddened Rib Eye with Pimiento Cheese, 238, **239**
Rib Roast in the Style of Gravlax, 245, **245**
Sirloin Steaks with Magic Green Sauce, 235
Sizzling Skirts with Lime, Basil & Sriracha, **236**, 237
Steak & Eggs with Salsa Verde & Fontina, 10
Tournedos Balsamico with Rosemary & Gorgonzola Dolce, 240–41
Tri-Tip Filet in Soy & Red Wine with Chinese Mustard, 244

Beets

"Beet" Broth, 99

Beets (*cont.*)
Beet Soup with Lemon Crème Fraîche, 77, **77**
Beets with Balsamic Syrup, Mint & Walnuts, 46
Beet Vinaigrette, 66
"Chipped Beets" & Beet Greens, 256–57
Magic Beets, 64
Veal Chops with Sage Butter, Sunflower Seeds & Beet Drizzle, 230, **231**
Berries. *See also* Blueberries; Cranberries; Raspberries; Strawberries
Fresh Ricotta with Lemon Curd & Blackberries, 293, **293**
Morning Fruit Soup with Tapioca, 22
Biscuits
Olive Oil Biscuits, 100
Blackberries
Fresh Ricotta with Lemon Curd & Blackberries, 293, **293**
Blueberries
Blueberries with Hibiscus Spice, Sugar Syrup, 290, **291**
Fresh Fruit Muffins: Blueberry, Cinnamon-Apple, or Pear, 28
Blue cheese
Grilled Romaine with Roquefort & Deviled Pecans, 58–59
Steamed Broccoli with Blue Cheese, Red Onion & Mint, 254, **255**
Tournedos Balsamico with Rosemary & Gorgonzola Dolce, 240–41
Watercress, Endive & St. Agur Blue Cheese, 53
Bluefish
Bluefish Salmoriglio with Red Pepper Julienne, 162
Bok choy
Asparagus, Bok Choy & Radicchio Salad, 48
Korean-Style Salmon "Bulgogi," Bok Choy & Shiitakes, **146**, 147
Bread pudding
Cheese Strata with Prosciutto, Basil & Spinach, 26, **27**
Breads and toasts
Barcelona Bread, 102
Basil-Scrubbed Toasts, 102
Caramelized Almond Toasts, 18, **19**
Emergency Crackers, 103

Fennel-Cumin Flatbreads, 103
Fresh Fruit Muffins: Blueberry, Cinnamon-Apple, or Pear, 28
Golden Raisin–Fennel Scones, 31, **31**
Olive Oil Biscuits, 100
Pappadams, 101
Peanut Butter–Granola Bruschetta, 21
Walnut-Onion Muffins, 101
Warm Buttermilk-Cheddar Scones, 30
Broccoli
Broccoli Soup with Lemon-Pistachio Butter, 90
A New Way to Cook Broccoli: Charred & Tossed with Chilies & Garlic, 256
Steamed Broccoli with Blue Cheese, Red Onion & Mint, 254, **255**
Broths
"Beet" Broth, 99
Corn Cob Broth, 98
Double-Strength Beef Broth, 98
Golden Chicken Broth, 99
Brussels sprouts
Jane Brody's Brussels Sprouts, 257
Roasted Brussels Sprouts with Medjool Dates, **258**, 259
Bulgur wheat
Overnight Tabbouleh with Hard-Boiled Eggs, 25
Burgers
Big Juicy Sun-Dried Tomato Burgers, 234
Bombay Turkey Sliders, Hurry-Curry Sauce, 204
Buttermilk
Lemon-Buttermilk Ice Cream, **326**, 329
Warm Buttermilk-Cheddar Scones, 30

Cabbage. *See also* Bok choy
Braised Black Sea Bass on Pancetta-Studded Cabbage, 159
Braised Red Cabbage with Cranberries, 275
Caramelized Cabbage & Noodles, 275
"Golden Robe" Salmon with Snow Peas & Red Cabbage, 145
Two-Cabbage Slaw, 62

Cakes
Almond Galettes with a Glass of Sherry, 310
Coconut "Macaroon" Cake, 315, **315**
Dutch Butter Ginger Cake, 311
French Yogurt Cake with Nutella, 312, **313**
The "Little Black Dress" Chocolate Cake, **316**, 317
Maple-Walnut Espresso Torte, Espresso-Lemon Syrup, 314
A Radically Simple Cheesecake, 318
Calabaza
Calabaza Soup with Celery & Crispy Sage, 96, **97**
Carrots
Carrot-Ginger Dressing, 66
Carrot Marmalade, 23
Carrot "Nib" Orzo, 259
Carrots-and-Onions in High Humidity, **260**, 261
Carrot Soup with Ginger & Crispy Carrot Tops, 87
Milky Carrot & Parsnip Puree, 261
Moroccan Carrots, 63
Oven-Steamed Halibut with Carrots, Lemon & Thyme, **154**, 155
Spring Mix with Carrot-Ginger Dressing & Prosciutto "Bacon," 50, **51**
Cashews
Swiss Chard with Lemony Tahina & Cashews, 264
Cauliflower
Cauliflower Vichyssoise with Chive Flowers, 82, **83**
Roasted Sliced Cauliflower with Cheddar & Rosemary, 262, **263**
Short Rigatoni with Cauliflower, Anchovies & Raisins, 124, **125**
Whole Cauliflower, Ras el Hanout Crumble, 262
Chard
Swiss Chard with Lemony Tahina & Cashews, 264
Cheddar cheese
Kimchee Frittata with Five-Spice Powder, 9
Pimento Mac, 119
Reddened Rib Eye with Pimiento Cheese, 238, **239**
Roasted Sliced Cauliflower with Cheddar & Rosemary, 262, **263**
Warm Buttermilk-Cheddar Scones, 30

index

Cheese. *See also* Blue cheese; Cheddar cheese; Feta cheese; Goat cheese; Parmesan
Baked Ziti in Bianco with Fontina & Salami, 120, **121**
Brie and Pear Soup, Brandied Cherries & Pears, 92
Castellane with Ricotta & Tomato-Marsala Sauce, 126–27
Cheese Strata with Prosciutto, Basil & Spinach, 26, **27**
Creamy Potato Gratin, 278
Fresh Ricotta with Lemon Curd & Blackberries, 293, **293**
Fruit & Cheese Pairings, 299
Homemade Cream Cheese, 22, **23**
Lemony Arugula & Sun-Dried Tomato Salad with Smoked Mozzarella, 55
Manchego Chicken with Prosciutto, Arugula & Pumpkin Seeds, 190
Pasta with Pepper, Pecorino & Pork Rinds, 108–9
A Radically Simple Cheesecake, 318
A Radically Simple Chicken Parmigiana, 180–81
Spaghetti with Aged Gouda & Frozen Olive Oil, 118
Spinach, Ricotta & Basil Puree, 271
Tomato, Buffalo Mozzarella & Fried Basil Salad, 44, **44**
Zucchini, Fresh Mozzarella & Sun-Dried Tomato Tart, 12
Cherries
Brie and Pear Soup, Brandied Cherries & Pears, 92
Pear, Cherry & Pine Nut Tartlets, 308
Chicken
"Almost Confit" Chicken with Melted Garlic, 192, **193**
Asian Chicken with Scallions, 180
Blistered Chicken, Tandoori-Style, 198–99
BLT Chicken with Cumin Seed & Lime Mayonnaise, 181
buying, 178
Cardamom Chicken with Chickpea & Orange Couscous, 184, 185
Chicken "Nuggets" with Sherry Vinegar & A Handful of Herbs, 191

Chicken Ras el Hanout with Tomato-Ginger Chutney, **196**, 197
Chicken Thighs with Rosemary & Two Paprikas, 194
Chicken with Chorizo, Peppadews & Fino Sherry, 195
Chicken with 40 Cloves of Garlic, Anisette & Greens, 201
Chicken with Goat Cheese, Basil & Lavender, 201
Chicken with Prosciutto, Tomatoes & White Wine, 199
Chicken with Za'atar, Lemon & Garlic, 200, **200**
Chicken Zahav with Blackened Onions & Turmeric, 194
Crisped Chicken with Chimichurri & Avocado, 182, **183**
Golden Chicken Broth, 99
Manchego Chicken with Prosciutto, Arugula & Pumpkin Seeds, 190
Miso Chicken with Fresh Ginger, 186
An Opinionated Way to Roast a Chicken, 203, **203**
Poulet au Crème Fraîche, 198
A Radically Simple Chicken Parmigiana, 180–81
Red Curry–Coconut Chicken, 186–87
Sautéed Chicken with Roasted Grapes & Grape Demi-Glace, 187, **188**
Velvet Chicken with Warm Asian Vinaigrette, 202
Chickpeas
Baby Romaine & Crispy Chickpeas with Hazelnut Vinaigrette, 56
Cardamom Chicken with Chickpea & Orange Couscous, **184**, 185
Chickpea Flour Soup from Provence, 78, 79
Couscous with Dates & Almonds, 63
"Thunder & Lightening," 126
Warm Wild Mushrooms on Hummus, 49
Chile peppers
A New Way to Cook Broccoli: Charred & Tossed with Chilies & Garlic, 256
Steamed Clams with Sake & Chiles, 170

Chocolate
All-Chocolate Velvet Tart, 309, **309**
Chocolate, Parmigiano-Reggiano & Red Grapes, 298, **298**
Chocolate-Chipotle Sorbet, **326**, 327
Chocolate-Coconut Fondue, Fresh Fruit, 295
Chocolate "Pousse," 305
French Yogurt Cake with Nutella, 312, **313**
Little Chocolate-Tahina Cups, 297
The "Little Black Dress" Chocolate Cake, **316**, 317
Nutella Sandwich Cookies, **322**, 323
Petit Pans au Chocolat, 29
Prunes and White Chocolate, Port Wine Reduction, 303
Watermelon "Carpaccio" with White Chocolate, 292
White Chocolate Mousse with Apricot Compote, 307
Cinnamon
Cinnamon-Sugar Crisps, 323
Clams
Steamed Clams with Sake & Chiles, 170
Coconut
Absurdly Easy Coconut Sorbet, 302, **302**
Beef Rendang, 246–47
Chocolate-Coconut Fondue, Fresh Fruit, 295
Coconut-Espresso Crème Caramel, 306
Coconut "Macaroon" Cake, 315, **315**
Cucumber-Coconut Bisque, 76
Pistachio-Coconut Rice, 274
Red Curry–Coconut Chicken, 186–87
Salmon with Lime Leaves, Poppy Rice & Coconut Sauce, 139
Warm Rhubarb Compote with Walnut-Coconut Crunch, 20, **20**
Cod
Braised Cod with "Sliced Tomato" Sauce & Fresh Oregano, 150–51
Crunchy Crumbed Cod with Frozen Peas, 150
500-Degree Cod with Macadamia Butter & Radicchio, 151
Sautéed Cod with Chorizo, Orange & Wild Arugula, Sherry Vinaigrette, 148, **149**

Coffee. *See* Espresso
Cookies
    Cinnamon-Sugar Crisps, 323
    A Giant Sugar Cookie, 319
    Hungarian Walnut Cookies, 319
    Nutella Sandwich Cookies, **322**,
        323
    Sesame Seed–Olive Oil Cookies,
        320
Corn
    Corn Cob Broth, 98
    "Green" Corn, 264
    Seared Tuna with Fresh Corn &
        Wasabi "Cream," 162–63
    Silky Corn Soup with Scallions &
        Green Apple, 88, **88**
Couscous
    Cardamom Chicken with Chickpea
        & Orange Couscous, **184**,
        185
    Couscous with Dates & Almonds,
        63
    Peas & Couscous with Curry Oil,
        267
Crabmeat
    Jade Soup with Lump Crab & Dill,
        82
Crackers
    Buttery Oatcakes, 100
    Emergency Crackers, 103
    Fennel-Cumin Flatbreads, 103
Cranberries and cranberry juice
    Braised Red Cabbage with
        Cranberries, 275
    Endive, Mâche & Cranberry Salad
        with Parmesan Frico, 54
    Leftover-Cranberry-Sauce Sorbet,
        328
    Seven Great Juice Blends, 4, **5**
    Two-Cabbage Slaw, 62
Crepes and pancakes
    Double-Rise Pancakes with
        Strawberries, Bananas &
        Almonds, 24
    Palacsintas with Apricot Jam &
        Powdered Sugar, 18, **19**
Cucumbers
    Apple Cider Cucumbers, 64
    Cucumber-Coconut Bisque, 76
    Plum Tomato Gazpacho, 81
    Salmon with Cucumbers &
        Blackened Lemons, 138
    Turkish Cucumbers, 64
Custards
    Chocolate "Pousse," 305
    Coconut-Espresso Crème Caramel,
        306

Pineapple Flan, **304**, 305
White Chocolate Mousse with
    Apricot Compote, 307

Dates
    Couscous with Dates & Almonds,
        63
    Grapefruit, Date & Arugula Salad
        with Parmesan Shards, 57, **57**
    Roasted Brussels Sprouts with
        Medjool Dates, **258**, 259
    Tahina & Date Syrup Swirl, Fresh
        Apple Slices, 294
Desserts. *See page 289 for list of recipes*
Drinks
    Apple-Ginger-Pear Martinis, 6
    "Bloody" Shrimp Cocktail, 7, **7**
    Seven Great Juice Blends, 4, **5**
    Vietnamese Coffee, 321, **321**

Eggnog
    One-Ingredient Eggnog "Crème
        Anglaise," 317
Eggplant
    Eggplant and Roasted Pepper
        Salad with Feta, 62
    Tian of Eggplant, Tomato &
        Herbs, 284
Eggs
    Capellini with Chili Paste &
        Crispy Egg, 114, **115**
    Creamy, Lemony Eggs with
        Prosciutto, 8
    Frittata with Pancetta, Red Onion
        & Mint, 9
    Glazed Salmon & Wok Eggs with
        Shiitakes, 17
    Kimchee Frittata with Five-Spice
        Powder, 9
    Overnight Tabbouleh with Hard-
        Boiled Eggs, 25
    Runny Eggs on Creamy Scallion-
        Bacon Grits, 11, **11**
    Scrambled Eggs with Leeks &
        Sable, 8
    Steak & Eggs with Salsa Verde &
        Fontina, 10
Endive
    Endive, Mâche & Cranberry
        Salad with Parmesan Frico,
        54
    Fig, Fennel & Endive Salad with
        Pistachio Vinaigrette, 58
    Watercress, Endive & St. Agur
        Blue Cheese, 53

Escarole
    Fusilli with Braised Escarole,
        Garlic & Ricotta Salata,
        130, 131
Espresso
    Coconut-Espresso Crème Caramel,
        306
    Maple-Walnut Espresso Torte,
        Espresso-Lemon Syrup,
        314
    Vietnamese Coffee, 321, **321**

Fennel and fennel seeds
    Fennel-Cumin Flatbreads, 103
    Fennel-Roasted Striped Bass, Tiny
        Tomatoes & Crispy Capers,
        157
    Fig, Fennel & Endive Salad with
        Pistachio Vinaigrette, 58
    Herring Salad with Fennel, Crème
        Fraîche & Toasted Bread
        Crumbs, 16, **16**
    Shaved Fennel with Parmigiano &
        Hot Pepper, 48
    Steamed Fennel & Red Peppers
        with Garlic Oil & Lemon
        Zest, 265
    Sweet Garlic-Fennel Bisque with
        Toasted Pine Nuts, 89
Feta cheese
    Cheese Strata with Prosciutto,
        Basil & Spinach, 26, **27**
    "Chipped Beets" & Beet Greens,
        256–57
    Eggplant and Roasted Pepper
        Salad with Feta, 62
    Watermelon Salad with Feta &
        Black Olives, 42
Figs
    Fig, Fennel & Endive Salad with
        Pistachio Vinaigrette, 58
    Fresh Figs & Shaved Halvah,
        Warm Honey Syrup, **296**, 297
    Lamb Shoulder with Figs, Lemon
        & Chartreuse, 223
    Prosciutto with Figs & Mint, 43
Fish. *See also* Cod; Halibut; Salmon;
        Swordfish; Tuna
    Bluefish Salmoriglio with Red
        Pepper Julienne, 162
    Braised Black Sea Bass on Pancetta-
        Studded Cabbage, 159
    buying, 136
    Chilean Sea Bass with Pistachio-
        Pesto Crust & Green Bean
        "Fries," 158, **158**

Fennel-Roasted Striped Bass, Tiny Tomatoes & Crispy Capers, 157
Golden Fettuccine with Sardines, Fennel & Saffron, **112**, 113
health benefits, 136
Herring Salad with Fennel, Crème Fraîche & Toasted Bread Crumbs, 16, **16**
Holy Mackerel, 160, **161**
Pasta Rustica with Sole, Greek Olives & White Wine, 127
Red Snapper with Pop-Pop Tomatoes, 153
Scrambled Eggs with Leeks & Sable, 8
"Silver Packet" Flounder with Miso Mayo, 152–53
Smoked Trout on Frisée with Warm Bacon-Maple Vinaigrette, 13
Sole Provençal with Petit Ratatouille, 152
Swordfish Steaks with Sardine "Bolognese," 168

Flounder
"Silver Packet" Flounder with Miso Mayo, 152–53

Frittatas
Frittata with Pancetta, Red Onion & Mint, 9
Kimchee Frittata with Five-Spice Powder, 9

Fruit. *See also specific fruits*
"Ceviche" of Spring Fruit with Sesame Seeds, 294
Chocolate-Coconut Fondue, Fresh Fruit, 295
Fruit Chaussons, 29
Fruit & Cheese Pairings, 299
Morning Fruit Soup with Tapioca, 22

Garlic
"Almost Confit" Chicken with Melted Garlic, 192, **193**
Chicken with 40 Cloves of Garlic, Anisette & Greens, 201
Chicken with Za'atar, Lemon & Garlic, 200, **200**
A Leg of Lamb & A Bottle of Chardonnay, 228
Stir-Fried Watercress with Garlic Chips, 274
Sweet Garlic-Fennel Bisque with Toasted Pine Nuts, 89

Ginger
Angel Hair with Ginger Butter & Chives, 114
Apple-Ginger-Pear Martinis, 6
Carrot-Ginger Dressing, 66
Carrot Soup with Ginger & Crispy Carrot Tops, 87
Dutch Butter Ginger Cake, 311
Ginger Bouillon with Enoki Mushrooms, 79
Miso Chicken with Fresh Ginger, 186
Rhubarb & Candied Ginger Compote with Coconut Sorbet, 302, **302**
Spring Mix with Carrot-Ginger Dressing & Prosciutto "Bacon," 50, **51**
Warm Sesame Noodles with Ginger & Snow Peas, 133

Goat cheese
Beets with Balsamic Syrup, Mint & Walnuts, 46
Chicken with Goat Cheese, Basil & Lavender, 201
Pea Shoots & Greens with Goat Cheese & Cumin Vinaigrette, **52**, 53
Smoked Salmon, Basil & Lemon Quesadillas, **14**, 15
Smoked Salmon with Petite Salade, Goat Cheese & Lime Vinaigrette, 38

Grains. *See also Rice*
Buttery Oatcakes, 100
Overnight Tabbouleh with Hard-Boiled Eggs, 25
Runny Eggs on Creamy Scallion-Bacon Grits, 11, **11**

Granita
Grapefruit-Framboise Granita, 328

Grapefruit and grapefruit juice
Grapefruit, Date & Arugula Salad with Parmesan Shards, 57, **57**
Grapefruit-Framboise Granita, 328
Seven Great Juice Blends, 4, **5**

Grapes
Chocolate, Parmigiano-Reggiano & Red Grapes, 298, **298**
Fennel Sausages with Wrinkled Grapes & Grape Extract, 218
Sautéed Chicken with Roasted Grapes & Grape Demi-Glace, 187, **188**

Green beans
Blasted Green Beans & Grape Tomatoes, 265

Chilean Sea Bass with Pistachio-Pesto Crust & Green Bean "Fries," 158, **158**
Three Green Vegetables in High Humidity, 273

Greens. *See page 35 for list of leafy green salads; specific greens*

Grits
Runny Eggs on Creamy Scallion-Bacon Grits, 11, **11**

Halibut
Halibut in Prosciutto Wrappers, Red Onions & Crispy Basil, 156–57
Oven-Steamed Halibut with Carrots, Lemon & Thyme, **154**, 155
Roasted Halibut with Tomatoes & Saffron Vinaigrette, 156
Tiradito, 37

Halvah
Fresh Figs & Shaved Halvah, Warm Honey Syrup, **296**, 297

Ham. *See Prosciutto*

Herring
Herring Salad with Fennel, Crème Fraîche & Toasted Bread Crumbs, 16, **16**

Ice cream
Lemon-Buttermilk Ice Cream, **326**, 329
Maple Ice Cream, **326**, 329

Kimchee
Kimchee Frittata with Five-Spice Powder, 9
Pot Roast with Burnt Onions & Kimchee, 247

Kiwifruit
Honeydew-Kiwi Sorbet with Chartreuse, 324, **325**

Lamb
Butterflied Lamb with Garam Masala, Yogurt & Lime, 226, **227**
Double Lamb Chops with Mint & Ginger Crust, 225
Lamb Chops with Smoked Paprika Oil, Cumin & Arugula, **224**, 225

Lamb (*cont.*)
Lamb Riblets with Sweet Asian
Flavors, 222
Lamb Shanks Provençal
with Cabernet & Dried
Mushrooms, 229
Lamb Shoulder with Figs, Lemon
& Chartreuse, 223
A Leg of Lamb & A Bottle of
Chardonnay, 228
Roast Rack of Lamb, Madeira-
Peppercorn Reduction,
222–23
Lemons
Fresh Ricotta with Lemon
Curd & Blackberries, 293,
293
Lemon-Buttermilk Ice Cream,
326, 329
Salmon with Cucumbers &
Blackened Lemons, 138
Lobster
Salt-Water Lobsters, Healthy
Drawn Butter, 175

Macadamia nuts
500-Degree Cod with Macadamia
Butter & Radicchio, 151
Mackerel
Holy Mackerel, 160, **161**
Maple syrup
Maple Ice Cream, **326**, 329
Maple-Mustard Vinaigrette, 66
Maple-Walnut Espresso Torte,
Espresso-Lemon Syrup,
314
Roasted Sweet Potatoes with
Whipped Butter & Maple
"Honey," 282
Smoked Trout on Frisée with
Warm Bacon-Maple
Vinaigrette, 13
Meat. *See* Beef; Lamb; Pork; Veal
Melon. *See also* Watermelon
"Ceviche" of Spring Fruit with
Sesame Seeds, 294
Honeydew-Kiwi Sorbet with
Chartreuse, 324, **325**
Miso
Garlic-Miso Pork Chops,
Orange Peppers & Arugula,
212–13
Miso Chicken with Fresh Ginger,
186
Steamed Asparagus with Wasabi-
Miso Butter, 254

Muffins
Fresh Fruit Muffins: Blueberry,
Cinnamon-Apple, or Pear, 28
Walnut-Onion Muffins, 101
Mushrooms
Ginger Bouillon with Enoki
Mushrooms, 79
Glazed Salmon & Wok Eggs with
Shiitakes, 17
Green Curry Swordfish with
Shiitakes & Basil, 168–69
Korean-Style Salmon "Bulgogi,"
Bok Choy & Shiitakes, **146**,
147
Lamb Shanks Provençal
with Cabernet & Dried
Mushrooms, 229
Tri-Tip Filet in Soy & Red Wine
with Chinese Mustard, 244
Veal Steaks "Stroganoff" with
Shiitakes & Portobellos, 233
Warm Wild Mushrooms on
Hummus, 49
Mussels
Sheet-Pan Mussels with Red
Curry–Garlic Broth, 170, **171**
Mustard
Maple-Mustard Vinaigrette, 66
1-Minute Mustard Sauce, 39

Nuts. *See also* Almonds; Pine nuts;
Pistachios; Walnuts
500-Degree Cod with Macadamia
Butter & Radicchio, 151
Swiss Chard with Lemony Tahina
& Cashews, 264

Oats
Buttery Oatcakes, 100
Olives
Pasta Rustica with Sole, Greek
Olives & White Wine, 127
Spiced Salmon on a Moroccan
Salad, 40, **41**
Watermelon Salad with Feta &
Black Olives, 42
Onions
Campanelle with Caramelized
Onions, Peas & Mint, 128, **129**
Carrots-and-Onions in High
Humidity, **260**, 261
Chicken Zahav with Blackened
Onions & Turmeric, 194
Onion Soup with Apple Cider &
Thyme, 86

Pot Roast with Burnt Onions &
Kimchee, 247
Walnut-Onion Muffins, 101
"Whole Buttered" Onion Soup, 86
Oranges
Arabic Orange Salad with
Nasturtiums, **60**, 61
Sautéed Cod with Chorizo,
Orange & Wild Arugula,
Sherry Vinaigrette, 148, **149**
Seven Great Juice Blends, 4, **5**
Shrimp Escabeche with Blood
Orange Mojo, 172
Spiced Salmon on a Moroccan
Salad, 40, **41**

Pancakes and crepes
Double-Rise Pancakes with
Strawberries, Bananas &
Almonds, 24
Palacsintas with Apricot Jam &
Powdered Sugar, 18, **19**
Pancetta
Braised Black Sea Bass on Pancetta-
Studded Cabbage, 159
Frittata with Pancetta, Red Onion
& Mint, 9
Parmesan cheese
Caesar-ette Dressing, 67
Chocolate, Parmigiano-Reggiano
& Red Grapes, 298, **298**
Eggless Caesar Salad with Green
Apple "Croutons," 59
Endive, Mâche & Cranberry Salad
with Parmesan Frico, 54
Grapefruit, Date & Arugula Salad
with Parmesan Shards, 57, **57**
Prosciutto with Pears &
Parmigiano, 43
A Radically Simple Chicken
Parmigiana, 180–81
Shaved Fennel with Parmigiano &
Hot Pepper, 48
Parsnips
Milky Carrot & Parsnip Puree, 261
Parsnip-Apple Soup with "Bacon
Candy," 93
Roasted Parsnip Fries, 268
Steamed Parsnips with Toasted
Almonds, **266**, 267
Pasta and noodles. *See also* Couscous;
page 107 for list of pasta recipes
Caramelized Cabbage & Noodles,
275
Carrot "Nib" Orzo, 259
Tortellini in Pesto Broth, 85

Pastries
  Fruit Chaussons, 29
  Petit Pans au Chocolat, 29
Peaches and peach nectar
  Peaches in Peach Schnapps with
    Basil, 290, **291**
  Seven Great Juice Blends, 4, **5**
Peanut butter
  Peanut Butter–Granola Bruschetta,
    21
  Warm Sesame Noodles with
    Ginger & Snow Peas, 133
Pears and pear nectar
  Apple-Ginger-Pear Martinis, 6
  Brie and Pear Soup, Brandied
    Cherries & Pears, 92
  Charred Tuna, Mizuna & Pear
    with Black Vinaigrette, **164**,
    165
  Fresh Fruit Muffins: Blueberry,
    Cinnamon-Apple, or Pear, 28
  Pear, Cherry & Pine Nut Tartlets,
    308
  Poached Pears with Marsala,
    Cinnamon & Vanilla, 303
  Prosciutto with Pears &
    Parmigiano, 43
  Seven Great Juice Blends, 4, **5**
Peas
  Campanelle with Caramelized
    Onions, Peas & Mint, 128,
    129
  Crunchy Crumbed Cod with
    Frozen Peas, 150
  "Golden Robe" Salmon with Snow
    Peas & Red Cabbage, 145
  Green Pea–Wasabi Soup with
    Mint, 84–85
  Peas & Couscous with Curry Oil,
    267
  Pea Shoots & Greens with
    Goat Cheese & Cumin
    Vinaigrette, **52**, 53
  Seared Scallops on Sweet Pea
    Puree, 174, **174**
  Sugar Snaps with Diced Bacon &
    Radishes, **272**, 273
  Three Green Vegetables in High
    Humidity, 273
  Warm Sesame Noodles with
    Ginger & Snow Peas, 133
Pecans
  Eggless Caesar Salad with Green
    Apple "Croutons," 59
  Grilled Romaine with Roquefort
    & Deviled Pecans, 58–59
  Jane Brody's Brussels Sprouts, 257

Sweet Potato–Rutabaga Soup with
    Toasted Pecans, 90–91
Pepper, freshly ground, for recipes, xi
Peppers. *See also* Chile peppers
  Bluefish Salmoriglio with Red
    Pepper Julienne, 162
  Chicken with Chorizo, Peppadews
    & Fino Sherry, 195
  Eggplant and Roasted Pepper
    Salad with Feta, 62
  Fragrant Asian Gazpacho, 80, **80**
  Garlic-Miso Pork Chops, Orange
    Peppers & Arugula, 212–13
  Ginger's No-Ginger Salmon, 144
  Pimento Mac, 119
  Plum Tomato Gazpacho, 81
  Reddened Rib Eye with Pimiento
    Cheese, 238, **239**
  Sautéed Peppers with Golden
    Raisins & Arugula, 270
  Sole Provençal with Petit
    Ratatouille, 152
  Steamed Fennel & Red Peppers
    with Garlic Oil & Lemon
    Zest, 265
Pesto
  Chilean Sea Bass with Pistachio-
    Pesto Crust & Green Bean
    "Fries," 158, **158**
  Linguine with Pesto Rosso, 109
  Summer Tomatoes with Za'atar
    Pesto, 45
  Tortellini in Pesto Broth, 85
Pineapple and pineapple juice
  "Ceviche" of Spring Fruit with
    Sesame Seeds, 294
  Pineapple Flan, **304**, 305
  Pineapple Shingles with Caramel
    & Pistachio Dust, 292
  Seven Great Juice Blends, 4, **5**
  Truffled Asparagus Soup with
    Pineapple Reduction, 95
Pine nuts
  Fennel Sausages with Wrinkled
    Grapes & Grape Extract, 218
  Fettuccine with Tahina, Pine Nuts
    & Cilantro, 110
  Pear, Cherry & Pine Nut Tartlets,
    308
  Summer Tomatoes with Za'atar
    Pesto, 45
  Sweet Garlic-Fennel Bisque with
    Toasted Pine Nuts, 89
  Tortellini in Pesto Broth, 85
Pistachios
  Arabic Orange Salad with
    Nasturtiums, **60**, 61

Broccoli Soup with Lemon-
    Pistachio Butter, 90
  Chilean Sea Bass with Pistachio-
    Pesto Crust & Green Bean
    "Fries," 158, **158**
  Fig, Fennel & Endive Salad with
    Pistachio Vinaigrette, 58
  Pineapple Shingles with Caramel
    & Pistachio Dust, 292
  Pistachio-Coconut Rice, 274
Pomegranate
  Lebanese Pomegranate Dressing,
    67
  Watermelon, Raspberry &
    Pomegranate Salad, 295
Pork. *See also* Bacon; Pork sausages;
    Prosciutto
  18-Hour Pork Shoulder with
    Fennel, Garlic & Lemon,
    216
  Garlic-Miso Pork Chops, Orange
    Peppers & Arugula, 212–13
  Pasta with Pepper, Pecorino &
    Pork Rinds, 108–9
  "Peking" Pork with Scotch &
    Scallions, 217
  Pork Chops & Apples, Madeira–
    Bay Butter Sauce, 214, **215**
  Pork Chops with Radicchio
    Snippets & Cornichon
    Vinaigrette, 212
  Pork Loin in Cream with
    Tomatoes, Sage & Gin, 219,
    220
  Sticky Country Ribs with Orange,
    Molasses & Vinegar, 213
Pork sausages
  Baked Ziti in Bianco with Fontina
    & Salami, 120, **121**
  Chicken with Chorizo, Peppadews
    & Fino Sherry, 195
  Fennel Sausages with Wrinkled
    Grapes & Grape Extract,
    218
  Gemelli with Sausage, Leeks &
    Barely Wilted Spinach, 132
  Sautéed Cod with Chorizo,
    Orange & Wild Arugula,
    Sherry Vinaigrette, 148,
    149
  Split Pea Soup with Soppressata &
    Fresh Oregano, 91
Potatoes. *See also* Sweet potatoes
  Bay-Smoked Potatoes, 276
  Creamy Potato Gratin, 278
  Crispy Shredded Potato Cakes,
    276, **277**

Potatoes (*cont.*)
    Olive Oil–Mashed Potatoes, 278
    Wasabi-Mashed Potatoes, 279
Poultry. *See* Chicken; Turkey
Prosciutto
    Cheese Strata with Prosciutto,
        Basil & Spinach, 26, **27**
    Chicken with Prosciutto, Tomatoes
        & White Wine, 199
    Creamy, Lemony Eggs with
        Prosciutto, 8
    Grilled Veal Chops with Prosciutto
        & Basil-Lemon Oil, 232
    Halibut in Prosciutto Wrappers, Red
        Onions & Crispy Basil, 156–57
    Manchego Chicken with
        Prosciutto, Arugula &
        Pumpkin Seeds, 190
    Pasta Cooked in a Bottle of Wine,
        119
    Prosciutto with Figs & Mint, 43
    Prosciutto with Pears &
        Parmigiano, 43
    Rolled-and-Tied Turkey Roast
        with Prosciutto, Prunes &
        Sage, 206, **207**
    Spring Mix with Carrot-Ginger
        Dressing & Prosciutto
        "Bacon," 50, **51**
Prunes
    Prunes and White Chocolate, Port
        Wine Reduction, 303
    Rolled-and-Tied Turkey Roast
        with Prosciutto, Prunes &
        Sage, 206, **207**
Pumpkin
    Manchego Chicken with
        Prosciutto, Arugula &
        Pumpkin Seeds, 190
    Pumpkin Ravioli with Crispy
        Sage & Walnut Butter, 111

Quesadillas
    Smoked Salmon, Basil & Lemon
        Quesadillas, **14**, 15

Radicchio
    Asparagus, Bok Choy & Radicchio
        Salad, 48
    500-Degree Cod with Macadamia
        Butter & Radicchio, 151
Radishes
    Perciatelli with French Breakfast
        Radishes, Bacon & Greens,
        122, 123

Roasted French Breakfast
    Radishes, 268, **269**
Sugar Snaps with Diced Bacon &
    Radishes, **272**, 273
Raisins
    Golden Raisin–Fennel Scones,
        31, **31**
    Sautéed Peppers with Golden
        Raisins & Arugula, 270
    Short Rigatoni with Cauliflower,
        Anchovies & Raisins, 124,
        125
Raspberries
    Double Raspberry Sorbet, **326**,
        327
    Watermelon, Raspberry &
        Pomegranate Salad, 295
Recipes, notes about, viii–xi
Red snapper
    Red Snapper with Pop-Pop
        Tomatoes, 153
    Tiradito, 37
Rhubarb
    Rhubarb & Candied Ginger
        Compote with Coconut
        Sorbet, 302, **302**
    Warm Rhubarb Compote with
        Walnut-Coconut Crunch,
        20, **20**
Rice
    "Creola" Rice, 285
    Pistachio-Coconut Rice, 274
    Riso in Bianco with Shrimp
        Scampi, 173
    Salmon with Lime Leaves, Poppy
        Rice & Coconut Sauce, 139
Rutabagas
    Rutabaga, Crème Fraîche &
        Havarti Torte, 279, **280**
    Sweet Potato–Rutabaga Soup with
        Toasted Pecans, 90–91

Sable
    Scrambled Eggs with Leeks &
        Sable, 8
Salad dressings, list of recipes, 35
Salads. *See also page 35 for list of salad*
    recipes
    Herring Salad with Fennel, Crème
        Fraîche & Toasted Bread
        Crumbs, 16, **16**
    Watermelon, Raspberry &
        Pomegranate Salad, 295
Salmon
    Fettuccine with Smoked Salmon,
        Crème Fraîche & Lemon, 110

Ginger's No-Ginger Salmon, 144
Glazed Salmon & Wok Eggs with
    Shiitakes, 17
"Golden Robe" Salmon with Snow
    Peas & Red Cabbage, 145
Korean-Style Salmon "Bulgogi,"
    Bok Choy & Shiitakes, **146**,
    147
Last-Minute Gravlax, 39
Salmon & Mint in Crispy Grape
    Leaves, Garlic Crème
    Fraîche, 140, **141**
Salmon with Cucumbers &
    Blackened Lemons, 138
Salmon with Lime Leaves,
    Poppy Rice & Coconut
    Sauce, 139
Smoked & Fresh Salmon en
    Chemise, **142**, 143
Smoked Salmon, Basil & Lemon
    Quesadillas, **14**, 15
Smoked Salmon with Petite
    Salade, Goat Cheese & Lime
    Vinaigrette, 38
Spiced Salmon on a Moroccan
    Salad, 40, **41**
3-Minute Wasabi Salmon, 138
Salt, for recipes, xi
Sardines
    Golden Fettuccine with
        Sardines, Fennel & Saffron,
        112, 113
    Swordfish Steaks with Sardine
        "Bolognese," 168
Sauces
    One-Ingredient Eggnog "Crème
        Anglaise," 317
    1-Minute Mustard Sauce, 39
Sausages. *See also* Pork sausages
    Homemade Turkey Sausage, 17
Scallops
    Scallop Carpaccio with Seaweed
        Salad & Lemon Oil, 36, **36**
    Seared Scallops on Sweet Pea
        Puree, 174, **174**
Scones
    Golden Raisin–Fennel Scones,
        31, **31**
    Warm Buttermilk-Cheddar
        Scones, 30
Sea bass
    Braised Black Sea Bass on
        Pancetta-Studded Cabbage,
        159
    Chilean Sea Bass with Pistachio-
        Pesto Crust & Green Bean
        "Fries," 158, **158**

index

Sesame seeds
 Cinnamon-Sugar Crisps, 323
 Sesame Seed–Olive Oil Cookies,
  320
Shellfish. *See also* Shrimp
 buying, 136
 Jade Soup with Lump Crab & Dill,
  82
 Salt-Water Lobsters, Healthy
  Drawn Butter, 175
 Scallop Carpaccio with Seaweed
  Salad & Lemon Oil, 36, **36**
 Seared Scallops on Sweet Pea
  Puree, 174, **174**
 Sheet-Pan Mussels with Red
  Curry–Garlic Broth, 170,
  171
 Steamed Clams with Sake &
  Chiles, 170
Shrimp
 "Bloody" Shrimp Cocktail, 7, **7**
 Riso in Bianco with Shrimp
  Scampi, 173
 Shrimp Escabeche with Blood
  Orange Mojo, 172
Sole
 Pasta Rustica with Sole, Greek
  Olives & White Wine, 127
 Sole Provençal with Petit
  Ratatouille, 152
Sorbet
 Absurdly Easy Coconut Sorbet,
  302, **302**
 Chocolate-Chipotle Sorbet, **326**,
  327
 Double Raspberry Sorbet, **326**, 327
 Honeydew-Kiwi Sorbet with
  Chartreuse, 324, **325**
 Leftover-Cranberry-Sauce Sorbet,
  328
Soups. *See also* page 71 for list of soup
  recipes
 Morning Fruit Soup with Tapioca,
  22
Spinach
 Cheese Strata with Prosciutto,
  Basil & Spinach, 26, **27**
 Fragrant Asian Gazpacho, 80, **80**
 Gemelli with Sausage, Leeks &
  Barely Wilted Spinach, 132
 Sheet-Pan Spinach, 270
 "Silver Packet" Flounder with
  Miso Mayo, 152–53
 Spinach, Ricotta & Basil Puree,
  271
 White Beans with Spinach,
  Tomatoes & Rosemary, 283

Split peas
 Split Pea Soup with Soppressata &
  Fresh Oregano, 91
Squash. *See also* Pumpkin; Zucchini
 Calabaza Soup with Celery &
  Crispy Sage, 96, **97**
Strata
 Cheese Strata with Prosciutto,
  Basil & Spinach, 26, **27**
Strawberries
 Double-Rise Pancakes with
  Strawberries, Bananas &
  Almonds, 24
 Orange Flower Strawberries &
  Mint Sugar, 290, **291**
Striped bass
 Fennel-Roasted Striped Bass, Tiny
  Tomatoes & Crispy Capers, 157
Sweet potatoes
 Roasted Sweet Potatoes with
  Whipped Butter & Maple
  "Honey," 282
 Sweet Potato Puree with Fresh
  Ginger & Orange, 282–83
 Sweet Potato–Rutabaga Soup with
  Toasted Pecans, 90–91
Swordfish
 Green Curry Swordfish with
  Shiitakes & Basil, 168–69
 Roasted Swordfish with Tomatoes-
  on-the-Vine & Rosemary
  Tartare Sauce, 169
 Swordfish Steaks with Sardine
  "Bolognese," 168

Tahina
 Fettuccine with Tahina, Pine Nuts
  & Cilantro, 110
 Grilled Tuna with Lemony Tahina,
  Greens & Pomegranate
  Seeds, 166, **167**
 Heirloom Tomatoes with Lemony
  Tahina, 45
 Little Chocolate-Tahina Cups, 297
 Swiss Chard with Lemony Tahina
  & Cashews, 264
 Tahina & Date Syrup Swirl, Fresh
  Apple Slices, 294
Tarts
 All-Chocolate Velvet Tart, 309,
  309
 E.A.T. (Easy Apple Tart), 310
 Pear, Cherry & Pine Nut Tartlets,
  308
 Zucchini, Fresh Mozzarella &
  Sun-Dried Tomato Tart, 12

Tomatoes
 Barcelona Bread, 102
 Big Juicy Sun-Dried Tomato
  Burgers, 234
 Blasted Green Beans & Grape
  Tomatoes, 265
 BLT Chicken with Cumin Seed &
  Lime Mayonnaise, 181
 Braised Cod with "Sliced Tomato"
  Sauce & Fresh Oregano,
  150–51
 Capellini with Spicy Fish Sauce
  Marinara, 111
 Castellane with Ricotta & Tomato-
  Marsala Sauce, 126–27
 Chicken Ras el Hanout with
  Tomato-Ginger Chutney,
  196, 197
 Chicken with Prosciutto, Tomatoes
  & White Wine, 199
 "Creola" Rice, 285
 Fennel-Roasted Striped Bass, Tiny
  Tomatoes & Crispy Capers,
  157
 Golden Fettuccine with Sardines,
  Fennel & Saffron, **112**, 113
 Heirloom Tomatoes with Lemony
  Tahina, 45
 Lemony Arugula & Sun-Dried
  Tomato Salad with Smoked
  Mozzarella, 55
 Linguine with Pesto Rosso, 109
 Pappa al Pomodoro, 94
 Pasta Rustica with Sole, Greek
  Olives & White Wine, 127
 Pink Tomato Frappés, 74, **74**
 Plum Tomato Gazpacho, 81
 Pork Loin in Cream with
  Tomatoes, Sage & Gin, 219,
  220
 A Recipe from 1841: Macaroni &
  Tomatoes, 120
 Red Snapper with Pop-Pop
  Tomatoes, 153
 Roasted Halibut with Tomatoes &
  Saffron Vinaigrette, 156
 Roasted Swordfish with Tomatoes-
  on-the-Vine & Rosemary
  Tartare Sauce, 169
 Summer Tomatoes with Za'atar
  Pesto, 45
 Sweet Tomato–Watermelon Soup,
  72, **73**
 Swordfish Steaks with Sardine
  "Bolognese," 168
 Tian of Eggplant, Tomato &
  Herbs, 284

Tomatoes (*cont.*)
Tomato, Buffalo Mozzarella &
Fried Basil Salad, 44, **44**
White Beans with Spinach,
Tomatoes & Rosemary, 283
Zucchini, Fresh Mozzarella &
Sun-Dried Tomato Tart, 12
Tomato juice
"Bloody" Shrimp Cocktail, 7, **7**
Overnight Tabbouleh with Hard-
Boiled Eggs, 25
Tomato-Anisette Soup with
Tarragon, 76
Tortillas
Smoked Salmon, Basil & Lemon
Quesadillas, **14**, 15
Tortilla Ribbons, 102
Trout
Smoked Trout on Frisée with
Warm Bacon-Maple
Vinaigrette, 13
Tuna
Black & Blue Tuna with Garlic
Asparagus & Yogurt-Caper
Sauce, 163
Charred Tuna, Mizuna & Pear
with Black Vinaigrette, **164**,
165
Chilled Asparagus Tonnato with
"Confetti," 46–47, **47**
Grilled Tuna with Lemony Tahina,
Greens & Pomegranate
Seeds, 166, **167**
Seared Tuna with Fresh Corn &
Wasabi "Cream," 162–63
Turkey
Bombay Turkey Sliders, Hurry-
Curry Sauce, 204
Homemade Turkey Sausage, 17
Rolled-and-Tied Turkey Roast
with Prosciutto, Prunes &
Sage, 206, **207**
Wined-and-Brined Turkey with
Bay Leaves & Oregano, 205

Veal
Grilled Veal Chops with Prosciutto
& Basil-Lemon Oil, 232
Veal Chops with Sage Butter,
Sunflower Seeds & Beet
Drizzle, 230, **231**
Veal Roast with Fresh Thyme &
Honey Mustard Jus, 232–33

Veal Steaks "Stroganoff" with
Shiitakes & Portobellos, 233

Walnuts
Beets with Balsamic Syrup, Mint
& Walnuts, 46
Hungarian Walnut Cookies, 319
Maple-Walnut Espresso Torte,
Espresso-Lemon Syrup, 314
Pumpkin Ravioli with Crispy Sage
& Walnut Butter, 111
Walnut-Onion Muffins, 101
Warm Rhubarb Compote with
Walnut-Coconut Crunch,
20, **20**
Wasabi paste or powder
Filet of Beef with Wasabi-Garlic
Cream, 242, **243**
Green Pea–Wasabi Soup with
Mint, 84–85
Steamed Asparagus with Wasabi-
Miso Butter, 254
3-Minute Wasabi Salmon, 138
Wasabi-Mashed Potatoes, 279
Watercress
Stir-Fried Watercress with Garlic
Chips, 274
Watercress, Endive & St. Agur
Blue Cheese, 53
Watermelon
Honeydew-Kiwi Sorbet with
Chartreuse, 324, **325**
Seven Great Juice Blends, 4, **5**
Sweet Tomato–Watermelon Soup,
72, **73**
Watermelon, Raspberry &
Pomegranate Salad,
295
Watermelon "Carpaccio" with
White Chocolate, 292
Watermelon Salad with Feta &
Black Olives, 42
White chocolate
Prunes and White Chocolate, Port
Wine Reduction, 303
Watermelon "Carpaccio" with
White Chocolate, 292
White Chocolate Mousse with
Apricot Compote, 307
Wine
Lamb Shanks Provençal
with Cabernet & Dried
Mushrooms, 229

A Leg of Lamb & a Bottle of
Chardonnay, 228
Pasta Cooked in a Bottle of Wine,
119
Poached Pears with Marsala,
Cinnamon & Vanilla, 303
Prunes and White Chocolate,
Port Wine Reduction,
303

Yogurt
Black & Blue Tuna with Garlic
Asparagus & Yogurt-Caper
Sauce, 163
Blistered Chicken, Tandoori-Style,
198–99
Breakfast "Surprise," 21
Butterflied Lamb with Garam
Masala, Yogurt & Lime,
226, **227**
Chicken Zahav with Blackened
Onions & Turmeric, 194
Cucumber-Coconut Bisque, 76
French Yogurt Cake with Nutella,
312, **313**
Tortellini with Yogurt, Mint &
Smoked Paprika Oil, 116,
117
Turkish Cucumbers, 64
Warm Rhubarb Compote with
Walnut-Coconut Crunch,
20, **20**

Za'atar
about, xi, 45
Chicken with Za'atar, Lemon &
Garlic, 200, **200**
Summer Tomatoes with Za'atar
Pesto, 45
Zucchini
Fragrant Asian Gazpacho, 80, **80**
Jade Soup with Lump Crab &
Dill, 82
Linguine with Zucchini, Lemon
Zest & Basil, 108
Sole Provençal with Petit
Ratatouille, 152
Three Green Vegetables in High
Humidity, 273
Zucchini, Fresh Mozzarella
& Sun-Dried Tomato Tart,
12